THE GREAT GENERALS SERIES

This distinguished new series features the lives of eminent military leaders who changed history in the United States and abroad. Top military historians write concise but comprehensive biographies including the personal lives, battles, strategies, and legacies of these great generals, with the aim to provide background and insight into today's armies and wars. These books are of interest to the military history buff, and, thanks to fast-paced narratives and references to current affairs, they are also accessible to the general reader.

Patton by Alan Axelrod

Grant by John Mosier

Eisenhower by John Wukovits

LeMay by Barrett Tillman

MacArthur by Richard B. Frank

Stonewall Jackson by Donald A. Davis

Bradley by Alan Axelrod

Pershing by Jim Lacey

Andrew Jackson by Robert V. Remini

Sherman by Steven E. Woodworth

Robert E. Lee by Noah Andre Trudeau

Marshall by H. Paul Jeffers

Custer by Duane Schultz

Washington

Lessons in Leadership

Gerald M. Carbone

For my father,
Robert A. Carbone

WASHINGTON
Copyright © Gerald M. Carbone, 2010.

First published in 2010 by PALGRAVE MACMILLAN® in the US–a
division of St. Martin's Press LLC, 175 Fifth Avenue, New York, NY
10010.

Where this book is distributed in the UK, Europe and the rest of the
world, this is by Palgrave Macmillan, a division of Macmillan Publishers
Limited, registered in England, company number 785998, of
Houndmills, Basingstoke, Hampshire RG21 6XS.

Palgrave Macmillan is the global academic imprint of the above
companies and has companies and representatives throughout the world.

Palgrave® and Macmillan® are registered trademarks in the United
States, the United Kingdom, Europe and other countries.

ISBN: 978-0-230-61707-0

Library of Congress Cataloging-in-Publication Data
Carbone, Gerald M.
    Washington : lessons in leadership / Gerald M. Carbone ; foreword by
General Wesley K. Clark.
        p.   cm.
    Includes bibliographical references and index.
    ISBN 0-230-61707-7 (alk. paper)
    1. Washington, George, 1732–1799—Military leadership.   2.
Command of troops—Case studies.   3. Political leadership—United
States—Case studies.   4. Generals—United States—Biography.   5.
United States. Continental Army—Biography.   6. United States—
History—Revolution, 1775–1783—Campaigns.   I. Title.
E312.25.C29   2009
973.4'1092--dc22

                                                            2009039963

A catalogue record of the book is available from the British Library.

Design by Letra Libre

First edition: January 2010
10   9   8   7   6   5   4   3   2   1
Printed in the United States of America.

Contents

Foreword

As the U.S. Army celebrated its bicentennial in 1975, it was a dark moment. The North Vietnamese had just overrun Saigon; in occupied Eastern Europe, the Soviet military was fielding an awesome new array of powerful weapons. And it seemed that the efforts and sacrifices of a decade in Vietnam were for naught. Students at the Army's Command and General Staff College—captains and majors, most veterans of multiple combat tours of duty—closely examined the ethics and character and origins of their Service. And it took us only the briefest moments of study to recognize that almost every value cherished and embodied in the Army of 1975 traced its origins to our first Commanding General, George Washington.

There's no better recounting of Washington's military thoughts, deeds, and values than this brisk and insightful biography by Gerald Carbone. To capture these insights from a life story so often retold and idolized as to have become almost hackneyed, is a work of real skill. His sharp focus on Washington's military experiences, judgments and character makes the book unique and Washington's military impact readily accessible.

America, in Washington's time, was the frontier. Armed conflict was but a few days walk away for most Americans. But military service was a personal choice. As a young man, Washington was apparently drawn to the military by complex motives—ambition, competitiveness, and insecurity, among others. Together they drove his determination to make his way forward in a society where he was on the fringes of those most privileged. And he had the sufficient natural talents and good luck to succeed, probably far beyond his greatest hopes.

In the American Revolution, Washington proved to be the one indispensable man. Having fought the Indians and the French and written about the experience, he was already a seasoned and celebrated warrior. And he had by marriage and hard work established himself among the top social rank of Virginia's landed class. From the outset, he was the obvious first and best choice for the highest command. And he proved to be a commander who had an instinct for the attack, who learned from his mistakes, who earned the loyalty of his subordinates (or most of them), and who won the admiration and affection of his countrymen for sharing the hardships and dangers of the campaign and battlefield. He emerged as the Father of Our Country—and also the father of our Army.

True, as Carbone notes, he may have lost more battles than he won—Brooklyn Heights and Manhattan, and Fort Washington may be the most notable. He juggled logistics, conflicting personalities, a meddlesome Congress, a civilian population who was fearful and sometimes riddled with sympathies for the enemy, and a volunteer soldiery to avoid defeat. The argument could be made that by not "losing" he was "winning." But in the vicissitudes of the eighteenth-century struggle between Britain and France, it took more than that to succeed. And he did far more than just hold the Army together. He had an aggressive nature and an "offensive" mindset which led to some remarkable actions, including his awesome winter crossing of the Delaware to defeat of the British at Trenton.

In this one battle, in the depth of winter, with an Army defeated in New York, pursued across New Jersey, and soon to be dismissed upon the completion of their service, he turned the course of history. Washington was a warrior. His determination, his judgments, and his personal courage in those terrible days were decisive. It was truly "victory or death," as his doodling suggests—for him and the nation. And in the victory was the turning point for American history. His judgment and skills improved, year by year of command, and in the end, his orchestration of the set-piece defeat of the British at Yorktown was truly classic.

But it is the revealed character behind the man which proved so powerful and enduring an influence on our Army. He was ambitious, though he took pains to cloak it with a modest demeanor. He had a strong sense of determination. He sought command as an adolescent—and in fact, had no adolescence by today's standards. He was not a genius, but instead struggled to understand tactics and strategy, and suffered humiliating and life-threatening failure as a young officer working with the British against the French and Indians. He could be doggedly self-interested in promoting his personal financial aims while in the "public" service along the frontier, but he learned that campaigns and war have their own logic, and can be bent to other ends only at great risk.

Washington brought incredible natural gifts to the task. First, his physical presence. He stood a head taller than most of his contemporaries, giving him a natural authority complemented by his own dignified—and well-planned—reserve. He also had unusual physical strength, skill and stamina. He was a gifted horseman, and was able to fight off the intense cold and prolonged fatigue that disabled many others.

He had a strong sense of fair play, perhaps founded on his own personal confidence. He had social charm and extolled discipline and advancement by merit. By his conduct and reserve, Washington created his own "moral authority" to undergird the legal authority bestowed by Congress. He shared hardships with his troops and exposed himself to battlefield risk, and had many close brushes with death. He took counsel of his fellow leaders, but could take decisive action if necessary. He instilled the offensive mindset in his troops. And though the military service was his profession, he subordinated his military judgment to the political authority and leadership of the Congress. And especially in the resignation ceremony at Annapolis in 1783, where he handed back his commission to the Congress, he enshrined, hopefully forever, the most fundamental principle for the army of a democracy—subordination of the military to civilian authority.

Washington's towering example still influences, and in some respects dominates, all those of us who have followed him in our military service. Physical vigor—stature if you have it; determined, diligent pursuit of military excellence; promotion by merit: firm, hard but fair discipline; open communication with "the troops." The offensive spirit. Promotion by merit. Respect for the opinions of others. Determination in the face of adversity. Leaders "made," not "born." Moral authority. Fair treatment of non-combatants and prisoners. Subordination to civil authority. Loyalty to country at great personal sacrifice.

Over two centuries have passed since his first shining moments in command around Boston, where he outmaneuvered the British and forced them to evacuate. We are still in awe of the man and his legacy. Here, in the sparse language of effective biography, you can read why, and feel again the power of extraordinary character which helped win our freedom and forge our Army.

—*Gen. Wesley K. Clark (Ret.)*

The Letter

THE TWO MEN HAD ONE DULL HATCHET BETWEEN THEM, AND they spent all of a December day on the banks of the Alleghany River taking turns swinging that dull blade to chop trees into logs that they then lashed together to form a raft.

In the blue glow of a winter's twilight in the waning days of 1753, they slid the raft across 50 yards of ice and then launched it into the powerful currents of the Alleghany. The river snatched their little raft, pulling them into a sluiceway of black, open water racing between jagged sheets of ice jutting out from either shore. Thick slabs had broken off these ice sheets and were now spinning adrift in the current, smashing heavily into each other, and into the raft, with the sounds of broken glass.

George Washington, then a 21-year-old militia major on a mission, and one of the two men on the raft, later wrote in his journal: "[B]efore we got half over, we were jamed in the Ice in such a Manner, that we expected every Moment our Raft wou'd sink, & we Perish."[1]

To avoid being crushed between floes of ice, Washington jabbed a long pole into the river bottom, 10 feet below, hoping to stop the raft so that the ice might pass by; as he leaned hard on the pole, the current snatched it. Washington plunged into the icy black waters of the Alleghany.

While Washington's head slipped beneath the surface of the river, his backpack, a rudimentary thing of canvas stretched across sticks, rested on the raft.

Nestled in the pack, beside his provisions of dried beef and corn, was the reason for this hazardous mission: a letter to Virginia's governor, Robert Dinwiddie.

⊹━━━⊹

Governor Dinwiddie, a rotund, moon-faced Scot with a mane of white hair, had given the young Washington a mission: Hike hundreds of miles through the wilds of the Ohio Valley until you find a French fort, then deliver a letter to the commander of that fort demanding that he leave the King of England's lands, then hike back to Williamsburg and deliver to the governor the French commander's response.

In giving an important assignment to this 21-year-old militia major, Dinwiddie had been quite specific in his commission: "You, the said George Washington, Esqr., forthwith to repair to the Logstown on the said River Ohio; and having there inform'd Your Self where the said French Forces have posted themselves, thereupon to proceed to such Place [. . .]"

Washington began this journey on the very day he received the commission, October 31, 1753. He collected a small party that eventually grew to six men and headed out for Logstown, an Indian trading village in Pennsylvania, 300 miles away; the band arrived there on November 24, after three fatiguing weeks of trudging through ankle-deep snows. There Washington met with three chiefs of the Six Nations tribes who, along with one of their best hunters, agreed to guide Washington's party. The Six Nations tribes had formed a tenuous alignment with the English in hopes that they would drive the French from the Ohio Valley and then leave these tribal lands alone.

From Logstown, the trip continued to be hard going through deep snows and cold rains that fell almost continuously. But a 70-mile slog through the snow paid off on December 4, when the party arrived at Venango, an old Indian town on a fork in the Alleghany; here Washington spied the French fleur-de-lis flying above a trading post that the French army had recently confiscated from a British fur trader.

Three French officers now lived in the Venango trading post, and they invited Washington's party to a dinner, where the wine flowed freely. The French, Washington observed in his diary, "dos'd themselves pretty plentifully" with the wine, and in their lightheadedness "soon banish'd the restraint which at first appear'd in their Conversation, & gave license to their Tongues to reveal their Sentiments more freely."

Washington was no teetotaler, but he remained sober to listen as the French told him "it was their absolute Design to take Possession of the Ohio, & by G—they wou'd do it." Washington earnestly absorbed strategic information as these French officers in their cups told him the location of seven forts up to Lake Erie and beyond; he learned about recent troop movements that left the French with a few hundred men garrisoning the forts in the Ohio; he heard the location of where "they lodge their goods at" and "the Place that all their Stores come from."[2]

The head of these three French officers, Captain Philippe Thomas de Joncaire, refused to accept Dinwiddie's letter from Washington; he also declined to take back the wampum that the French had earlier given to the Indians to seal a pact, telling both Washington and a Seneca-raised chief named Tanacharison—the "Half King"—to continue on up to Fort Le Boeuf, near Lake Erie, where the commander there had more authority to deal with them. So the party slogged on, covering 60 miles in four days, their progress retarded, Washington wrote, "by excessive rains, Snows, & bad traveling, through Mires & Swamps."[3]

Finally on December 11, some 43 days after they'd set out, Washington's little party reached the gates of Fort Le Boeuf. Early the next morning, Washington prepared to meet with the commander, Jacques Le Gardeur, sieur de Saint-Pierre, a 52-year-old knight of the order of St. Louis who struck the young Washington as "an elderly gentleman."[4] Washington gave the French captain his passport and showed his commission, but when he tried to press Dinwiddie's letter on Gardeur, the captain refused it, telling Washington to wait another day till the captain from the Presque Isle fort on Lake Erie arrived.

Late on the thirteenth, the French officers finally received Governor Dinwiddie's letter, taking it into a private war council to draft a response. Washington took advantage of this delay to reconnoiter the fort, taking its dimensions, counting the cannon (eight six-pounders and a four-pounder), their location, the height of the bastions (12 feet), and the location of the barracks, stables, and blacksmith's furnace. He could only guess at the number of men stationed there, but he took a count of the canoes: 50 of birch bark and 170 of pine.

Snow fell all the next day. While Washington impatiently awaited a reply to his letter, he ordered a man to take the packhorses toward home, unloaded, for they were too weak now to carry any weight.

Finally on the fourteenth, Washington wrote in his journal: "This Evening I receiv'd an Answer to His Honour the Governor's Letter from the Commandment."[5] While handing him their sealed reply, the French officers promised to lend him a canoe and guides to paddle as far as Venango, some 130 miles as the river winds, through a drafty, snow-choked valley.

The paddle toward home was hard going. Several times the canoes stove against rocks and were nearly swamped; in places shallow shoals forced the men to wade for nearly an hour in icy water. Washington's clothing stiffened with ice.

It took a week to rendezvous with the packhorses in Venango, where Washington determined that they were still too weak to carry baggage. He decided to split up his little party: Four of the men would take the horses at a leisurely pace on a path along the Ohio, while Washington and a seasoned guide, Christopher Gist, would don backpacks and hike the shortest route to Virginia through the wilderness on foot. Washington wrote: "I took my necessary Papers, pull'd off my Cloths; tied My Self up in a Match Coat; & with my Pack at my back, with my Papers & Provisions in it, & a Gun, set out with Mr. Gist, fitted in the same manner."[6]

<hr/>

The next day, Washington and Gist reached Murthering Town or Murdering Town, where (according to Gist's telling of the story) they met an Indian who agreed to guide them on the shortest route to the next town. After a march of eight or ten miles, both Washington and Gist began feeling uneasy about their Indian guide. His course was more northerly than it should have been; he became "churlish," in Gist's words, and overly eager to press on. Then, in a meadow white with snow, the Indian guide whirled about and fired his gun at Washington and Gist. When he fired, the Indian was just 12 or 15 paces from Washington; somehow he missed.

"Are you shot?" Washington asked Gist.

"No."

The two men saw their guide running for a big white oak where he stopped to jam another ball down the barrel of his gun. Washington and Gist ran to him and wrestled away the gun.

"I would've killed him," Gist wrote, "but the Major [Washington] would not suffer me to kill him."[7]

Instead they gave their guide a cake of bread and told him to go; then Washington and Gist pressed on through the night, trying to distance themselves from the hostile Indian, lest he return with more men.[8] They hiked until they came to the banks of the Alleghany, where they camped a night before spending all of the next day building and launching their little raft.

The sun was long down when Washington plunged from the raft and the black waters of the river closed above his head. But Washington was young, tall, strong, and stubborn; he quickly managed to grab one of the raft's logs and hauled himself back onto the platform, where he and Gist tried mightily to pole the raft to one bank or the other. Try as they might, the Allegheny's current bore them along until it spat out the raft in shallow waters at the tip of an island; they plunged into the icy, waist-deep water, donned their wood-and-canvas backpacks, and waded ashore. They spent that night in wet clothes, camped on an island while the temperatures dramatically dropped. Gist's fingers suffered frostbite but, he noted, "the cold did us some service"—by the time a pale sun rose on Sunday, December 30, the night's deep freeze had frozen the river thickly enough to let the two men walk across from the island to the opposite shore.

On New Year's Day, 1754, Washington bought a horse and saddle at Fraser's trading post; two weeks after that he rode into Virginia's capital, Williamsburg, with detailed plans of Fort Le Boeuf, solid intelligence about French personnel and installations in the Ohio, and a letter bearing a defiant reply from the French to Dinwiddie's demand that they withdraw from the North American frontier.

Le Gardeur de Saint-Pierre's reply—"As to the summons you send me to retire, I do not think myself obliged to obey it"—was a polite way of thumbing his nose at English authority.[9] Dinwiddie wasted no time in publishing both the response and Washington's journal of his epic, months-long journey into the Ohio wilderness. The story had everything an eighteenth-century reader could want: councils with the Indians; meetings with drunken, perfidious French; near-death experiences. Newspapers throughout the colonies printed the journal, bringing the young Washington a measure of fame and a payment of £50 from Virginia's grateful House of Burgesses.

Washington's eyewitness report of French forces massing in the Ohio with plans to sweep through the valley in the coming summer touched off what American colonists came to call the French and Indian War. That war would give Washington a crash course in combat and command, but already his journey through the wilderness had strengthened aspects of his character that would shape everything that was to follow:

- *Discipline.* In refusing offers to drink liberally with the French officers at Venango, Washington, a 21-year-old with a fondness for wine, showed a maturity beyond his years. Throughout his journey, he acted like a sponge, single-mindedly absorbing intelligence, from firsthand observation of the terrain to thorough interviewing of French deserters who spelled out the locations of French fortifications down the Ohio all the way to New Orleans. For a young militia officer, Washington displayed an uncanny ability for zeroing in on intelligence of importance without being distracted by the superfluous.

- *Patience.* From the first day of his trip, Washington realized the urgency of his mission—the sooner British colonial governors got intelligence of French plans to dominate the Ohio frontier, the sooner they'd be able to mobilize against those plans. But the Six Nations chiefs who traveled with him had a different sense of time than he did; twice they asked him to delay his departure from Logstown, and both times he gave in to their wishes while silently chafing. The French commander at Fort Le Beouf deliberately stalled the Indians' departure by promising them guns and liquor if they would remain in the fort until after Washington left. Again Washington swallowed his impatience and waited out the French, though it taxed every fiber of his being to tarry at Fort Le Boeuf when so much awaited his return. Of the forced wait at the fort he wrote: "I can't say that ever in my Life I suffer'd so much Anxiety as I did in this affair."[10]

- *Stamina.* The round trip from Williamsburg to Fort Le Boeuf covered more than 700 miles through winter's darkest days. It required crossing the Blue Ridge Mountains, fording icy rivers, and portaging canoes across the snow. Gist, a seasoned guide, did not want Washington to walk with him through the wilderness "Indian style," because Washington lacked backcountry experience. But, Gist noted, Washington "insisted on it," and persevered.
- *Resolve.* Above all, what Washington's journey demonstrated was a fierce devotion to duty. When George Washington resolved to do a thing he would do it, or die trying. And as events of the journey demonstrated, George Washington was a hard man to kill.

CHAPTER 1

"Something Charming in the Sound"

Wɪᴛʜ sᴏʟɪᴅ ᴇᴠɪᴅᴇɴᴄᴇ ᴛʜᴀᴛ ᴛʜᴇ Fʀᴇɴᴄʜ ɪɴᴛᴇɴᴅᴇᴅ ᴛᴏ ᴄʟᴀɪᴍ ᴀ good chunk of North America from Lake Erie to Louisiana, Governor Robert Dinwiddie appealed to the 13 colonies for militia to oppose this scheme. He had little success. The colonies rarely acted in concert on anything, and were as apt to be rivals as allies. Even Dinwiddie's own colony of Virginia was luke-warm to the idea of a confrontation with the French; many in the House of Burgesses suspected the governor of trying to manipulate the militia in a self-ish bid to protect wealthy cronies who had invested heavily in settling those frontier lands through a venture called the Ohio Land Company.

In February 1754, Virginia's House of Burgesses reluctantly agreed to spend £10,000 on sending an armed expedition into the Ohio and a race was on for the "Forks of the Ohio," site of present-day Pittsburgh, where the Alleghany and the Monongahela flow together to form the Ohio River. Washington had identified this as the perfect place to build a fort in the region, and the natural advantages were so obvious that the English colonies had to hurry before the French built there first.

Washington volunteered to be "among chief officers of this expedition" to fortify the Forks. He knew that at age 22 he was too green in the military arts to actually lead the expedition, writing: "The command of the whole forces is what I neither look for, expect, nor desire; for I must be impartial enough to confess it is a charge too great for my youth and inexperience to be intrusted with." [1]

Washington became second in command for this foray to the Forks, receiving his commission as lieutenant colonel on March 15, 1754. Even as second in command, he was over his head. Some expeditions, blessed with good luck and good planning, click like clockwork; others are beset with problems from the beginning, where error compounds error, officers snipe at each other, and troop morale sinks into the mire. This expedition was of the latter stripe; for Washington it was a horrible experience but an excellent education. If his epic journey through the wilderness in 1753 set the foundation for his military career, this expedition toward the Forks of the Ohio framed it.

Even before Washington stepped off at the head of his troops, he learned an age-old lesson in the problems of supply. From Colonel William Fairfax's lavish estate of Belvoir, where Washington was welcomed thanks to his half brother's marriage to Fairfax's daughter, Washington wrote to Dinwiddie in early March: "We should be glad to have so many Tints [tents] sent up as can be spard, for there is no proper Linnen to make them of here and would be difficult to get done if there was[.] We also are much in want of Cutlasses, Halbards, Officer's half pikes, Drum's &ca . . . that Drum which was sent up with the Artillery being very bad is scarcely worth the trouble of carrying." [2]

Besides tents, weapons, and drums, Washington's gathering army required clothing, preferably uniforms with red coats to impress Indian allies and strike fear into their foes. For the Indians, red "is compard to Blood and is look'd upon as the distinguishing marks of Warriours," Washington wrote Dinwiddie. "It is my acquaintance with these Indians and a study in their Tempers that has in some measure let me into their Customs and dispositions."

⊶━━⊷

Through his journey to Fort Le Boeuf, Washington had learned something of the "Customs" of the Indians; the Seneca Chief, Tanacharison, had even given him an Indian name: Conotocarious, meaning "town taker" or "devourer of villages."[3] Tanacharison knew that this had been the Indian name of Washington's grandfather, John Washington, who had proven to be adept at taking Indian land not by force of arms but through force of law. Washington's own father, Augustine, had been a Virginia planter, land speculator, and iron forge owner who died when George was 11. He had left a large family—three sons with his first wife (one of whom died in childhood) and four sons and a daughter with his second, Mary Ball, among whom the eldest was George.

In the first six years of Washington's life, his family moved three times, finally settling at the Ferry Farm Plantation near Fredericksburg, where they were living when his father died. This is where Washington spent his boyhood, receiving tutoring from an unknown teacher or teachers in all of the fields that a planter's son would be expected to master: mathematics, accounting, an understanding of legal instruments such as deeds and wills.

Augustine Washington left enough money to keep his families comfortable, but it was George's older half brother, Lawrence, who lifted the family into the upper tier of Virginia society by marrying Ann Fairfax of the rich and influential Fairfax family. Lawrence Washington had received a liberal education in England, a luxury not available to George after the family's fortunes fell with his father's death; Lawrence moved comfortably in the upper strata of society and showed George how to do the same.

At the age of 19, George accompanied Lawrence on a trip to Barbados intended to improve Lawrence's health (he suffered from tuberculosis), the only sea voyage Washington ever made. Washington contracted smallpox on this trip, which made him immune to the recurrent epidemics of the 1770s; it also may have rendered him sterile.

Through his brother's connections with the Fairfax family, George, at the age of 20, won a lucrative sinecure as a county surveyor—in his studies he had demonstrated a natural talent for the field; Lord Thomas Fairfax had previously hired a 16-year-old Washington to accompany a survey party across the Blue Ridge Mountains in 1748 to document Fairfax's vast, ancestral holdings in the Shenandoah Valley. Washington, a precociously ambitious young man, used some of the £400 he earned as a surveyor to buy 2,300 acres of his own in the Shenandoah.

Following his brother's death in 1752, Washington took Lawrence's place as an adjutant in the Virginia militia, earning another £100 a year. With his military and surveying incomes, plus receipts from tobacco grown on his Shenandoah Valley lands, Washington was doing all right for a 21-year-old.[4]

But lands west of the Appalachian Mountains, such as Washington's Bullskin Plantation, were then at the nexus of a growing dispute among France, England, and the Native American tribes that had long lived there. By the mid-1700s, both the French and the English realized enormous profits trading in furs and deerskin with the tribes, and they understood that the Ohio River Valley was key to tapping into the Mississippi and controlling the vast continent's interior.

+>==+

On April 2, 1754, George Washington marched out of Alexandria, leading two companies totaling 167 officers and men. He was a tall man, somewhere between six feet and six-foot-two, slender but broad-shouldered and strong, with blue eyes, thin eyebrows, thin lips, sandy hair, and a barn owl's wide face.[5] His regiment climbed the Blue Ridge Mountains, crossing through Vestal Gap, then ferrying across the Shenandoah. Less than three weeks into their march, word came that 1,000 French with 18 artillery pieces had come down the Ohio in canoes and ordered a few dozen members of the Ohio Company erecting a fort at the forks to leave. They did, and a primary objective of the mission, securing the Forks of the Ohio, had been lost.

At his camp on Wills Creek in the Appalachians of western Maryland, Washington held a council of war to determine what to do next. He took stock of his situation: He had in camp 167 troops plus a few dozen men from the Ohio Company whom he had deputized as militia—men who turned out to be more liability than asset. The French toward whom he was marching had about 1,000 men.

"It was thought a Thing impractical to march towards the Fort without sufficient strength," Washington wrote in his diary. But the Seneca Chief, Tanacharison, made a strong case before the war council that his warriors needed to see English troops gathering in the region to buck up their spirits.

And, Washington figured, help was on the way: The overall commander of this expedition, Colonel Joshua Fry, was crossing the Blue Ridge with 10 cannon and 100 men to round out the Virginia regiment of nearly 300. Two independent companies paid and equipped by King George II had also been raised to head for the Ohio and together they'd bring another 300 men commissioned as regular troops. North Carolina had also raised 400 men under Colonel James Innes, and Tanacharison had pledged fidelity from the Six Nations tribes and their allies in the region; with artillery, 1,000 men, plus assistance from the Indians, it looked like the English could gather a credible threat.

From Wills Creek, Washington decided to press on: He pushed his troops deeper into the backcountry toward Redstone Old Fort, more than 80 miles distant on the Monongahela River. There the Ohio Company had already built a blockhouse that could be used for a fort to meet the French threat. In order to clear the way for the troops and artillery that he was sure would follow him, Washington had his men chop a road through the wilderness, slowing their progress to a mere two or three miles a day.

By May 9, they had cut through two dozen miles of forest to a place called the Little Meadows; there Washington dismissed the Ohio Company laborers he had deputized. They had become a sullen drag on the camp after having their wages cut to 8 pence per day, the same rate as Washington's volunteers. His detachment was now down to about 160 men, but Washington was as optimistic as he was indefatigable—he continued to push on, eventually pitching camp in the Great Meadows, a boggy clearing in the forest between two hulking mountains.

Naturally, the French learned of a detachment of English encamped about 50 miles south of the Forks; with advance scouts from both sides prowling the woods, conflict was a distinct possibility.

As heavy clouds descended just before sundown on May 27, 1754, a mounted messenger galloped into George Washington's camp bearing news from Tanacharison, the Half King: He had followed the tracks of two men toward what Washington described in his diary as a "low obscure Place" in the woods, where the footprints merged with the tracks of many. Tanacharison was sure a party of French was hidden in a glen there, about seven miles northwest of Washington's camp.

Washington immediately ordered 40 men under arms for a nighttime march toward Tanacharison's camp. They stumbled through the rain, men bumping into each other in the darkness, frequently losing the path then finding it again; they wandered into the Indian camp around daybreak, where they united with 13 warriors and hiked in single file toward the secluded glen. When they reached the glen, they encircled it. Down in the hollow, a few of the French soldiers had emerged from their bark-over-stick lodgings to light smoky fires of wet wood for their breakfasts.

"We were advanced pretty near to them . . . when they discovered us," Washington wrote in his diaries, "whereupon I ordered my Company to fire."[6]

+══─══+

In pulling his trigger, Washington provided the casus belli for France and England to resume long-standing hostilities. The resumption of war between these two European powers, sparked in an obscure glen in western Pennsylvania, drew in their allies overseas and ignited the Seven Years' War, a global conflagration that would burn for more than seven years and eventually engulf France, England, Spain, India, Austria, several German states, and dozens of American Indian nations with battles fought as far away as the Philippines.[7] The boom of musket fire lasted less than 15 minutes, but the controversy over who started it lasts till this day.

From Washington's point of view, the French party of 35 men were "spies" sent to gather intelligence about his troop strength and to reconnoiter the roads, rivers, and landscape all the way to the Potomac. He had surprised them in their camp and, as he wrote to Dinwiddie days after the skirmish, "Fir'd briskly till they were defeated."

When the smoke cleared, 1 of Washington's men was dead and 3 were wounded. All 35 of the French but 1 were captured or killed. From Washington's viewpoint, a hostile force skulking about near his encampment had gotten what it deserved.

Among the French dead was the party's commander, Joseph Coulon de Villiers, sieur de Jumonville. From the French point of view, Jumonville was on an ambassadorial mission to present Washington with a summons demanding that he quit the area, similar to the summons that Washington had delivered to Fort Le Boeuf. The ambush of an ambassadorial party was an egregious war crime.

When the firing began one French soldier, a Canadian named Monceau, managed to slip out of the noose of English and Indian troops and escape. According to Monceau, the French troops were surprised in their camp at around 7 A.M., when the English poured two volleys into their ranks. Jumonville then successfully called for a cease-fire. He gave his summons to the English and gathered his troops peacefully around him while awaiting their reply. Monceau did not wait for the answer; he made his way barefoot through the woods to the Monongahela, where he had stashed a little canoe.

The last Monceau knew, when the firing ceased, Jumonville was still alive. How did he die? One of Tanacharison's warriors said that he knew. Days after the skirmish, the warrior appeared before the French erecting a fort at the Forks and told their commander that during the cease-fire, Washington's troops shot Jumonville through the head in cold blood. The "English" would have killed all of the surviving French "had not the Indians who were present, by rushing between them and the *English,* prevented their design."[8]

Two other accounts of the skirmish at what became known as Jumonville's Rocks surfaced, one told by a man who was there and another told by one of Washington's soldiers who was not present in the glen but who shared campfires with, and heard the story time and again from, those who were. In several key aspects, these stories aligned: When the firing ceased, Jumonville was wounded but alive, and he did send over a summons. While Washington pored over the document, Tanacharison, the Half King, approached the wounded Jumonville and said something in French. According to a deserter from Washington's camp, an Indian warrior named Denis Kaninguen, Tanacharison said, "Thou art not yet dead, my father." Then he cleaved Jumonville's head with a hatchet, reached into the skull, and pulled out his brains.[9] At this, Tanacharison's warriors ran amok, killing all of the wounded French, taking their weapons, accoutrements, and scalps.

This last version has the ring of truth. The warrior sent to the French camp to blame Jumonville's death on the English had an obvious agenda: to ingratiate Tanacharison's warriors with the most powerful army in the Ohio.

And Washington's terse account failed to reconcile the impossibly high ratio of French dead to French wounded, variously stated by Washington as 10 to 1 or 12 to 0. The muskets of that time were neither accurate nor lethal enough to engender that kind of ratio—after any battle or skirmish, the tally of wounded to dead almost always ran between 2 or 3 wounded for every 1 killed. (Washington had suffered 3 wounded and 1 killed.)

Denis Kaninguen's account makes the most sense of them all. As a Six Nations chief, Tanacharison's power base was in the Finger Lakes region of

New York; he had been steadily losing his authority over the Ohio region tribes to the south, and he desperately wanted help from those tribes to remove the French from the Ohio.[10] To get their attention, he needed French booty and scalps as tangible evidence of English power and will to drive off the French.

Tanacharison often played the part of the obsequious Indian; but he was older than Washington, had far more experience, and had shrewdly summed up the young colonel as "a good-natured man" who "had no experience."[11] When Tanacharison's warriors fell on the French wounded, standard tactics for Iroquois warriors, the 22-year-old Washington in his first combat command could do nothing but watch.

In his first after-action report to Governor Dinwiddie, Washington wrote: "[A]fter an Engagement of 15 Minutes we killd 10, wounded one and took 21 Prisoner's, among those that were killd was Monsieur De Jumonville the Commander." In his diary, Washington dryly noted: "The *Indians* scalped the dead."[12]

Technically, everything that Washington wrote was almost true: It was more like 13 French killed with 1 or none left wounded; and the Indians did scalp the dead. But his report left out so much as to appear untruthful, a lie to cover up what Europeans would view as a massacre. Only after Governor Dinwiddie expressed his approbation of the killing and capturing of the French (he even ordered medals struck for the occasion) did Washington 'fess up a little; in a follow-up letter to Dinwiddie, he wrote: "There were 5, or 6 other Indian[s], who servd to knock the poor unhappy wounded in the head and believ'd them of their Scalps."[13] In a letter written from Great Meadows to his brother John, Washington boasted about the fighting: "I fortunately escaped without a wound, tho' the right Wing where I stood was exposed to & received all the Enemy's fire and was the part where the man was killed & the rest wounded. I can with truth assure you, I heard Bulletts whistle and believe me there was something charming in the sound."[14]

CHAPTER 2

Fort Necessity

THE DAY AFTER THE MASSACRE AT JUMONVILLE'S ROCKS, AN EXPRESS rider thundered out of Washington's camp at Great Meadows bound for Winchester, Virginia, a trip of nearly 70 miles across the wide Potomac and over the Blue Ridge Mountains.

The rider carried an urgent letter from Washington to the commander of this foray into the Ohio, Colonel Joshua Fry, who in civilian life was an Oxford-educated professor at the College of William and Mary in Williamsburg. In his letter, Washington pleaded for Fry to hustle up from Winchester with his artillery and the rest of the Virginia Regiment.

Colonel Washington was now in a vulnerable spot, and he knew it. He heard rumors that the new French fort at the Forks of the Ohio had received reinforcements and was now more than 1,000 men strong. Washington was aware that one man had escaped from Jumonville's camp and had no doubt that he would carry word of the French defeat back to the fort, now christened Fort Duquesne. Soon a large party of French bent on revenge would be spilling out of the fort and marching his way.

Washington wrote Fry: "If there does not come a sufficient Reinforcement we must either quit our gd [ground], & retn to you or fight very unequal Number's which I will do before I will give up one Inch of what we have gaind."[1]

George Washington liked to gamble, and judging from the detailed financial ledgers that he routinely kept with his numerous notations of money lost "at cards," he was not particularly good at it.[2] He was now about to take a gamble with the lives of his troops. Rather than retreat and yield even an inch of ground, he would hope that fate would deal him reinforcements before turning up the French.

In his diary entry for May 30, 1754, Washington wrote from Great Meadows: "Began to raise a Fort with small Pallisadoes, fearing that when the *French* should hear News of the Defeat, we might be attacked by considerable forces." Two days later his diary entry read: "We are finishing our Fort."[3]

As might be expected of a fort that took few days to build, it was small and not very formidable. It was built of white oak logs, each about 7 feet tall and 10 inches round; they were split, with the flat sides facing out. The log wall formed a circle 53 feet in diameter, a space large enough to hold only 50 or 60 men. In case of attack, most of the Virginia Regiment would have to take cover in a circular entrenchment that formed a ring about 8 yards outside of the walls.

Washington called his little fort in Great Meadows "Fort Necessity," and he was quite proud of it, writing Dinwiddie on June 3: "We have just finish'd a small palisadod Fort in which with my small Number's I shall not fear the attack of 500 men."[4] Tanacharison had a different opinion of Fort Necessity; he called it "that little thing upon the meadow"[5] and resolved that his people would never be caught dead in it.

A week after Washington sent his express rider over the mountains to Winchester, he received a reply: The rest of the Virginia Regiment was heading his way, but Colonel Fry would not be leading them. En route from Winchester, Fry had been thrown from his horse and died. Command of all the armies in the expedition passed to Colonel James Innes, who was supposed to lead 400 North Carolina volunteers and two independent companies from New York into Washington's camp. He never did; Innes and his men never came within 30 miles of Fort Necessity. This left young Washington in full command of the Virginia Regiment.

Washington did receive some reinforcements: on June 9, the Second Division of the Virginia Regiment finally joined his 160 men, dragging with them nine swivel guns—small, horse-drawn cannon that could fire two-pound balls. And a few days after that, Captain James Mackay marched in with 100 red-coated members of the South Carolina Independent Company, professional soldiers who drew their commission directly from King George II. Since he drew his commission from the king, Mackay thought himself and his company superior to Washington and his Virginians.

Mackay refused to accept even the most basic orders from Washington, such as what the day's password should be for going to and from the fort. After a few days of living side by side but separately with the Independent Company, Washington grew impatient. Rather than wait for a French attack that had not materialized, he would take his nearly 300 Virginians and press on for Redstone Old Fort, nearer to the 1,100 men in the French fort at the Forks. Washington possessed a boldness of spirit, an edgy audacity that time and wisdom tempered but, to his credit, never dulled.

Washington still believed that Colonel Innes was going to come up with the North Carolinians and the New York Independent Companies and 10 pieces of heavier artillery; he and his Virginians would cut them a nice road to Redstone Old Fort and would welcome them there. Captain Mackay refused to send men on this road-building expedition on the grounds that real soldiers do not build roads.

So Washington, his men, and wagons carrying equipment, baggage, and the swivel guns set out toward the French garrisoned in Fort Duquesne. They did not get far. The terrain was so hilly, steep, and ribbed with ledge that wagons broke on the newly cleared road and horses dropped dead of exhaustion. The local tribes—Delaware, Shawnee, and Mingo—assessed the two opposing powers—the 1,000-plus French in their strong fort versus the 400 English with their broken wagons and starving horses—and dropped hints to Washington that they would be going over to the French. Even Tanacharison, who complained that Washington was "always driving them to fight by his directions," gathered up his followers and ran away.[6]

On June 28, Washington called for a council of war at the house of Christopher Gist, his former frontier guide, just 13 miles north of his new fort in Great Meadows. Mackay, chastised by a letter from Governor Dinwiddie stressing that he was fourth in command and Washington was second, had reluctantly marched his 100 Independents over the steep, rocky road that Washington had carved out to Gist's. There the officers met an Oneida chief who had spent two days traveling from the French fort. He confirmed reports of reinforcements arriving there, saying he had "heard them declare their Resolution to march and Attack the English with 800 of their own men and 400 Indians."[7]

Washington had strayed far beyond the limits of his supply lines; his camp had received no bread or meat in nearly a week, and knew of no plans to deliver any. So the war council decided: It was time to head back to Fort Necessity, to await provisions.

The retreat went slowly. With most draft horses dead from overwork, the men had to haul the swivel guns over what one officer called the "roughest and most hilly road of any on the Alleghany Mountains." For food, all they had was a ration of parched corn. Naturally the Independent Company refused to haul swivel guns or baggage, or serve as scouts along the road, which, one captain observed, "had an unhappy Effect on our men."[8]

For parts of three days the men labored, finally reaching Great Meadows on July 1, 1754, where they hoped to find fresh supplies. There were none. Later that day a convoy arrived, but it carried only a few bags of flour to supplement the corn.

Meanwhile, a strong force of 600 French regulars and Canadian militia, plus 100 Indians, had left Fort Duquesne, paddled upstream against the northward-flowing Monongahela, and began to march from Redstone Creek. At their head was Captain Louis Coulon de Villiers, the late Jumonville's older brother. He had specifically asked for this command to avenge his brother's death.

⊹⊱═⊰⊹

In the predawn darkness of July 3, the French marched down the road that Washington had cut between Gist's settlement and Great Meadows. "We marched the whole Day in the Rain, and I sent out Scouts one after another," Villiers wrote in his journal. "I Stopped at the Place where my Brother had been assassinated."[9] Some dead lay there still, unburied and partially eaten by animals.

At 9 A.M., Washington's scouts reported a large party of French soldiers only four miles away. After the hard march to Fort Necessity, his returns that morning showed only 284 men fit for duty;[10] these troops dug furiously into the black muck of the meadow, throwing up embankments in front of their ring of trenches, which were cut only two feet deep. They dug for two hours until they saw columns of French regulars and Indians filing down a wooded hill. Washington hoped that his enemy would charge across a cleared field in an attempt to storm his fort, but there was no reason for them to—he had not made the clearing wide enough, and the edge of the woods provided cover within easy musket range of the fort. At one point the woods came as close as 60 yards, and the enemy forces began to concentrate there. Washington ordered his troops to march in regular formations on the open field in hopes of driving the French and Indian forces off this closest wooded slope.

As Washington's troops marched into the meadow, a couple of dozen Indians ran at them; the head of the second division, Lieutenant Colonel George Muse, called to his men to halt. Concerned that the French would sneak into the fort behind him (or so he later said), Muse ordered his division into the fort, saving his skin but leaving a flank of Mackay's regulars unprotected. Two volleys from the regulars drove the Indians back, but rather than continuing a fight with his flank exposed Mackay withdrew his men into the trenches, dashing Washington's hopes of flushing the French out of the woods and onto the open field.

All of Washington's 284 fighting men were within easy range of muskets trained on them by French soldiers and Indian warriors firing from behind trees and downed logs. The woods flared with musket fire. Washington's men fired back. "We continued this unequal Fight, with an Enemy sheltered behind the Trees, ourselves without Shelter, in Trenches full of Water," Washington and Mackay wrote in a joint letter to Dinwiddie.[11]

The hard rains of the night before resumed, flooding the trenches in black, muddy water, which also filled with blood. The French and Indians shot at anything that moved, downing all of Washington's horses and cattle, shooting even the camp dogs.

By dusk, a third of Washington's men lay wounded or killed. Washington's men were covered in mud and blood, and Washington's powder was wet, his cattle were killed, and musket balls were whistling in from all sides. And then the firing ceased. The French called for a parley, a meeting to discuss terms of Washington's surrender. Unwilling to let French negotiators into his fort, where they could see how truly desperate his situation was, Washington sent two negotiators into the woods to discuss terms there.

In the lull of negotiations, some of the fort's survivors broke into the rum supply, a necessary staple for taking the edge off the hard living of an eighteenth-century army camp, and dipped liberally from the two hogsheads—big, chest-high barrels that Dinwiddie had recently sent. "It was no sooner dark than one-half of our men got drunk," wrote a captain, Adam Stephen.[12]

After some back-and-forth discussions, negotiators brought Washington a rain-soaked copy of the articles of capitulation, written with poor penmanship in French. Using a flickering candle for light, Jacob Van Braam, a 29-year-old captain of the Virginia Regiment, attempted to translate the surrender terms.[13] Van Braam, a native speaker of Dutch, knew only passable French and even less English.

The articles insisted that Washington confess to the "assassination" of a French officer, Jumonville. But somehow, Van Braam failed to point this out to Washington. He read the assassination of Jumonville as "the death" or "loss" of Jumonville. Washington absolutely would not have accepted terms in which he admitted to being an assassin. He later suspected that Van Braam deliberately avoided using the word "assassination" so that Washington would accept the surrender terms and the captain could get out of Great Meadows alive; but it is more likely that a native speaker of Dutch translating French into English from a muddy scrap of paper by candlelight had no idea that Villiers was demanding that Washington confess to assassinating an emissary.[14] Other than that, the articles were fairly favorable to Washington: At daybreak, his men could march from the fort with anything they could carry; Villiers even granted "the honors of war," which allowed the men to march with drums beating, carrying their colors, and hauling one ceremonial swivel gun.

To his men's relief and to his own lifelong regret, Washington signed the document.

<hr>

From the Governor's Palace in Williamsburg, a brick mansion of 10,000 square feet surrounded with gated fences, orchards, and gardens, Governor

Dinwiddie had no conception of what camp life was like for Washington and his troops. After surrendering Fort Necessity, the army—minus the 30 men who died fighting in Great Meadows—trudged the 50 miles back to Wills Creek, hauling some of their 70 wounded in makeshift litters. Among the wounded was one of Washington's slaves, who later died of his wounds.[15] By the time the men reached Wills Creek, most had worn through their shoes and stockings; they were barefoot and without hats or blankets or any reliable way of receiving provisions. They withdrew to Alexandria, with troops deserting daily; deserters are as bad as spies to an army, perhaps worse, for they carry off weapons, reduce manpower, and deliver intelligence into the wrong hands. Washington wanted to lash or hang deserters but could not, for they had enlisted as militia and were not under the same regulations as regular troops; militiamen could not be severely punished, while troops could be whipped or even executed.[16]

The French, however, were living well. Villiers had avenged his brother's death, burned Fort Necessity, blown up the Ohio Company's blockhouse at Redstone Creek, and marched his men triumphantly into well-stocked Fort Duquesne. Many of the Indians who marched with him were Washington's former allies; the French now firmly controlled the Ohio River Valley, and Dinwiddie could not stand it.

On August 1, 1754, not one month after the defeat at Fort Necessity, Dinwiddie, ensconced in his mansion, ordered Washington to cross the Alleghanies again with his defeated, demoralized troops and drive the French from their fort. The order was ludicrous and Washington said so, not to Dinwiddie but in a letter to Colonel Innes, whose troops still had not pushed beyond Winchester. In a second letter to Innes, Washington showed devotion to duty even when orders defy common sense, writing: "If you think it advisable to order me in the shatterd Condition we are in to March up to you, I will, if no more than ten Men follows me (which I believe will be the full amount.)"[17]

Innes agreed that there was no reason for Washington to come up. Finally, Virginia's House of Burgesses, which held the army's purse strings, put an end to Dinwiddie's scheme by refusing to grant any more supplies to the expedition, bringing a close to the campaign of 1754 with the French in firm control of the Ohio Valley.

Public perception plays an important role in a military officer's career, and there was some grumbling about Washington's handling of his first field command.[18] One way of viewing Washington's performance was that he had allowed warriors under his command to massacre defenseless, wounded soldiers—and covered it up; that he recklessly marched his men toward a decidedly superior force and placed them in an untenable position where they were soundly beaten, thus losing the entire strategic objective of his command; and that he inadvertently confessed to assassinating an emissary from a country with which he was not at war.

Governor Dinwiddie and other influential Virginians had a vested interest in casting Washington's story in a more charitable light. They wanted the French gone from the Ohio Valley, and they needed assistance from London and the other provinces to drive them out. So the House of Burgesses made heroes out of Washington and his men, passing a resolution honoring all of the officers—except for Van Braam and Muse—"for their late gallant and brave Behaviour."[19]

Washington rode into Williamsburg on October 21, 1754, the proud owner of a medal cast for the Jumonville Rocks affair and a bona fide "gallant," honored as a hero by the House.

Two weeks later, Dinwiddie abolished the rank of colonel in his state's militia, effectively demoting Washington. In redeploying the Virginia troops for the next year's campaign, the governor decided that rather than have a single colonel, he would break the regiment into 10 independent companies of 100 men each, and the heads of these companies would hold the rank of captain. Washington could have had one of these captaincies, but any officer with a king's commission would have been his superior; thus he would have been reduced to taking orders from some of the very men he so recently commanded.

Rather than accept a demotion, Washington resigned his colonel's commission and moved into the Potomac River farmhouse he was leasing, and soon would inherit, from the estate of his recently deceased half brother Lawrence.

Washington explained his resignation to William Fitzhugh, a man who had served with the late Lawrence Washington in the British navy under Admiral Edward Vernon. Lawrence had admired Vernon so much that he had named his simple farmhouse perched on a bluff overlooking the Potomac River "Mount Vernon" after him.

Washington wrote Fitzhugh:

> I must be reduced to a very low Command and subjected to that of many who acted my inferior Officers. In short, every Captain, bearing the King's Commission; every half-pay Officer, or other, appearing with such commission, would rank before me; for these reasons, I choose to submit to the loss of Health, which I have, however, already sustained . . . and the fatigue I have undergone in our first Efforts; than subject myself to the same inconveniences, and run the same risque of a second disappointment. I shall have the consolation, itself, of knowing, that I have opened the way when the smallness of our numbers exposed us to the attacks of a Superior Enemy; that I have hitherto stood the heat and brunt of the Day, and escaped untouched, in time of extreme danger; and that I have the Thanks of My Country, for the Services I have rendered it.

Still, Washington wrote Fitzhugh, he hated quitting the service: "My inclinations are strongly bent to arms."[20]

CHAPTER 3

Braddock's Defeat

AFTER GEORGE WASHINGTON RESIGNED FROM THE ARMY, HE found himself busy with domestic affairs. He was charged with equitably dividing the 62 slaves left by Lawrence Washington—Lawrence's widow received 31 people, and the other 31 were split among Washington and his surviving brothers. The division was made by assigning each enslaved person a monetary value, then distributing them so that all parties received an equal share of strong and weak slaves. The child slaves were assessed no value but were distributed by height. For example, Doll, at 3 foot 7 inches, was assigned to the widow; and Prince, at 3 foot 7.5 inches, was assigned to the brothers.[1]

As surely as Washington did not wish to resign from the military, the powers prosecuting the war did not wish for him to leave. Although he was only 22 years old when he resigned his commission in 1754, he was an experienced leader who had fought this enemy on this ground; he knew the country as far as Fort Le Boeuf, and could draw a decent map of it from memory. Washington would be a good man to have in camp.

On February 20, 1755, three ships flying the Union Jack anchored in harbor at Hampton, Virginia; aboard the *Norwich* was General Edward Braddock, the new commander of all English troops in North America.[2] At first blush, Braddock looked like an answer to Dinwiddie's prayers: He was a long-serving, 59-year-old major general sent by King George II with two regiments of regulars to flush the French out of the Ohio Valley.

Braddock and his aide, Robert Orme, wasted no time in calling on Dinwiddie at Williamsburg to learn the lay of the land. Naturally Washington's name came up, and on March 2, Orme sent Washington a polite proposal: "The General [Braddock] having been informd that you exprest some desire to make the Campaigne, but that you declind it upon some disagreeableness that you thought might arise from the Regulation of Command, has ordered me to acquaint you that he will be very glad of your Company in his Family, by which all inconveniences of the kind will be obviated."[3]

By offering Washington a slot in Braddock's military "family" as a volunteer aide-de-camp, Braddock had placed him above the reach of captains or anyone else. Only Braddock could give orders to his aides, and it was the business of the aides to pass on the orders to subordinates.

In ingratiating himself with authority, Washington could be unctuously solicitous, as he was in his reply to Braddock's proposal; after calling Braddock a man of "great good Character" Washington wrote: "To be plain, Sir, I wish for nothing more earnestly, than to attain a small degree of knowledge in the Military Art: and believeing a more favourable opportunity cannot be wishd than serving under a Gentleman of his Excellencys known ability and experience it <does as you may reasonably> suppose, not a little contribute to influence me in my choice."[4]

Washington delayed joining Braddock's army until April 24, 1755, when he rode off from Mount Vernon against his mother's wish that he stay out of harm's way. He rode in no hurry, convinced that Braddock's troops would move slowly with all the baggage and the train of artillery that they were attempting to haul into the woods and over the mountains on freshly cut, steep, stumpy roads.

Braddock's train of artillery would be wonderful for razing a frontier fort like Fort Duquesne—if he could get it there. The train consisted of four 12-pound cannon—each one weighing more than a ton and requiring seven horses to pull it; six 6-pound cannon, generally weighing 1,300 pounds apiece and requiring at least a four-horse team; four 8-inch howitzers, heavier even than the 12-pound cannon; and 15 Coehorn mortars, weighing 86 pounds apiece, plus shot, shells, and powder. The mortars and supplies were placed on about three dozen wagons, each pulled by teams of six. The artillery train alone required more than 300 horses consuming enormous amounts of forage as they labored to pull one-ton cannons up mountain faces that scaled 3,000 feet.[5]

In early May, Washington caught up to Braddock at Frederick, Maryland, where the general had been delayed trying to obtain horses and wagons. With Braddock, he crossed the Potomac into Winchester, Virginia, a town of four cross streets and 60 houses that Washington described as a "hole"; here they waited till the second division of the artillery caught up with them on its way to the campaign's staging area at Wills Creek.

Finally, on May 14, Braddock, Washington, and the other aides arrived at Wills Creek, where troops had been employed since winter building a square fort, with log walls 120 feet long and 12 feet high, enclosing a house for Braddock, four storehouses, and a powder magazine. They called it Fort Cumberland (modern-day Cumberland, Maryland) after the Duke of Cumberland, one of King George II's sons. Braddock's quartermaster, Sir John St. Clair, found it a miserable fort, poorly placed on low ground with no key transport route; although St. Clair tended to be negative about everything and everyone he saw in America, his judgment of Fort Cumberland was spot on.

<hr/>

Washington's first impression of Braddock was good; he wrote his mother in early May: "I am very happy in the Genrals Family, as I am treated with a complaisant Freedom which is quite agreeable." But within a month, Washington had come to see Braddock as short-tempered, impatient, imperious, and given to "rudeness."[6]

Braddock railed against Virginians and Marylanders for failing to send wagons and forage for his troops; the Pennsylvanians curried favor thanks to Ben Franklin, who promised to deliver 150 wagons with horses and 1,500 packhorses.

The wait for all of the horses and forage to come into camp was interminable, but important developments were taking place in the camp. A delegation of possibly friendly Indians came in to negotiate with Braddock; six chiefs of the Ohio tribes were still on the fence—the French seemed to be the stronger power, but to these chiefs they appeared too strong, powerful enough to settle the Ohio and drive the natives from their long-established villages. The Indians were willing to help Braddock beat the French if he would promise to leave them enough hunting grounds to support themselves and their families.

Braddock sincerely wanted the Indians on his side, but his nature ran more toward bluntness than duplicity. He had no plans to grant the Indians the land they wished to retain and rather than lie he told them so, replying: "No savage shall inherit the land."[7]

When Braddock's reply reached tribes in the valley, many warriors went over to the French.[8]

By June 7, the army was 2,900 men strong, but among them were only 7 Indian warriors, a weakness because the Indians had a far better knowledge of the ground and wilderness fighting tactics. After three days on the road, the army, encumbered by heavy artillery, had covered but 5 miles; Braddock called a council to reconsider his transportation. His intended march from Fort Cumberland to Fort Duquesne was 110 miles; at the rate they were going, they'd be there in September—and time was of the essence. Before Braddock had sent them away angry, Indians had tried to warn Braddock that nearly 1,000 French reinforcements were flocking to Fort Duquesne. Braddock had not believed them, but Washington did;, as he wrote to William Fairfax: "[W]e are assur'd that 900 Men has certainly passed Oswego, to reinforce[e]e the French on Ohio, so . . . we have reason to believe we shall have more to do than go up the Hills to come down again."[9]

To move things along, all of the officers, including Washington, agreed to give up some of their baggage in order to free up packhorses and lighten the wagon loads. They also sent back to Fort Cumberland 4 of the six-pound cannon, 6 of the smaller mortars, the 16 heavy-duty wagons that King George had sent (they were too heavy for backcountry horses to pull), some powder, and some stores.

Still, their progress was tediously slow. On June 15, as the army straggled on for Little Meadows, its wagon train stretched five miles from beginning to end. The first brigade had begun the march eight days earlier and had scarcely covered two dozen miles. "The horses grew every day fainter, and many died," wrote Robert Orme, Washington's fellow aide.

Washington himself was also growing fainter and fainter, as he plunged into the throes of what he called the "bloody flux"—dysentery. He was "seizd with vio[lent Fevers] and P[ains]" in his head. Still, when Braddock came to him outside Little Meadows to ask his "private opinion" of what to do next, Washington was yet lucid enough to lay out a scheme that Braddock adopted: An advance division would move forward as quickly as it could without waiting for the baggage train, which would be left under the care of about 800 men commanded by Colonel Thomas Dunbar. Dunbar's train of artillery and supply wagons lacked enough horses to move all at once—he'd move half his supplies, then send the horses back to bring up the rest. Under this scheme, the baggage train fell farther and farther behind.

Washington's bloody flux made him too sick so sit a horse, so he rode with the advance division in a covered wagon—but the jolting of wagon wheel over rocky road proved too much to bear. About 21 miles north of Little Meadows, Braddock left Washington on the road with a guard, where they waited two days for the baggage train to collect them. A pinch of "James's Powder"—a mixture of lime phosphate and oxide of antimony—brought immediate "ease," Washington wrote to his brother John, "and removed my Fevrs and other Comp[laints] in 4 Days time."[10]

Even when his fever settled some, Washington was still too weak to ride a horse; but when Braddock ordered some covered wagons forward with supplies, Washington jumped into one for a rocky, tooth-rattling ride to the front.

Washington's wagon arrived in Braddock's camp on July 8. The advance division of the army was now about a dozen miles from Fort Duquesne, and Braddock was tantalizingly close to pulling off a miraculous journey of 110 miles through the wilderness with enough heavy artillery to blow a fort to smithereens.

The camp came to life at 2 A.M. on July 9, as a vanguard of about 350 troops under Lieutenant Colonel Thomas Gage began to march down Sugar Run to the Monongahela River. The approach plan called for crossing the Monongahela to the west bank, then re-crossing it, climbing an incline cut through a sandy bank, and making a beeline for the fort through a natural corridor with the river to the left and a wooded hill rising to the right.[11]

In a midsummer drought, the river crossings were easy. Washington felt well enough to mount a horse for the first time in weeks, though he still felt "very weak and low"; he padded his saddle with pillows to reduce the shock of hooves striking ground, mounted, and joined Braddock in the line of march.[12]

Not long after noon, everyone had crossed the second ford and the column moved through the narrows in the finest formation, beating the grenadier's march. At the head were 7 Indian scouts and a frontiersman; then came Gage with his 350, many of them regulars from the 44th Foot. Then came Horatio Gates with 100 men from the New York Independent Companies, out in front of 250 carpenters and pioneers, chopping and sawing to clear a road 12 feet wide.

The road clearing was easier than it had been in days. Sir John St. Clair, the quartermaster overseeing the road-building party, had noted that the woods in the frontier were so dark and thick with undergrowth that "one may go twenty Miles without seeing before him ten yards."[13] In the narrows between the river and the hill, all that underbrush had been burned away so that you could drive wagons around and between the trees. St. Clair did not know it, but the Indians had burned off this land with controlled fires to create tender shoots of new growth that lured animals in, while the clearing provided Indian hunters with fine site lines for shooting.

Braddock's party had blundered onto an Indian hunting ground and was about to become the prey.

+==+

On July 9, 1755, George Washington rode next to General Braddock, sandwiched between the carpenters and pioneers clearing the road in front of them and 500 red-coated regular soldiers moving in two columns behind. Beyond the regulars came 30 troops of light horse, 11 artillery pieces, 50 camp women, cattle, pack animals, and dozens of supply wagons; and behind them came a rear guard of 100 Virginia provincials. The whole party from beginning to end stretched nearly a mile. Their flanks were securely protected by 60 men patrolling the woods down to the river on their left and another 60 combing the rising woods to their right.

Around 1 P.M., scouts spotted French and Indian soldiers moving toward them through the woods. The enemy was about 200 yards off, out of effective musket range; still, Gage's vanguard fired three thundering volleys, and a lucky shot felled the party's captain, Daniel Li'enard de Beaujeu.

Beaujeu had been sent from Fort Duquesne that morning with a detachment of 72 French regulars, 146 Canadian militia, 36 officers, and 637 Indian warriors from more than a half dozen tribes. He was supposed to ambush Braddock's column at one of the river fords, but Braddock had stolen the march on him with his 2 A.M. departure, and Beaujeu had been late to the field. Now he was dead, an auspicious beginning for Braddock.

Losing a field commander would be enough to spread confusion among troops of British regulars, who looked to their officers for direction. But most of Beaujeu's party was made up of Indian warriors; they did not need anyone to tell them how to fight on this ground.

At the sound of firing, Braddock ordered half of his 500 regulars forward, where they ran into the 250 unarmed laborers, who dropped their tools and fled to the rear. Gage's vanguard of 300 and the flanking parties of 60 men each were also being driven back by heavy musket fire from the French and Indian forces.

The confused men, about 900 strong, converged under withering fire, some being ordered forward, others reflexively flinching from the fire pouring in from the front. Braddock ordered the colors of the two regiments brought forward as rallying posts, but the men of those regiments couldn't or wouldn't follow in regular formation.

The 600-plus Indians filed down the riverbank on the left and atop the thickly wooded high ground to Braddock's right, forming a horseshoe around Braddock's train. On either side, frightful war whoops filled the woods; most of the regulars had never seen combat, and those who had fought had never seen tactics like this on the battlefields of Europe. Braddock's train was stalled in a crossfire; the shooting from the high ground was particularly heavy.

St. Clair, his clothes bloody from a wound, staggered up to Braddock and begged him "for God-Sake . . . gain the rising ground" on the right—then he fainted from loss of blood.[14]

The most maddening thing was that the English could not see their enemy. The Indians used trees, brush, rocks, and ravines to their advantage, rarely firing from the same place twice.

Braddock and his aides—Washington, Orme, Captain Robert Morris, and a secretary, William Shirley Jr. (a son of the Massachusetts governor)—

made conspicuous targets for the 637 Indians. With the crack of bullet on bone Shirley got blown off his horse, a musket ball lodged fatally in his head; Orme and Morris also went down early, Orme with a shot through his thigh, Morris with his nose clipped by a bullet. Gage had one eyebrow singed by a slug. Braddock had four horses shot out from under him; Washington's horse with the padded saddle went down, forcing him to remount—and his second horse was killed too. He mounted a third and rode on with Braddock.

Braddock could not easily remove his men through a nearly mile-long gauntlet of musket fire. The troops were now clustered in knots, firing through a haze of smoke at the dark spaces between trees. When their shots hit anything at all, they most frequently struck their own men; of every three balls that surgeons extracted from wounds, two were the larger British balls, one was the smaller ball of the French.[15]

For more than two hours, troops stayed in the field. Several of the Virginia officers had served with Washington at Fort Necessity and had seen this kind of fighting before; they knew how to load and fire from the cover of trees and ground, and they managed to keep the wagon train from being encircled.

Only when Braddock was knocked off his horse by a bullet passing through his back and into his lungs did the troops begin to break in panic from the field. Washington spied a small, horse-drawn baggage cart that he ordered emptied so that the general, wounded but still giving orders, could be hauled back beyond the second ford they had crossed on that long-ago morning.

As Washington was Braddock's only unwounded aide, the responsibility of issuing orders fell on him. He rode south to the first ford to order retreating men back to where Braddock still hoped make a stand; he found a wounded Thomas Gage trying to rally a force there and so Washington rode back toward the general; as he did, he saw Braddock's little cart rolling toward him—the general had decided to withdraw. He told Washington to take two guides and ride back to the supply camp to order the immediate dispatch of wagons bearing food and medical supplies. The slow-moving baggage train had fallen 50 miles behind the advance forces; to reach it, Washington would have to ride through the forest all night.

Washington had begun that morning "weak and low" from a long bout with dysentery; he'd spent all day in the saddle, save for the moments when he'd been unhorsed by dying mounts; his coat had been shredded by four musket balls that had passed through its flaps; now he needed to ride 50 miles on a night so dark that his guides often dismounted and felt the ground with their hands in order to find the soft, churned ground of the trail.

As his horse plodded through the ink-black night, Washington heard the pleas, cries, and death rattles of wounded men. It was amazing how many miles some of them had crawled before lying down to die.

"The shocking Scenes which presented themselves in this Nights march are not to be described," Washington later wrote. "The dead—the dying— the groans—lamentation—and crys along the road of the wounded for help . . . were enough to pierce a heart of adamant."[16]

+══+

The long retreat back to Fort Cumberland was slow and painful. Not much could be done for those too wounded to walk. Of the 1,469 men who took the field that morning, 66 percent were casualties: 426 dead, 520 wounded— 946 men. Seven of the 50 camp women were captured; the rest were killed.

On the night of July 13, in camp at Great Meadows, Braddock joined the ranks of the dead. Colonel Dunbar put Washington in charge of the burial party, and the next morning Washington ordered a hole dug in the wagon road about a mile from the blackened remains of Fort Necessity. Braddock's body, held in a sling of two blankets, was lowered into the road; men filled the grave, and such wagons as were left and all of the men trudged over it, ensuring that the Indians would never claim the general's scalp.

On July 17, a full eight days after Braddock's Defeat, the troops straggled back into Fort Cumberland, where Washington heard a report of his own death. Taking quill in hand, he wrote to his brother John at Mount Vernon:

> As I have heard since my arrivl at this place, a circumstantial acct of my deth and dying Speech, I take this early opportunity of contradicting both, and of assuring you that I < have not. As yet, composed the latter, But by the all powerful dispensatns of Providence, < I have been > protected beyond all human expecatation; I had 4 Bullets through my Coat, and two Horses shot under and yet escaped unhurt.[17]

In his letters home, Washington placed blame on the rout not on Braddock but on his enlisted men, "*chiefly* of the English soldiers," he wrote his mother, "who were struck with such a panick, that they behavd with more cowardice than is possible to conceive; The Officers behav'd Gallantly."

To Dinwiddie, he was even harsher in his assessment of the English regulars, calling them "cowardly dogs of Soldier's."[18] Washington was unduly harsh on men who stayed on the field through cross-flanking fire for hours, withdrawing only after their commander was down; they suffered casualties at the same high rate as the officers, suggesting that they were on the field fighting as best as they could, not running away. But this is immaterial. What matters is what Washington thought. The impressions left on him were that British regulars were not necessarily good troops, and that when enlisted men lost discipline under fire, officers died and everyone suffered. Discipline, he was now convinced, was the key to a good fighting force.

+≡═≡+

On July 26, 1755, Washington straggled into Mount Vernon to recover from the dysentery that still left him weak. From the comfort of the governor's mansion, Dinwiddie was ready for the troops to fight again. On the day Washington arrived home, Dinwiddie wrote him a letter: "But pray Sr, wth the Numbr of Men remaing is there no Possibility of doing somethg the other Side of he Mounts. Before the Winter Months?"[19]

The army had been so thoroughly beaten that its men wanted no more of the French and their Indian allies this season; there was no possibility of crossing the mountains and fighting again before the snow flew. Most of the troops had followed Colonel Dunbar to Philadelphia, where they had taken permanent winter quarters—"in *July*," Washington noted to Dinwiddie with disgust. Couriers continued to deliver congratulatory letters to Washington's door, wishing him a speedy recovery and thanking him for his gallant conduct.

On August 5, Dinwiddie convened a meeting of the state's legislature, and the next day, the House of Burgesses voted to raise a regiment of 1,200 men—a fourfold increase of the regiments that 22-year-old Lieutenant Colonel Washington had led to Great Meadows the previous summer. This large Virginia Regiment would need a colonel to lead it, and all eyes turned to Washington.

Charles Lewis, Washington's cousin, sent a message from Williamsburg, 80 miles distant, offering "Notice of the good Opinion the Governour Assembly &c. entertain of yr Conduct, I assure You Sir scarce any thing else is talk'd of here. . . . People in these Parts seem very desirous of serving under the brave Colo. Washington, and want nothing more to encourage 'em out, but yr Declaration of going to command them."[20]

Though he'd taken three trips to the Ohio Valley and had nearly drowned, been shot at, and sickened, Washington was not ready to quit; as he wrote to his half brother Augustine: "I am so little dispirted at what has happen'd, that I am always ready, and always willing, to do my Country any Services that I am capable off; but never upon the Terms I have done."[21]

Washington would serve, but not as anyone's inferior; nor would he stay on as unpaid aide. The young soldier had seen and learned a lot, and he was now ready to employ some of his experiences. If he were to command the regiment, he would need to have a say in choosing his officers; he would need a "military chest" or ready cash to pay for provisions, and intelligence, and the sundry expenses that arise at camp.

Even if he were offered those terms, Washington wrote back to his cousin, with his usual modesty, "I am unequal to the Task, and assure you it requires more experience than I am master of to conduct an affair of the importance that this is now arisen to."[22]

After negotiations, the governor and the House of Burgesses did agree to Washington's terms: He would have a say in choosing his second in command (his former captain, now lieutenant colonel, Adam Stephen) and in picking captains to head each of the regiment's 16 companies; he would also have a military chest of £10,000. With these terms secured, Washington accepted the commission as colonel of the Virginia Regiment on August 15, 1755.

+≡══≡+

In the fall of 1755, the Virginia backcountry was in a panic—settlers streamed east across the Blue Ridge Mountains into Winchester bringing horrific tales of Indian massacres. Some of the stories were even true—there really were scalped, wolf-eaten corpses strewn by burned-out farmhouses. Braddock's Defeat left no forces in the region to stop Indian raiding parties, and members of several tribes, egged on by the French, killed settlers, captured women, burned their farms, and razed their corn. Washington's job was to stop them.

Sometimes Indian attacks galvanized recruitments, but in this case Washington found that recruiting men for an army when the Indians were on the attack was extraordinarily hard. Washington had to chastise one of his recruiters for busting into houses, kidnapping eligible men while they slept, then confining or torturing them until they agreed to enlist.[23] By mid-September, the Virginia Regiment reported 1,008 men, including officers and their assistants, scattered at three recruiting centers and in Fort Cumberland.

In October, Washington rode into Winchester and found the people so frightened about reports of marauding Indians that they would not cooperate with even the simplest requests: He tried to assemble a small party of militia to investigate reports of an Indian war party advancing on the town, but people wouldn't even lend him horses to complete the task.

"In all things I meet with the greatest opposition," he wrote to Dinwiddie from Winchester, "no orders are obey'd but what a Party of Soldier's or my own drawn Sword Enforces." Even at the point of Washington's sword the people were reluctant to help out, although Washington pledged not to back down "unless they execute what they threaten i, e, to 'to blow out my brains.'"

By the time Washington assembled the bulk of his regiment at Winchester, the Indians had moved on. This proved to be a frustrating pattern—the Indians traveled in small bands of a few dozen warriors who struck quickly and slipped away. It was tough to find and engage them.

Through the winter of 1755–1756 there were only a few skirmishes, and soldiers of the Virginia Regiment grew restless. Issues about command surfaced again—a captain heading a detachment of 30 Marylanders in Fort Cumberland claimed that he outranked all of the Virginians, even Washington, on the basis of having held a king's commission in 1746. The claim was absurd; the captain, John Dagworthy, had been paid a lump sum in exchange for that commission years before, but his assertion caused so much trouble that Dinwiddie finally authorized Washington to travel all the way to Boston to resolve the issue.

In Boston, Washington met with Massachusetts governor William Shirley, who was in charge of all the king's forces in North America. Washington had come in hopes of securing a king's commission for himself and his

Virginia Regiment, putting them on equal footing with regular, professional soldiers. Shirley, the consummate politician, could not grant him that, but he did send Washington home happy—he gave him a letter stating that Washington outranked Dagworthy and that Dagworthy should either leave Fort Cumberland or get used to it.

⊹⇒⚬⇐⊹

On his return to the fort, all the problems of an idle army continued to plague Washington. He wrote to a captain of his short-lived Ranger corps: "There are continual complaints to me of the misbehaviour of your Wife; who I am told sows sedition among the men . . . If she is not set from camp . . . I shall take care to drive her out myself."

Another captain, John Stewart, "keeps a Disorderly and riotous Assembly about him," Washington complained in his orders. "I do Order, that, for the future, he shall not presume to Sell any Liquor to any Soldier or any other Person whatsoever, under the pain of severest punishment."

When yet another officer got caught cheating at cards, Washington wrote an "Address" to his officers, a manifesto outlining his guiding managerial philosophy: He would notice and reward merit, would punish those who deserved it, and would not let personal ties sway him either way. In his address of January 8, 1756, he wrote:

> I am determined . . . to observe the strictest discipline through the whole economy of my Behaviour. On the other hand; you may as certainly depend upon having the strictest justice administred to all: and I shall make it the most agreeable part of my duty, to study merit, and reward the brave, and deserving. I assure you, Gentlemen, that partiality shall never biass my conduct; nor shall prejudice injure any; but throughout the whole tenor of my proceedings, I shall endeavour, as far as I am able, to reward and punish, without the least diminution.[24]

When Washington said that he would punish, he meant it. In November, the House of Burgesses put the Virginia Regiment under military law, which allowed whippings for cursing and execution for desertion or theft. Washington and his officers made liberal use of the lashings clause; his lieutenant colonel, Adam Stephen, wrote from Fort Cumberland: "We catchd two [soldiers] in the very Act of desertion and have wheal'd them till they pissd themselves and the Spectators Shed tears for them."[25]

Washington also used his power to execute; on June 27, 1755, all the soldiers in Winchester turned out on Washington's orders to witness Henry Campbell, a chronic deserter, face the firing squad.

For two years, Washington kept the Virginia Regiment on a defensive footing. He had neither the men nor the cannon required to march back into the Ohio for an attack on Fort Duquesne, so he reverted to Plan B: building a chain of 25 frontier forts from the northern end of western Virginia to the south, a stretch of 350 miles. He garrisoned companies of his men in each fort, where they patrolled the backcountry and skirmished with Indians. Through 1756 and 1757, the Virginia Regiment, drilling together, fighting together, living together, became an amazingly proficient army for a provincial force. Washington was so impressed with them that he tried a second time to get commissions for them and himself as regular troops, appealing now to John Campbell, Earl of Loudoun, who had taken command of Britain's North American troops from Governor Shirley.

In his petition to Loudoun, Washington wrote:

> We cant conceive, that being Americans shoud deprive us of the benefits of British Subjects; nor lessen our claim to preferment: and we are very certain, that no Body of regular troops ever before Servd 3 Bloody Campaigns without attracting Royal notice. . . .
>
> If it shou'd be said, the Troops of Virginia are Irregulars, and cannot expect more notice than other Provincials, I must beg leave to differ and observe in turn, that we want nothing but Commissions from His Majesty to make us as regular a Corps as any upon the Continent.[26]

Washington had a point: Some in his Virginia Regiment had fought at Fort Necessity and at Braddock's Defeat, and the whole body had been in dozens of bloody skirmishes with the Indians on the frontier; unlike other provincials, they continuously remained in the field, drilling, training, and living the disciplined lives of soldiers. But Loudoun, a stocky Scot who had planted the trees on his estate to resemble an infantry regiment drawn up in review, did not see the point: Not only did he deny Washington's request, he made the Virginia Regiment subordinate to regular Colonel John Stanwix, who headed a battalion of the Royal American Regiment in Pennsylvania; Stanwix promptly ordered Washington to hand over 100 barrels of gunpowder and 12,000 flints.[27]

Loudoun's contentious command in America lasted barely a year; after squabbling with provincial governments from Massachusetts to Virginia, he was dismissed just in time for the campaign of 1758, when the British strategy again included an attack on Fort Duquesne.

This time, the expedition to the Ohio would be lead by Brigadier John Forbes, a 50-year-old doctor turned officer who had proven to be a good and capable leader. Washington heard of this latest expedition to the Ohio in March 1758, one of the lowest periods of his life. His friend and patron, Colonel William Fairfax, had recently died; his quartermaster had embezzled goods then deserted; he and Governor Dinwiddie were thoroughly sick of each other; and for half a year, Washington had again been battling the bloody flux. This time, though he was only 26, the disease almost killed him.

The dysentery struck him at headquarters in Winchester, coming on so hard that a friend wrote Dinwiddie to report: "the day before yesterday he was seiz'd with Stitches and violent Pleuretick Pains upon which the Docr Bled him and yesterday he twice repeated the same operation."

On doctor's orders, Washington returned to Mount Vernon, but by March 4, his spirits were so low that he wrote his commanding officer, Colonel Stanwix: "My constitution I believe has receivd great Injury, and as nothing can retrieve it but the greateast care, & most circumspect Conduct—As I now see no prospect of preferment in Military Life—and as I despair of rendering that immediate Service which this Colony may require of the Person commanding their Troops, I have some thought of quitting my Command."[28]

Washington left the next day for Williamsburg, where he intended to see doctors, to straighten out some military accounts, and perhaps to resign. According to his grandson, while en route to Williamsburg, Washington stopped at the mansion of a family named Chamberlayne, where a wealthy young widow, Martha Dandridge Custis, happened to be staying. Her grandfather had been an immigrant merchant, but at 18, she had married John Parke Custis, a 37-year-old never-married bachelor who hailed from an eccentric family of incredible wealth. Despite his crazy father and grandfather, Custis proved to be a steady, loving husband who managed the family's plantations well. He and Martha had four children, two of whom lived, and for seven years Martha was a pretty young mother who liked fine, colorful clothes. They had been married fewer than eight years when John Custis took ill and quickly died, leaving Martha a young, stylish widow in control of a fortune. Colonel Washington met her as a guest at the Chamberlayne mansion; he liked her, the feeling was mutual, and the relationship they kindled resulted just 10 months later in marriage.[29]

Stanwix's brief reply to Washington's threat to quit the service caught up with him at Williamsburg—and it must have acted as salve to his worn spirits: "I am much concern'd to hear [your health] is in so bad a Condition as to put you upon resigning your Command. . . . am sorry to tell you that I hear Lord Loudon is to go home & . . . that a very large Fleet is expected & seven Thousand men."[30]

Stanwix was right: A large fleet was bringing soldiers to America. Nearly 50,000 men would be sent in three expeditions against the French that summer, including 7,000 soldiers on a mission to take Fort Duquesne. Virginia was raising a second regiment to buttress Washington's First Virginia Regiment on this campaign. Bloody flux and all, there was no way Washington was going to miss this.

CHAPTER 4

The Fall of Fort Duquesne

Two weeks after threatening to resign his colonel's commission due to sickness, Washington wrote a cousin in March of 1758: "I am now in a fair way of regaining my health."[1] Soon he was riding for army headquarters in Winchester, where he set about trying to ingratiate himself with John Forbes, the commander of the latest and largest expedition into the Ohio.

Washington wrote to his old comrade Thomas Gage, "I wou'd now, altho' I think modesty will scarcely permit me to ask it, beg the favour of you to mention me to Genl Forbes. . . . I only wish to be distinguished in some measure from the general run of provincial Officers, as I understand there will be a motley herd of us!"[2]

Forbes knew well who Washington was, and he did want him to participate in the coming campaign; upon hearing this, Washington sent Forbes a solicitous letter praising his "universal good character" and officiously offering advice about how to please Indian allies. Forbes, more than Braddock, recognized the importance of Indian warriors; on behalf of Forbes, an aide,

Brigade Major Francis Halkett—a friend of Washington's who had lost both his father and his brother while fighting beside them at Braddock's Defeat—thanked Washington for his advice. Forbes, wrote Halkett, did not "debar any body from telling their way of thinking, when at the same time he only makes use of that part of their way of thinking, which corresponds with his own."[3]

By summer's end, Washington's way of thinking did not correspond with Forbes's on a crucial point: the path that the 7,000-man army would take to reach Fort Duquesne. Washington assumed that Forbes would use the same road that Braddock had taken, a road that was supplied by the Potomac River and ran through the Virginia backcountry, where influential members of the Ohio Company were heavily invested and Washington himself owned a tobacco plantation.

Washington had an extra reason for wanting to ingratiate himself with Virginia's influential men of property—its voters—that summer; he had thrown his hat into the ring for a seat in the House of Burgesses, an election held on July 24. Washington did not leave the army camp at Fort Cumberland to campaign at the Frederick County polling place, but he did have a campaign team outside the polls. On election day, his team spent nearly £40 buying 40 gallons of beer, more than a hogshead of rum, 35 gallons of wine, a few pints of brandy, and dinner for the county's voters. The expenditure paid off: Washington easily topped a four-man field to win the county's seat in the Virginia House, drawing 310 votes to 240 for his nearest competitor.

Forbes was well aware of the troubles Braddock had encountered on the road Washington and his friends favored; not surprisingly, he wanted a better route—and he believed he had found one. By cutting a new road from Raystown, Pennsylvania, to the west, Forbes would save 45 miles (100 miles versus 145), have better pasturage for horses and cattle, have fewer streams to ford, and pass through a more open country less prone to ambushes. But the new road would favor Pennsylvania suppliers and land speculators at the expense of those from Virginia.

In early August, Lieutenant Colonel Henry Bouquet told Washington that he favored the Pennsylvania route; Washington went wild: "If Colo. Bouquet succeeds in this point with the General—all is lost!" Washington wrote to Major Halkett. "All is lost by Heavens!—our Enterprize Ruind."[4]

On that same day, August 2, 1758, Washington wrote a long and reasoned letter to Bouquet explaining why he felt the Braddock Road was the better route to Fort Duquesne, concluding with: "I have nothing to fear but for the general Service, and no hopes but the advantages it will derive from the success of Our Operations; therefore cannot be supposed to have any private Interest or Sinester views." Washington made a good case that it would take so much time to cut a new road that the troops would never reach Fort Duquesne before winter; he truly may have had nothing but the success of the expedition in mind, but even after Forbes made it clear they were taking the Raystown route, Washington pressed the point with an impertinence that bordered on insubordination.

Washington's insistence that the Raystown Road could never work almost gave him a rooting interest against the expedition's success; on one hand, he yearned to see the fall of Fort Duquesne; on the other, the successful investment of that fort would prove him wrong about the Raystown Road. In much of his private correspondence and even in some of his official dispatches, he could not resist taking digs at Forbes's selection of the Raystown Road, going so far as to call Forbes and Bouquet "dupes" of "Pennsylvanian Artifice."

The fact was, Forbes was nobody's dupe. He had carefully researched the roads before narrowly deciding to build a new one; he was doing the best that he could, and he was seriously sick with skin lesions and a case of dysentery that eventually killed him. He grew tired of Washington's constant carping, and when the Virginia regiments marched into Raystown in mid-September, Forbes summoned Washington and Colonel William Byrd to his headquarters. Byrd, the well-heeled colonel of the Second Virginia Regiment, had also been overly disappointed in the selection of the Pennsylvania road, and Forbes lit into them, saying "their weakness in their attachment to the province they belong to" had made them blind to "the good of the service."[5]

Washington's obstinacy led Forbes to mistrust him; on another issue, he wrote to Bouquet: "Consult Colonel Washington, although perhaps not follow his advice as his behavior about the roads was no ways like a soldier."[6]

John Forbes did not hold a grudge against George Washington—he couldn't afford to: Washington was an experienced officer at the head of good troops, and Forbes needed him. Even on the day that he dressed down Washington and Byrd, he complimented Washington on the behavior of the Virginians, who had been part of a detachment of 800 men under the command of Major James Grant. Against orders, Grant had stupidly marched his men from a fort called Loyalhanna, 50 miles from the gates of Fort Duquesne; there they goaded the French and Indians to sally by openly reconnoitering the works and playing reveille. Only the Virginians prevented Grant from being surrounded by French and Indian forces, allowing his men to escape with the loss of one-third of their forces.

Work on the Raystown Road went slowly; as cold weather settled into the mountains, it appeared more and more as if Washington had been right all along—Forbes's troops would never reach Fort Duquesne before the snow flew. To his credit, Washington did not gloat; in fact, the more likely it seemed that this mission would result in yet another failure, the more Washington became reflective and mature.

To Washington's relief, the irritating Governor Dinwiddie had been recalled to London and replaced by Francis Fauquier, a 55-year-old Renaissance man whose father had worked with Sir Isaac Newton. On October 30, after frost had killed much of the pasturage that the horses needed, Washington wrote to Fauquier from the outpost of Loyalhanna: "Our affairs, as I observed in my last, are drawing to a crisis. . . . [W]e expect to move on in a very few days—encoutering every hardship, that an advanced season, want of clothes, and indeed (no great stock of Provisions) will expose us to. But it is no longer a time for pointing out difficulties—and I hope my next will run in a more agreeable strain."[7]

A week after that, Washington and the second in command of this expedition, Lieutenant Colonel Bouquet, met by candlelight in the latter's tent; Bouquet sought Washington's opinion on an aggressive plan: leaving behind all the tents and baggage, even the artillery, marching 50 miles to the fort, and storming it as quickly as possible.

Washington listened—and he was so troubled by this "scheme" that when he got back to his own tent, he lit a candle and wrote Bouquet a thoughtful response:

> How far then do you believe our Stock of Provisions—to say nothing of other matters—will allow you to execute this plan? . . .

Now suppose the Enemy gives us a meeting in the Field and we put them to the Rout what do we gain by it? . . . [T]o risk an Engagement when so much depends upon it, without having the accomplishment of the main point in view, appears to my Eye, to be a little imprudent.[8]

In the summer of 1756, the newly minted Colonel Washington had rashly pushed his 300 men toward the gates of Fort Duquesne, then been forced to withdraw to Fort Necessity, where he had suffered humiliation and defeat; now, two years later, he was advising a commissioned lieutenant colonel of the British army against doing the same thing. As a man and an officer, he had matured.

A council of war held on November 11 supported Washington's judgment: "the risks [of attacking] being so obviously greater than the advantages there is no doubt as to the sole course that prudence dictates": a retreat. Washington had been right all along: Building the Raystown Road had taken too long, and there would be no flushing the French from Fort Duquesne this year.

+≔═≕+

The day after the council of war issued its edict to withdraw, Forbes sent out a detachment to do duty as the "Grass Guard," basically guarding the cattle as it grazed on the frostbitten meadows. Near nightfall, this detachment came under attack from about 200 French and Indians.

On hearing the shooting, Forbes ordered men from either the First or the Second Virginia Regiment to reinforce the Grass Guard. Accounts from the time indicate that Washington was sent out with a detachment from the First Regiment; years later, Washington recalled that Colonel Hugh Mercer was sent out with the Second. Whatever the case, the initial regiment on the scene skirmished with the French and Indians and managed to take three prisoners, two of whom were Indians.

As evening grew darker, Forbes sent out another detachment of Virginians—Washington said he was sent out at this time with his First Regiment. Regardless of who was sent to relieve whom, the fact is that in the gloaming, looking at silhouettes of soldiers and seeing Indians, both Virginia regiments mistook each other as the enemy; both regiments had trained in marksman-ship, and both fired upon each other with disastrous effect. According to Washington's account, when he realized what was happening, he stepped in front his line of men firing and receiving fire; with his sword, he knocked their musket muzzles up.

A Captain Thomas Bullitt of the Second Virginia Regiment recalled that he was the first man to notice the troops were firing on each other, and he ran between the two parties waving his hat. Bullitt's assessment was "Colonel Washington did not discover his usual activity and presence of mind upon the occasion."[9]

The Virginians paid dearly for driving off the enemy—a colonel and 13 or 14 soldiers were killed—but their capture of prisoners made the price worthwhile. The prisoners revealed that Fort Duquesne "was very scarce in provisions, as well as weak in Men."[10] Armed with this knowledge, Forbes overrode his council of war; he ordered his men to leave their baggage behind for a quick march on the fort. He did haul his artillery, and felling trees to clear a road for that forced a slow pace. After 12 days, the army had moved 40 miles, bringing it within 10 miles of Fort Duquesne. Forbes ordered "the greatest Silence" to be observed in camp at night, even ordering the camp dogs hanged to quiet their barking. He need not have worried; on the night of November 24, a great blast shook the forest. The French had touched off kegs of gunpowder to blow up Fort Duquesne. By the light of the burning walls, they slipped away in canoes down the Ohio River.

On November 25, George Washington finally stood in the ruins of Fort Duquesne at the Forks of the Ohio. He had nearly drowned east of this spot in 1754; had been humiliated at Fort Necessity in 1755; had had horses shot from under him at Braddock's Defeat; and had recently stood between lines of his own men firing at each other outside Loyalhanna. But he had lived to see the fall of Fort Duquesne. Now it was time to go home.

<hr>

For the Virginia regiments, the march back home to Winchester was about 160 miles through mountains, in December, without proper clothes or enough food. Eight or nine men died of hypothermia at Raystown, 60 miles short of their goal. Forbes, still suffering from dysentery, was carried on a litter back to Philadelphia, where he died; Washington, too, fell sick at the end of this campaign, and in a low moment he it slip to his friend and doctor, James Craik, that he intended to resign.

Word of Washington's intended resignation spread, and on New Year's Eve, 1758, his officers sent him an "Address" asking him to stay on for another year:

> In our earliest Infancy you took us under your Tuition, train'd us up in the Practice of that Discipline which alone can constitute good Troops. . . .
>
> Your steady adherence to impartial Justice, your quick Discernment and invarable Regard to Merit . . . first heighten'd our natural Emulation, and our Desire to excel.[11]

Couched in flowery, hyperbolic language, what the officers said was essentially true: Nearly three years earlier, Washington had pledged "to reward and punish" on the basis of merit, not on connections or personality. He had done that, and his men had responded.

Despite the plea of his officers, Washington carried through with his plans to resign his commission. He had plenty of reasons for resigning: Once again a long campaign had left him ill; no matter how well his troops performed, he could not win a regular commission for them and for himself; he had achieved his objective in seeing the French driven from the Ohio; and he had fallen in love with the wealthy young widow, Martha Dandridge Custis. They had met, possibly twice, at the Chamberlayne mansion and had had no chance to see each other while he was riding the frontier with the Virginia Regiment. If they carried on a courtship by writing, no authentic letters of it survive. But by January 1, 1759, he was in Williamsburg handing in his commission; five days later, he got married.

Washington's marriage to Martha made him one of the richest men in America. Her late husband had owned plantations in six counties covering 17,880 acres; with their slaves, these lands were valued at £30,000; plus he'd held a credit surplus with British merchants of £10,000. Washington also had his own plantations and slaves at Mount Vernon, his mother's Ferry Farm, and the Bullskin Plantation on the western slopes of the Blue Ridge Mountains.

The newlyweds settled in at Martha's "White House" plantation, about 25 miles from Williamsburg, where, on his twenty-seventh birthday, Washington joined the House of Burgesses for its February session.

After the House finished its session, Washington wrote to a white servant at Mount Vernon to get the place spruced up: "You must have the House very well cleand . . . You must get two of the best Bedsteads put up . . . you must also get out the chairs and Tables, & have them very well rubd & Cleand."[12]

Finally, after three years at war, George Washington was bringing home his bride.

CHAPTER 5

"A Sword Sheathed in a Brother's Breast"

WASHINGTON SETTLED INTO MARRIED LIFE AT MOUNT VERNON in the spring of 1759. Martha came with a ready-made family—her two surviving children, a boy and a girl, from her first marriage, Jackie, five, and three-year-old Patsy.

For Washington, expanding the house and acreage of Mount Vernon became an obsessive hobby; within 10 years of his marriage to a wealthy widow, he nearly tripled Mount Vernon from 2,126 acres to 5,790, with a commensurate increase in the number of slaves.

Washington kept his seat in the House of Burgesses but missed the final weeks of the May 1765 session in which a fiery young lawyer named Patrick Henry gave a rousing speech against the recently passed Stamp Act, requiring the colonies to purchase and affix tax stamps to nearly everything, from bottles of rum, to every sheet of paper in a court filing. Like most of the burgesses, Washington had left that year's session before adjournment as it was planting season and there was little of interest left on the agenda. In the session's waning days, while Washington was at home sowing hemp seeds, word came to Williamsburg of the British Parliament's plan to tax the colonies.[1] Washington shared Henry's revulsion to the Stamp Act, viewing it as an unconstitutional abuse of power by Parliament.

In September 1765, Washington wrote to Martha's uncle, Francis Dandridge, then living in London: "The Stamp Act Imposed on these colonies by the Parliament of Great Britain engrosses the conversation [of the colonists] who look upon this unconstitutional method of Taxation as a direful attack upon their Liberties, & loudly exclaim against the Violation—what may be the result of this—& some other (I think I may add) ill judgd Measures, I will not undertake to determine."[2]

In April 1769, Washington wrote a radical letter to his neighbor George Mason, an intelligent man who suffered frequent, painful bouts of gout and spent his convalescences reading from his extensive library. In his letter, Washington complained about the Townshend Acts, a series of revenue-raising laws that Parliament had recently passed to replace the despised Stamp Act. The Townshend Acts put a tax on many goods, such as paper, glass, and tea; and they created vice admiralty courts, centered in Boston, to collect the revenue. The taxes were not high, but it wasn't the amount that rankled Washington—he believed that Parliament lacked constitutional authority to tax the colonies at all. Many shared his view; in Boston, rioters drove the judges of the vice admiralty courts to seek safety on a British warship in the harbor.

Washington wrote Mason:

> At a time when our lordly Masters in Great Britain will be satisfied with nothing less than the deprivation of American freedom, it seems highly necessary that something shou'd be done to avert the stroke and maintain the liberty which we have derived from our Ancestors; but the method of doing it to answer the purpose effectually is the point in question.
>
> That no man shou'd scruple, or hesitate a moment to use a—ms [arms] in defence of so valuable a blessing, on which all the good and evil of life depends; is clearly my opinion; Yet A—ms I wou'd beg leave to add, should be the last resource.[3]

This was a radical stance, to suggest fighting Great Britain with arms; but before rushing to war, Washington thought that Virginia should embrace a nonimportation act, essentially a boycott of certain British goods. Merchants in Boston, New York, and Philadelphia had already taken nonimportation pledges. For two days, Mason and Washington huddled at Mount Vernon, hashing out details of their proposal for fellow planters and merchants. Then in May, Washington rode to Williamsburg for a session of the House of Burgesses.

On May 16, 1769, Washington voted with the majority of burgesses to adopt resolves asserting their sole right to levy taxes in Virginia, and renouncing British attempts to remove agitators in Boston and ship them to England to stand charges of treason. The governor of Virginia, now Lord Norborne Berkeley Botetourt, overreacted to these symbolic resolutions—the next day he ordered the House of Burgesses dissolved. When the burgesses were turned out of the Capitol Building, Washington joined them in marching down Duke of Gloucester Street to the Raleigh Tavern, where they overwhelmingly passed the nonimportation articles that Mason had drafted after consulting with Washington.

By now, British officials had identified Massachusetts and Virginia as the two most radical colonies[4]—and Washington was one of the most radical men in Virginia, already (though privately) declaring his willingness to use arms against England.

＋＞＝＝＜＋

When George Washington pulled the trigger at Jumonville's Rocks in 1754, he lit the fuse that was now burning toward the American Revolution. In firing at Jumonville, Washington had sparked the French and Indian War, which created the volatile conditions that made the American Revolution possible.

Because the French and Indian War weakened the French presence in North America, the colonists no longer needed regiments of British regulars to protect them against a French threat; by 1769, the regulars at Boston had gone from being welcome protectors to an occupying force. The war had also put Great Britain deeply in debt, debts that it tried to recoup in part through measures such as the Stamp and Townshend acts, which fomented dissent.

The French and Indian War also showed the American colonies the benefit of working together, though they never really perfected it; more importantly, it taught a whole generation of Americans, Washington's generation, how to fight while simultaneously showing them that British regulars were not invincible.

+⊷⊶+

Governor Botetourt could not abolish the House of Burgesses forever; when sessions resumed in November 1769, Washington was there, listening to the governor explain that while most of the Townshend Acts had been repealed, the tax on tea would remain. Therefore, a boycott of English goods would continue in Virginia, and Washington played a key role in an "association" of planters and merchants who drafted arcane rules on which goods were subject to the boycott.

The governor also had some good news in that fall session: The king had agreed to move the boundary line separating the colonies from Cherokee Country farther to the west, thus allowing Virginia to make good on a pledge to give western lands to veterans of the 1754 campaign, the one that had ended with Washington's unintentional confession of "assassination" at Fort Necessity. For the next two years, Washington spent considerable time on the west side of the Blue Ridge Mountains surveying those lands and ensuring that the government made good on its pledge. His actions were partly an altruistic endeavor to ensure that his soldiers from that campaign got their due and partly because he wanted what was promised him. Eventually he obtained more than 20,000 acres west of the Blue Ridge Mountains, lands that in later years added substantially to his wealth.

In the spring of 1772, a fashionable young portrait artist, Charles Willson Peale, rode into the courtyard of Mount Vernon, where he had come to paint portraits of the Washington family. He spent several weeks trying to capture the figure of the colonel, George Washington, and although the painting is not Peale at his mature best, he did capture Washington's build as Washington himself had described to a tailor a decade before—six feet tall with long arms and thighs, though no longer "Slender . . . for a person of that highth."[5] Peale portrayed Washington as broad across the hips with a slight paunch (it's possible that Peale added girth to suggest healthfulness, which was standard in portraits of that time) and a youthful-looking face for a 40-year-old.

What is most telling about Peale's 1772 portrait is what Washington decided to wear while posing: the uniform of an officer in the First Virginia Regiment, with its blue coat, silver facing, and bloodred waistcoat. He carried a musket and sword. In donning his military uniform, was Washington looking into his past—or at his future?

While at Mount Vernon, Peale earned an additional £26 for painting miniatures of Martha and her 16-year-old daughter, Patsy. This would be the last representation of the girl, who suffered a lifelong seizure disorder. On June 19, 1773, Washington wrote of Patsy to a friend: "She rose from Dinner about four Oclock, in better health and spirits than she appeard to have been in for some time; soon after which she was seized with one of her usual Fits, & expird in it, in less than two Minutes, without uttering a Word, a groan, or scarce a Sigh."[6]

The death, Washington wrote in that same letter, "has almost reduced my poor Wife to the lowest ebb of Misery; which is encreas'd by the absence of her Son," Jackie, who had just gone off to King's College (present-day Columbia University) in New York. On hearing of his sister's death, Jack wrote to Washington that he "could not withstand the Shock, but like a Woman gave myself up entirely to melancholy for several Days."[7]

Jack was then engaged to Eleanor Nelly Calvert, who lived across the Potomac in Maryland; though Washington had tried to talk the two teens into delaying their wedding for a few years to give Jack a chance to complete his studies, that December the two decided they would wait no more: they would be married in February 1774, at Eleanor's parents' Mount Airy estate. Washington tossed his reservations aside and sailed across the Potomac on February 3 to attend the wedding.

⊹══⊹

In mid-May, Washington rode into Williamsburg for a session of the House of Burgesses that again proved short-lived: On May 24, 1774, the House passed a resolution calling for a day of fasting and prayer in protest of the Boston Port Acts—a series of punitive acts taken against the people of Boston in order to force them to pay for shiploads of tea that some had recently dumped into the harbor as a tax protest. The value of the tea was considerable—about £100,000 worth—and though Washington did not agree with the tea's destruction, he sympathized with the reasons for it. Now Parliament was not only taxing tea—an illegal measure in Washington's opinion—it was allowing the East India Company to ship tea into America without paying duty on it in London, thus allowing the politically connected company to undercut all other shippers of tea that did pay the duty.

Once again the governor of Virginia, now Lord John Murray Dunmore, dissolved the House of Burgesses for its relatively benign proclamation, and again members repaired to the Raleigh Tavern to resume business. This time they resolved to pass a nonimportation act, the details of which would be worked out by committees in the various counties.

Washington chaired Fairfax County's committee; on July 17, George Mason spent a night at Mount Vernon, enlisting Washington's help in putting the fine points on the Fairfax County Resolves that were adopted the next day in Alexandria. Unlike the benign proclamation of the House of Burgesses, the Fairfax County Resolves were truly radical. Right from the opening word the resolves were militaristic: "1. Resolved that Colony and the Dominion of Virginia can not be considered as a conquered Country; and if it was, that the present Inhabitants are the Descendants not of the conquered, but of the Conquerors."[8]

The Fairfax Resolves included the specifics of a nonimportation act and called for the creation of a congress "from all the Colonies, to concert a general and uniform Plan for the Defence and Preservation of our common rights."

These resolves were detailed and influential; by late summer, all of the colonies but Georgia were on board for a meeting of the First Continental Congress at Philadelphia in September. Washington was named as one of Virginia's seven delegates to the Continental Congress, a post that came with expense money of £90; on August 31, a carriage left Mount Vernon carrying Washington and fellow delegates Patrick Henry and Edward Pendleton to Philadelphia.

In nearly two months of meetings at Carpenters Hall, the First Continental Congress did not accomplish much; it passed a nonimportation agreement to begin on December 1 and threatened a nonexportation agreement to begin the following year if the Boston Port Bill Acts were not withdrawn; the congress also agreed to meet again the following May. By then, things would be changed utterly.

+===+

In the predawn darkness of April 21, 1775, the British schooner *Magdalene* slipped up the James River and dropped off a detachment of marines. The soldiers marched a half dozen miles through the night to Williamsburg where, using a key given to them by the governor, they opened the door to the magazine where the local militia stored gunpowder, firelocks, muskets, and flints.

The governor, Lord Dunmore, wanted to remove the powder from an increasingly belligerent populace that had recently raised four new militia groups; all of the groups had asked Washington to command them, and though he had accepted no command, he had agreed to review the troops.

In congratulating his brother John Augustine Washington for leading one of the newly raised companies, Washington wrote in March 1775: "it is my full intention to devote my Life & Fortune in the cause we engagd in, if need be."[9]

The marines managed to load 15 half barrels of gunpowder onto a wagon before someone sounded an alarm. As the day brightened, an enraged mob grew outside the governor's mansion, but the marines managed to spirit their wagonload of gunpowder out of Williamsburg to a warship off Norfolk.

A similar attempt by British soldiers to secure the gunpowder stored in Concord, Massachusetts, had not been as successful. At daybreak of April 19, 1775, a detachment of British soldiers sent from Boston to capture the stores were met in Lexington by a few dozen American militiamen forming a line across the village green. After a thunderous exchange of musket fire, seven militiamen lay dead on the blood-spattered green. The redcoats marched on for Concord. They managed to destroy the gunpowder stocked there, but their success came at a price. On their 16-mile march back to Boston, the British faced a gauntlet of armed minutemen nearly 4,000 strong. For hours the minutemen blasted the long British column with more than a shot a second,[10] killing 68 and wounding 168 more.

The news of events at Lexington and Concord reached Virginia in late April, as Washington was making plans to set out in his chariot for the Second

Continental Congress in Philadelphia. This time he packed his bloodred breeches, waistcoat, and blue jacket—the uniform of the First Virginia Regiment. From Philadelphia, he wrote in detail of Lexington-Concord to his friend and former neighbor George William Fairfax, now living in London, adding: "Unhappy it is though to reflect, that a Brother's Sword has been sheathed in a Brother's breast, and that, the once happy and peaceful plains of America are either to be drenched with Blood, or Inhabited by Slaves. Sad alternative! But can a virtuous Man hesitate in his choice?"[11]

In Philadelphia, Washington bought five "Military Books," a cartouche box for carrying bullets and powder, a tomahawk, coverings for his holsters, and a silk sash to be worn with an officer's uniform.[12] He attended sessions of the Second Continental Congress dressed in his uniform, cutting an impressive, martial figure. Here was a man wealthier than any, bigger than most, an experienced warrior yet still virile enough to handily beat younger men at games of strength. "He seems discret & Virtuous, no harum Starum ranting Swearing fellow but Sober, steady, & Calm," observed Connecticut representative Eliphalet Dyer.[13]

Congress, now meeting in Philadelphia's State House in proceedings of utmost secrecy, had voted to "adopt" the motley militia camped outside Boston as one army and to raise 10 companies of riflemen from Virginia, Maryland, and Pennsylvania to join it. This multicolonial army would need a general to lead it.

At a session in early June, John Adams—a portly, midsize Massachusetts man with a grave air—rose to nominate a general.[14] Since secrecy was part of the process, there is no official record of the proceedings, only Adams's written recollection of the event:

> I had no hesitation to declare that I had but one Gentleman in my Mind for that important command, and that was a Gentleman from Virginia who was among Us and very well known to all of Us, a Gentleman whose Skill and Experience as an Officer, whose independent fortune, great Talents and excellent universal Character, would command the Approbation of all America, and unite the

cordial Exertions of all the Colonies better than any other Person in the Union.[15]

Washington modestly slipped through a side door into the library to give congress an unfettered chance to discuss his merits. A few spoke against Washington's appointment, reasoning that since most of the troops around Boston were New Englanders, they ought to be led by a New Englander, such as Artemas Ward, who had been a militia colonel in the French and Indian War. Congress deferred voting that day; in informal discussions, those who had raised objections were persuaded to vote for Washington, and on June 15, he stayed away from proceedings while the rest of the congress appointed him general by unanimous consent. The next day Washington accepted the commission, stating:

> Mr. President, Tho' I am truly sensible of the high Honour done me in this Appointment, yet I feel great distress, from a consciousness that my abilities & Military experience may not be equal to the extensive & important Trust. . . .
>
> I do not think myself equal to the Command I am honored with.[16]

Every time Washington earned a commission, he made some equally humble statement. Fellow delegate Patrick Henry later recalled that in a private meeting with Washington after the vote, tears had come to Washington's blue eyes as he said: "Remember, Mr. Henry, what I now tell you: from the day I enter upon the command of the American armies, I date my fall, and the ruin of my reputation."[17]

Washington sent his horses and chariot back to Mount Vernon, then bought a lighter, faster phaeton and five horses to carry him to Boston. Before leaving, Washington sat down to write Martha, whom he called by the pet name of Patsy, explaining that he was going off to war and that he had made a will. This is one of only three of his letters to her that she did not burn after his death:

> You may beleive me my dear Patcy, when I assure you, in the most solemn manner, that, so far from seeking this appointment I have

used every endeavour in my power to avoid it, not only from an unwillingness to part with you and the Family, but from a consciousness of its being trust too great for my Capacity and that I should enjoy more real happiness and felicity in one month with you, at home, than I have the most distant prospect of reaping abroad, if my stay was to be Seven times Seven years. But, as it has been a kind of destiny that has thrown me upon this Service, I shall hope the undertaking of it, is designd to answer some good purpose.[18]

CHAPTER 6

Washington Takes Command

A SKY OF GRAY FLANNEL THREATENED RAIN AS GENERAL GEORGE Washington began the final leg of what had been an exhausting, nine-day trip from Philadelphia to the outskirts of Boston. He felt tired but anxious, eager to see how his troops were situated in respect to the British troops who had recently encamped on a piece of high ground known as Bunker Hill.

Washington had received scant news of a battle fought between the men he would soon be commanding and the British forces on Bunker Hill, just north of Boston; he had been so curious about that battle that during his trip to Boston, he had broken the seal on a letter carrying news of the battle from Boston to the president of the Continental Congress. He apologized to the president, John Hancock, for this transgression; by the time he reached Boston, Washington had learned that British troops had lost more than 1,000 men in taking that hill.[1]

Washington arrived at Cambridge on July 2, 1775, accompanied by a ceremonial troop of horsemen from the town of Marlborough. His journey had been slowed by elaborate, interminable shows of pageantry staged by locals in the cities and towns where he had stayed, and it must have been with some relief that he ditched the ceremonial escort and got down to the business of inspecting his troops.

Boston was built on a peninsula centered between two other peninsulas—Charlestown, just to its north, and Dorchester, flanking it on the south. The Charlestown and Dorchester peninsulas were humped with hills, green now in summer.

Boston was set in a basin, and American troops had encamped on most of the nearby hills forming a nine-mile-wide arc around the town, cutting off all land traffic to the British troops besieged there. In a letter to London, General Thomas Gage wrote of Boston: "I wish this Cursed place was burned . . . its the worst place either to act offensively from, or defencively."[2]

Washington rode into Cambridge, a quintessential New England village with a white church on a big green and the solid brick buildings of Harvard University framing Harvard Yard. A small ceremony to welcome the general had been called off on account of the rain, which was just as well—Washington had business to conduct.[3]

He rode a half mile through the rain to the American camp on Prospect Hill; at his side rode his second in command, Major General Charles Lee, an eccentric but knowledgeable military man who had recently been drawing half pay as a British officer. From Prospect Hill, the two peered through the rain toward Bunker Hill, not a mile away, but through the fog and rain they could not see much.

The next day dawned blue and clear; Washington issued his first orders: Regimental commanders were to report on the number of men and amount of ammunition they had, a seemingly simple request. He spent the next two days riding his lines to review the troops, and his presence seemed to boost morale. Washington had honed his horsemanship by hunting fox in Virginia, and on horseback he cut a splendid figure. James Thacher, a 21-year-old military surgeon, wrote in his journal: "I have been much gratified this day with a view of General Washington. His Excellency was on horseback, in company with several military gentlemen. It was not difficult to distinguish him from all others; his personal appearance is truly noble and majestic; being tall and well proportioned. His dress is a blue coat with buff colored facings, a rich epaulette on each shoulder, buff under dress, and an elegant small sword; a black cockade in his hat."[4]

On July 4, Brigadier General Nathanael Greene wrote home to Rhode Island's governor: "[H]is Excellency General Washington has arrivd and is universally admird. The excellent Charactor he bears, and the promising Genius he possesses gives great spirit to the Troops."[5]

Washington's appearance may have boosted the morale of the troops, but the looks of the troops around Boston did little to improve Washington's. He had expected greatness from these New England troops—they had driven the British from Concord to Boston, killed them en masse on Bunker Hill, and captured Fort Ticonderoga up on Lake Champlain—yet they were the most unsoldierly people he had ever seen.

As he rode along his lines from Roxbury to Plowed Hill, Washington took in most unpleasant sights and smells. The camps were not the neatly arrayed tent cities of a Virginia regiment—far from it. Most didn't even have tents—they lived in shantytowns of cast-off lumber and sailcloth; few units had uniforms, and the men looked slovenly and disheveled. They did not dig proper latrines, and their camps smelled.

Even the simple order that Washington had first issued—count your men and muskets and tell me how many you have—went unfilled. He had expected returns the next morning; he did not receive them for more than a week, and even then, many were incomplete or fudged.

There was a culture clash between this proud Virginian and the citizen-soldier New England Yankees from Massachusetts, New Hampshire, Rhode Island, and Connecticut.[6] Massachusetts men mistrusted standing armies of professional soldiers; the British had forced them to barrack troops in their homes, and they were sick of soldiers. Some of the Rhode Island militias chose their officers by popular vote. Most officers won their rank based on the number of men they recruited, and to recruit men, they made promises, cajoled, and in short acted the part of the politician to win popular support. Such officers would never whip their men, and in Washington's eyes, men who could not be whipped could not be disciplined.

In Virginia, enlisted men tended to be poor or bound men ordered into service by masters; their officers, appointed by aristocracy from aristocracy, were of different social strata. Officers could, and would, discipline with impunity. This was not merely a cultural issue—Washington believed, based on his reading about European practices and on his own experience, that a hierarchical army functioned more effectively.

When Washington finally received accurate numbers, he found that he had about 16,500 men—not the 20,000 he'd been led to believe by the count of his officers. And only about 14,000 were fit for duty; the rest were ill, unarmed, or away from camp.

The British in Boston had more than 6,000 ready, regular troops with the best training and the best weaponry in the world. Washington estimated that if they armed the slaves, free blacks, and Tories left behind in Boston, the British could mount a fighting force of 12,000—plus they had cannon on warships and on floating batteries that could strike any of the American positions. On July 10, 1775, Washington confided to a friend, Virginia Congressman Richard Henry Lee: "Between you and me I think we are in an exceeding dangerous Situation."[7]

The same day, Washington confided in President Hancock. His troops had few tents, no clothes, no training, no artillery regiment, no engineers, no commissary, no quartermaster general, too few entrenching tools, no hospitals, and no money. What Washington had was an ill-tempered army in its infancy, an army that could not feed or clothe itself, could not move in a coordinated fashion, and indeed could not even go to the bathroom without making a mess. His job was to raise this army within musket shot of a superior, disciplined enemy.

"I flatter myself that in a little Time we shall work up these raw Materials into good Stuff," he wrote to one of his major generals, Philip Schuyler, who was then holding Fort Ticonderoga. "I must recommend to you, what I endeavor to practice myself, Patience and Perseverance."[8]

The day he took command, Washington had asked for counts of men and ammunition, and though it took eight days to get the manpower count, the reply from the Massachusetts Committee of Supplies had been swift: It had collected 308 barrels of gunpowder in the province. In late July, Washington asked for gunpowder to make up bullet cartridges; the committee told him it had only 36 barrels left. Though they had collected 308 barrels, they'd fired off most of that at the Battle of Bunker Hill in June.

On August 3, Washington called for a council of war at 9 A.M. in his Cambridge headquarters, a large gray mansion that had been seized from John Vassal Jr., a local Tory. The place was suitably impressive for a headquarters, with 12-foot ceilings, 8-foot doors, and carved moldings. Each general was to bring a tally of gunpowder at every station and post under his command. The returns were not good—together, all the provincial troops had 90 barrels of powder, enough to furnish men with only 9 rounds apiece.[9] By contrast, the British soldiers were then carrying 60 bullets per man.[10] When Washington heard this, he was shocked; if the British attacked his lines now, they would be shredded. He bit his tongue; for 30 minutes as the clock ticked in his office, he silently seethed while his officers watched, waiting for him to speak.[11]

Raising an infant army would indeed take "patience and perseverance," the last being Washington's strongest character trait. It would also take experience, the kind that Washington had earned in three years of hard campaigning on the Ohio frontier; and it would also take discipline.

No one else could have done it.

⊬━━━⊢

"As the Health of an Army principally depends upon Cleanliness; it is recommended in the strongest manner, to the Commanding Officer of Corps, Posts, and Detachments, to be strictly diligent in ordering the Necessarys to be filled up once a Week and new ones dug," Washington wrote in his orders in mid-July.[12]

Sweep the barracks every morning, he wrote; keep clean kitchens. And when the commander in chief or any of his generals pass your guard post, turn out and meet them respectfully with musket stocks resting on the ground. The custom seemed to be that guards would either sullenly stare as generals passed or else challenge them with muskets primed and pointed.

Washington was starting from scratch; he would even have to invent the insignia. Sergeants would be distinguished by a stripe of red sewn onto their right shoulder, corporals by green; field officers would wear on their hats cockades of red or pink; and privates who messed up could be whipped.

There was also the question of prisoners of war—captives taken at Bunker Hill and at some later skirmishes. The British had thrown American prisoners, including officers, into a common jail, where an imprisoned civilian named John Leach observed in his journal that wounded soldiers plucked from the battlefield at Bunker Hill "fare very hard, are many days without the Comforts of Life. . . . [T]hey had no Bread all Day and the day before." Festering wounds forced jailhouse amputations. When complaints were raised on behalf of the wounded soldiers, the jail provost replied they could "eat the nail heads and gnaw the plank and be damned."[13]

Washington wrote to the British commander in chief, Thomas Gage, with whom he had served at Braddock's Defeat:

> My duty now makes it necessary to apprize you, that for the future I shall regulate my conduct towards those Gentlemen who are or may be in our Possession, exactly by the Rule which you shall observe, towards those of ours, who may be in your Custody. If Severity & Hardship mark the Line of your Conduct, (painful as it may be to me) your Prisoners will feel its Effects: but if Kindness & Humanity are shewn to ours, I shall with Pleasure consider those in our Hands, only as unfortunates, and they shall receive the Treatment to which the unfortunate are ever intitled.[14]

Besides dealing with all the innumerable details of rank and insignia, supplies of food, clothes, and powder, of treating with prisoners of war, Washington had to keep his eye on the big-picture strategy: what to do about the 6,000 British regulars occupying the town of Boston. At a council of war in July, all of the generals agreed that they should stay on a defensive footing: continue to strengthen their works, prevent supplies from reaching Boston by land, and hope to starve the British out.

Washington also hoped to intercept supplies coming by sea, sending a small detachment from his army aboard the schooner *Hannah* to intercept supply ships. He instructed the crew to treat any prisoners they may capture "with Kindness & Humanity,"[15] and to this day the *U.S. Army Field Manual* requires humane treatment of prisoners.

He gave similar instructions to a detachment of 1,100 men that he sent, per Congress's orders, on an attempt to capture Canada—a large country of strategic importance, for it gave Great Britain secure ports at Halifax and near the head of the Hudson River. Most Canadians were French Catholics, though living under British rule. Washington warned his detachment: "As the contempt of the Religion of a Country by ridiculing any of its Ceremonies . . . has ever been deeply resented," the men were to "protect & support the free Exercise of the Religion of the Country."

The strategy to attack Canada was Congress's, but Washington had concurred; the route that this detachment had chosen to reach Quebec—crossing 350 miles through mountainous central Maine in late fall—was Washington's, an operational blunder as poorly planned as Braddock's attempt on Fort Duquesne. Benedict Arnold, then a colonel, somehow managed to push 700 of his original force all the way to Quebec, where they joined with an army of Continentals led by General Richard Montgomery; their attempt to take the city ended with the loss of nearly 500 men killed (including Montgomery), captured, or wounded (including Arnold, who suffered a serious leg wound).

<hr />

Washington agreed with the defensive strategy adopted for the troops outside of Boston—at first. But in Colonial New England, winter came early; by the first week of September, he could feel the tang of frost in the air, and on September 8, he sounded out his generals on the advisability of attacking Boston. Washington was by nature an aggressive commander who exercised patience only with great restraint. He clearly favored an attack to get this business over with before winter.

The troops would need barracks and thousands of cords of wood to last a winter; the men had no winter clothes, and blankets were scarce. Worst of all, troop enlistments would begin expiring on December 1, and no one was bound to stay on after January 1. If the Americans were still attempting to hold lines outside Boston in January, they'd have to recruit and train an entirely new force within easy shot of the enemy, an impossible task. "These among many other reason's which might be assigned, induce me to wish a speedy finish of the dispute," Washington wrote to his generals.[16]

On September 11, eight of Washington's generals trooped into his headquarters; after meeting briefly in the dining room, the generals were unanimous in their opinion: "it was not expedient to make the Attempt"[17] on Boston. They had reined in Washington's aggressive impulses—this time.

On September 21, the British cannon on Bunker Hill fired all day, kicking up the earth where American fatigue parties were trying to entrench on Plowed and Prospect hills. One American private noted in his journal that cannon fire "wounded two of Col[onel] Doolittle men brook one of the mens thigh and took the Calf off the others Leg."[18]

British cannon thundered for much of that week, but because of a lack of gunpowder, Washington could respond with only sporadic fire from his camps. With winter coming on, the battle for Boston had turned into a siege, with both sides miserable and unable to move. The British lacked the manpower and, after what happened on Bunker Hill, the will to try and take the entrenched hills. In Boston, British troops were dying at the rate of about 30 per week due to dysentery; since the Battle of Lexington-Concord, about 2,500 redcoats had died in battle or from disease.[19] Smallpox also broke out in town; when civilians sick with the pox began streaming out of Boston, Washington accused the British of using them as biological warfare to infect his troops.[20]

By mid-November, Washington had no confidence in his artillery colonel, Richard Gridley, who was too old for hard service and was in over his head. Even with a competent artillery colonel, Washington would not have had nearly enough powder or cannon to blast the British out of Boston. He decided to rectify both situations. After consulting with Congress, he replaced Gridley with a new artillery commander, the soon-to-be colonel Henry Knox.

Knox, a 26-year-old, Boston-born bookstore owner, had trained in artillery with the local militia since he was 18. He stood about 6 foot 2, weighed over 250 pounds, and had blown off two fingers of his left hand with a fowling piece. His future father-in-law, Thomas Flucker, was a wealthy and well-connected Tory who abhorred Knox's political leanings. As an olive branch to his 17-year-old daughter, Lucy, Flucker had offered to buy the love of her life a coveted commission in the British army. Knox turned it down.[21]

On November 16, 1775, Washington ordered Knox to go plead for more cannon before a congressional committee in New York, then to ride up to Fort Ticonderoga and: "Get the remainder [of cannons] from Ticonderoga, Crown Point, or St. Johns—if it should be necessary from Quebec . . . the want of them is so great, that no trouble or expence must be spared."[22]

Knox had no luck persuading the congressional committee of the dire need for cannon; on November 27, he wrote Washington: "I shall set out by land tomorrow morning for Ticonderoga & proceed with the utmost dispatch k[nowing] our whole dependence for heavy cannon will be from that part."[23]

It took Knox a week to reach Fort Ticonderoga, where he laid eyes on his challenge: 78 cannon, 6 mortars, 3 howitzers, lead, and 30,000 musket flints with a total weight of 119,000 pounds. He needed to haul these down Lake Champlain, across the Hudson River, and over the Berkshire Mountains to Boston, 200 miles away—in winter.

While Knox wrestled with that problem, Washington struggled to overcome insurmountable problems of his own—principally, enlisting a new army while dismissing the old one. By late November, just days before the first of the enlistees were entitled to go home, Washington had enlisted but 3,500 men for the campaign of 1776.

In a moment of despair, Washington wrote in late November to his friend and former secretary Colonel Joseph Reed: "could I have foreseen what I have, & am like to experience, no consideration upon Earth should have induced me to accept this Command."[24]

On December 17, Knox wrote Washington from Fort George with a progress report on his mission: "I have sent for the sleds & teams to come up & expect to begin to move them to Saratoga on Wednesday or Thursday next trusting that between this & that period we shall have a fine fall of Snow which will enable us to proceed further & make the Carriage easy—if that should be the case I hope in 16 or 17 days to be able to present your Excellency a Noble train of Artillery."[25]

In late December, Martha arrived at Washington's headquarters with her son, Jack, and daughter-in-law Nell, pregnant with their first grandchild. The big mansion on Brattle Street was now full to the rafters with Washington's staff, servants, and slaves. On Christmas Eve, fires blazed in the mansion's many fireplaces as a blizzard flung snow against the tall windows. By Christmas morning, a foot of snow had fallen in Boston and fell still in the Berkshire Mountains, providing good, slippery sledding for Henry Knox to haul his train of artillery over the peaks.

⊹⇒⋅⇐⊹

On New Year's Eve, 1775, George Washington counted his troops and found he had 9,650 men, down from a summertime peak of more than 16,000 and not half the more than 20,372 troops that Congress had authorized.[26] To help stem losses, he overrode a congressional committee's recommendation that "Negroes . . . be rejected all together" for enlistment in the new army. Free blacks had been fighting alongside Washington's troops; in order to stem manpower losses and to prevent his black soldiers from switching sides, Washington asked for, and received, Congress's permission to ignore the committee's recommendation—free black soldiers could continue fighting in Washington's army.

On New Year's Day, 1776, Washington ordered the new "Union Flag" hoisted over the American camps, a flag of 13 red-and-white stripes with the British Grand Union in the upper-left corner.

When the redcoats in Boston saw a flag resembling the British Grand Union rise over the American troops, they felt a palpable sense of relief; they thought the flag signaled that the "Rebels" had read copies of the king's latest speech—in which he pledged to send 30,000 troops to quash the rebellion in spring—realized that resistance was futile, and were showing allegiance to the crown. They were mistaken. Copies of the king's speech had not yet made it to headquarters in Cambridge; in fact, many copies never made it beyond the front lines, where American troops set them afire.

January 1, 1776, essentially marked the birth date of the American army, in Cambridge, Massachusetts. The troops no longer answered to the provinces that had raised them but to the Continental Congress, and their enlistments ran until the end of the year. In his general orders of January 1, Washington wrote: "This day giving commencement to the new-army, which in every point of View is entirely Continental; the general flatters himself, that a laudable Spirit of emulation, will now take place, and pervade the whole of it."[27]

Despite its new footing, the Continental Army was still undermanned, undersupplied, and under the gun.

"It is not in the pages of History perhaps, to furnish a case like ours," Washington wrote Hancock, "to maintain a post within Musket Shot of the Enemy for Six months together without—and at the same time to disband one Army and recruit another, within that distance, of Twenty odd British regiments, is probably more than ever was attempted."[28]

By mid-January, Washington was so worried about his army's exposed condition that he lay awake next to a sleeping Martha, watching the firelight play upon the tiles of their bedroom fireplace while wondering what he could do to prevent disaster. He wrote to his friend Reed: [W]e are now without Money in our treasury—Powder in our Magazines—Arms in Our Stores . . . Engineers—Expresses. [T]he reflection upon my situation, & that of this Army, produces many an uneasy hour when all around me are wrapped in sleep."[29]

When pushed into desperate straits, Washington's default mode was to go on the attack. Even in this plaintive letter to Reed, Washington regretted not having attacked Boston sooner. Two days later, he called a council of war at his headquarters and told them that with 30,000 enemy troops heading their way come spring, they needed to make "a Bold attempt to Conquer the Ministerial Troops in Boston" now.

"The Council agreed unanimously, that a Vigorous attempt ought to be made," read the minutes of the meeting, and a call went out for 4,000 militia to assemble at Cambridge by February 1.[30]

A week before the militia was supposed to arrive, Washington had second thoughts about the attack. The Boston peninsula connected to land by only a thin neck, and the British could easily mow down his troops if they tried to march across it. British warships controlled the harbor, making an amphibious assault prohibitively dangerous. Boston Harbor needed to freeze thickly so his army could encircle the town and march on it, but by late January, there was still no ice.

True to his word of keeping Congress apprised of the military's actions, he wrote on January 24 to President John Hancock: "[N]o man upon Earth wishes more ardently to destroy the Nest in Boston, than I do—no person would be willing to go greater lengths than I shall to accomplish It, If it shall be thought advisable—but if we have neither Powder to bombard them with, nor ice to pass on, we shall be in no better situation than we have been in all year."[31]

The next day, word came into Cambridge that Knox's train of artillery had arrived in Framingham, just 10 miles away. Washington finally had enough artillery to conduct a proper siege, but he still lacked powder to "feed" the cannons.

By mid-February, the harbor had frozen, and Washington was again eager to press an attack. On February 16, he told his council of war "that a Stroke well aim'd at this critical juncture, might put a final end to the War."[32]

His generals, minus Nathanael Greene, who was sick with jaundice, took stock of their situation: By Washington's estimate, the British had 5,000 regular soldiers plus armed Loyalists in a fortified garrison (in fact, reinforcements had given them closer to 9,000 regulars.)[33] The Americans had 12,600 men, one-quarter of them militia, and not enough muskets for all. They had little gunpowder for the cannon. Faced with a lack of men, gunpowder, and arms, Washington's generals once again pulled him back from the brink. They resolved that "a Cannonade & Bombardment will be expedient and advisable as soon as there shall be a proper Supply of powder & not before . . . in the mean Time, preparations should be made to take possession of Dorchester Hill," the high ground on the peninsula just south of Boston.[34]

Washington reluctantly accepted their advice, writing to Reed: "behold! Though we had been waiting all year fir this favourable Event, the enterprise was thought too dangerous! Perhaps it was—perhaps the irksomeness of my Situation led me to undertake more than could be warranted by prudence—I did not think so."[35]

Washington hoped that if he put troops and cannon on top of the hills on Dorchester's peninsula, the British would sally out in an attempt to take the hill, precipitating another Bunker Hill–type battle.

Fortifying Dorchester's heights would be dangerous and exhausting. Like Boston, Dorchester was connected to land only by a thin causeway that could be enfiladed by British fire from Boston. Teamsters would have to goad oxen into climbing 150 feet[36] from sea level up hard, frozen hills, where men with pickaxes would have to break the ground to make earthworks to protect the gunners. Much of the protection would come from prefabricated chandeliers and fascines—frames of lumber filled with woven branches stuffed with hay to deflect shot and to screen troop movements.

With promises of gunpowder being sent from New York, Washington decided to blow off the last of his stores. On Saturday night, March 2, he ordered Knox's artillery to begin bombarding Boston from Roxbury and from the hills north of Boston. Washington's bombardment was a feint to draw British attention away from Dorchester Neck—and it worked. The British fired back, shaking the ground and lighting the night sky with shot and shell, most of which fell harmlessly on Roxbury and Prospect Hill.

Washington resumed his covering bombardments on Sunday and Monday nights, and in the predawn hours of Tuesday, March 5, 4,000 men set the protective fascines along Dorchester Neck and moved, undetected, to Dorchester Heights. Teams of oxen, 800 strong, hauled the cannon and wagons full of shot, shell, and gunpowder. In a single night, under cover of a furious bombardment from the north, the Americans set up a 20-gun artillery park. When the sun rose, the British could see the barrels of heavy cannon lording over their garrison.

+══──══+

General William Howe, who had taken Gage's post as commander in chief in October 1775, ordered his troops to capture that hill—a battle Washington was eager to fight. Washington and Howe had many superficial qualities in common: both were tall, were painfully plagued by bad teeth, and won sterling reputations in the French and Indian War. But while Washington preached against the vices of alcohol and gambling in army camps, Howe—the illegitimate son of King George I—reveled in them. In Boston, he frequented gambling tables with his blond mistress Elizabeth Loring, whose husband, Joshua, tolerated the arrangement in exchange for a lucrative sinecure as commissary of prisoners.

By noon of March 5, 1776, transport ships loaded with redcoats were shoving off from the wharves of Boston for the brief sail to Castle Island, where they would stage for a nighttime attack.

From Dorchester, regimental surgeon James Thacher observed:

> Our breast works are strengthened, and among the means of defence are a great number of barrels, filled with stones and sand, arranged in front of our works; which are to be put in motion and made to roll down the hill, to break the ranks and legs of the assailants as they advance. These are the preparations for blood and slaughter! Gracious God! If it be determined in thy Providence that thousands of our fellow creatures shall this day be slain, let thy wrath be appeased, and in mercy grant, that victory be on the side of our suffering, bleeding, country.[37]

But providence, or at least the weather, determined that thousands would not be slain that day. All that day the wind picked up; by nightfall, it was blowing at least a heavy gale,[38] making it impossible for the transports to load and unload troops. Wind and rain held through the weekend; with the bad weather—and the lingering memory of Bunker Hill sapping the morale of his troops—Howe called off the attack and began evacuating Tories and troops from Boston.

Howe never formally announced the evacuation, but from his posts, Washington could see redcoats withdrawing cannon from Bunker Hill, ships taking on soldiers at the wharves, stores being destroyed. The British ships hoisted their sails on March 17 and slipped away from Boston, only to drop anchor nine miles south in Nantasket Road, where they sat for a week. The ships' lingering presence put Washington in a bind: He wanted to reposition his troops to New York City, which he correctly surmised would be the next theater of the war. But as long as those warships loomed off Boston, he could not risk a wholesale redeployment to New York; he compromised, sending regiments of riflemen from Pennsylvania and Maryland to New York while keeping the bulk of his troops in Boston.

Finally, on March 27, 1776, the British ships sailed over the horizon, and Washington could claim victory in the siege of Boston. For him, the victory had come the hard way, not through the aggressive tactics that he favored by nature, but through patience; he had respected Congress's civil authority and accepted its rulings on everything from regulations to promotions and tactics, and he had listened to his generals, consenting with their reasoned opinion even when it contradicted his own. Through patience, mature deliberation, industriousness, and the creative spark of wrestling the guns from Fort Ticonderoga, Washington had taken his undisciplined infant army, imposed order, and won round one. The next round of the American Revolution would be infinitely more difficult.

CHAPTER 7

New York

JOHN ADAMS WAS SO EXCITED ABOUT THE SUCCESSFUL SIEGE OF Boston that he convinced his fellow congressmen to have a gold medal struck featuring an absurdly large Lady Liberty leering suggestively at Washington while grabbing his arm.[1] That design was terrible and never was struck, but it captured the exuberance of the moment.

In an April 1 letter, written from Philadelphia, Adams congratulated Washington and all "Friends of Mankind" on the successful siege; but Adams knew as well as anyone that in the big picture, Boston held little strategic advantage. New York was the most advantageous place to hold, with Adams himself calling it "a Kind of Key to the whole Continent."[2] The Hudson River, stretching all the way up from New York to Lake Champlain, provided water access almost into Canada. All communications between New England and the southern colonies eventually had to cross the Hudson. So whoever controlled New York would control the river. If the British took it, they could move their Canadian and New York troops up and down the river corridor, neatly severing New England from the colonies that supplied it with wheat and flour and sundry other goods.

As early as August of 1775, Lord Dartmouth suggested that General Gage forget about Boston and "make Hudson's River the Seat of the War."[3] By January 1776, Washington realized that a British occupation of New York would be an "evil, almost irremediable, should it happen."[4] He resolved not to let it happen.

On April 4, Washington set out for New York, with two of his aides-de-camp and his adjutant general, Horatio Gates; they rode over spring-thawed roads churned to mud by the thousands of troops that had preceded them. Eight days later, they clomped across the wooden King's Bridge over the Hudson and onto Manhattan, a patchwork of woods and streams and plowed fields stitched together by split-rail fence.

Washington rolled his way over the rocky headlands in the northern part of the island, then descended through farms and some vast, country estates, riding a full 10 miles before coming to the edge of the city—a square mile of 4,000 buildings set on wide streets. At 1 Broadway, Washington made his headquarters. On the adjacent Bowling Green stood a 15-foot-high statue of King George III on horseback, a lead figure gilded in gold. The statue provided stark symbolism that in New York, Loyalists ruled. Fully two-thirds of the city's residents held Loyalist sympathies, making New York a much tougher position for the Americans than Boston.

Topography made New York an impossible place to defend; Manhattan was, after all, an island propped up between the wide Hudson River to its west and the narrower, wilder East River dividing it from the cliffs of Long Island. To defend an island, a general needed to control the surrounding water, and Washington did not; he scarcely had a navy, while the British had the largest navy on Earth.

Washington formed his army into five brigades, each one under the command of a brigadier general. He wanted to put his best general on Long Island, where he had to hold the high ground in order to keep New York.

On April 29, Washington selected Brigadier General Nathanael Greene to command the brigade on Long Island—a curious choice. At age 32, Greene was the youngest of Washington's generals. He had never seen combat. Just a year ago, at the outbreak of hostilities at Lexington-Concord, Greene had been a private in a Rhode Island militia. He had sought a commission as a militia officer, but his peers felt that Greene—a bookish, gimp-kneed, asthmatic son of a Quaker preacher—did not have the right stuff to lead them.

But Nathanael Greene possessed qualities that did not immediately meet the eye—though informally educated, he was intelligent, and he had been the foreman of his family's ironworks, a place that employed more than 100 men. When Rhode Island's General Assembly voted to raise an army to send to Boston, they recognized Greene's leadership abilities and made him its general. At Boston, Washington had been impressed by Greene's camp, its neatness and orderliness, and Greene's strict attention to detail.

At the end of April, Greene moved onto Long Island with his three Rhode Island regiments plus two temporary regiments and a company of Pennsylvania Rifleman, an elite if rowdy company of men picked for their size and shooting ability.

As Long Island was the key to protecting New York, Brooklyn was the key to holding Long Island. A little village of less than a dozen houses and a Dutch church, Brooklyn was built on the backside of a bluff that looked across the East River and down on New York just a mile away. If the British built a park of artillery on the bluff, they could easily bomb the Americans out of New York. To defend Brooklyn, Greene continued to strengthen a chain of five forts connected by a mile-long trench that formed a wall across the approach to Brooklyn.

Washington also had fatigue parties busily fortifying posts overlooking the Hudson River, one on the New Jersey side of the river and one almost directly across from it on Manhattan. These posts, later christened Fort Lee and Fort Washington, stood on rocky cliffs more than 200 feet above the Hudson, in good position to harass any ships that might try to sail upriver to surround Manhattan. From New Jersey to Long Island, and in the streets of New York, soldiers worked like beavers, shoveling earth into the great timber frames of the chandeliers, building redoubts, hauling heavy cannon into place for an expected attack.

Washington had read the speech in which King George III pledged to send 30,000 troops to America come spring, but he could only guess where and when they might arrive. In his general orders of April 16, 1776, Washington warned his men: "If the British troops which evacuated Boston, or any part of them, are destined for this place, their Arrival may be very soon expected."[5]

Washington was wrong. The first warships did not ghost up to Sandy Hook, just south of Long Island, until June 29.

+=+

Washington had established a signal post on the Staten Island highlands: If lookouts there spied 6 or fewer ships, they'd fly one large flag of red and white stripes; if 6 to 20 ships showed, they'd raise two flags on two poles; for an armada of more than 20 ships, three striped flags on three poles. As the sun rose over Long Island on June 29, signal guns thundered from Manhattan. On the Staten Island highlands, all three flags snapped in the breeze. By noon, 40 ships had rounded Sandy Hook and dropped anchor behind the hook's protective arm. A Pennsylvania rifleman stationed on Long Island peeped through the half-moon of an outhouse door and saw a thicket of masts "resembling a forest of pine trees trimmed," he wrote. "I declare that I thought all London was afloat."[6]

By midafternoon, 100 British ships had arrived carrying 10,000 men. Washington appeared calm. Even his orders for that day speak of a sanguine pragmatism: Each private to be equipped with 24 rounds of powder and ball; all carthorses to be delivered to Colonel Knox for use of the artillery; all rowboats to be docked and ready at the Albany Pier. But his situation was desperate, and he knew it; the ink was barely dry on a letter he had written to President Hancock the previous day: "I could wish Genl Howe & his Armament not to arrive yet, as not more than a Thousand militia have yet come in, and our whole force Including the Troops at all the detached posts . . . is but small and inconsiderable when compared with the extensive lines they are to defend."[7]

Washington included a return with that letter that showed he had 9,301 officers and men fit for duty. He had split them into five divisions strung out from posts atop cliffs in New Jersey to manning a mile-long series of forts on the highlands of Long Island and in batteries down in Manhattan. It was bad form for Washington to split his troops; by doing so, they could be exposed to defeat in detail—rounded up one small detachment at a time. It's easy to criticize his troop deployment as the bumbling first attempt of an amateur; it's more difficult to suggest a better strategy. What else could he have done?

His aide, Joseph Reed, suggested in private letters that the Americans retreat and avoid a general action, but given the strategic importance of New York, this was politically unacceptable.

Washington had no idea where the British would strike first: Manhattan, Long Island, or farther up the Hudson. He had correctly identified Long Island's Brooklyn Heights as the key to holding New York. He would remain at headquarters in Manhattan and let Greene handle Long Island.

+≡≡≡+

From the sound of his general orders, Washington was in a pensive mood on July 2, 1776, the one-year anniversary of his taking command of the troops. A year before, he had never commanded anything larger than a regiment; now he had some 20,000 regular troops and militia under his command in a theater of war that stretched from Lake Champlain in present-day Vermont to Savannah, Georgia. On that day, he had these orders read aloud to his men:

> The time is now near at hand which must probably determine, whether Americans are to be, Freemen, or Slaves; whether they are to have any property they can call their own; whether their Houses, and Farms, are to be pillaged and destroyed, and they consigned to a State of Wretchedness from which no human efforts will probably deliver them. The fate of unborn Millions will now depend, under God, on the Courage and Conduct if this army. . . . Let us therefore animate and encourage each other, and shew the whole world, that Freeman contending for Liberty on his own ground is superior to any slavish mercenary on earth.[8]

On that same day, Congress was secretly approving the final draft of a Declaration of Independence. Congress announced its approval on July 4, 1776, the same day that Washington learned the details of the formidable force that Great Britain had sent to fight him.

Four British sailors captured that day at the Narrows were sent to Nathanael Greene for a nighttime interrogation. They yielded that the fleet anchored off Manhattan contained 120 sailing ships holding 10,000 men plus some Scottish Highlanders who had joined the fleet en route from Halifax; they were led by Generals William Howe, Robert Pigot, Lord Hugh Percy, James Grant, and Daniel Jones. Most astoundingly, the men said that the fleet now in the harbor would soon be joined by a larger fleet of 150 sail carrying 20,000 additional troops.

The admiral leading the overall fleet was General Howe's brother, Lord Richard Howe, whose sobriquet "Black Dick" reflected the dark complexion he shared with his brothers, one of whom had died an American hero at Ticonderoga in the French and Indian War.

Greene's intelligence was solid. Every day brought a new wave of ships; in all, the Howe brothers would have at their disposal 427 ships armed with 1,200 cannon; they carried 34,000 regular troops and seamen—a population as large as Philadelphia, America's largest city; they were stuffed with artillery, shot, shell, powder, provisions, and the horses to draw them.[9]

John Hancock formally broke the news about the Declaration of Independence to Washington in a letter that arrived at headquarters on July 9; Hancock wrote: "[T]he Congress have judged it necessary to dissolve the Connection between Great Britain and the American Colonies, and to declare them free and independent States; as you will perceive by the enclosed Declaration, which I am directed to transmit to you, and to request you will have it proclaimed at the Head of the Army."[10] Enclosed was an incomplete broadside of one of the first printed copies of the Declaration of Independence.

In his morning orders of July 9, Washington ordered troops to line up by brigades on their parade grounds at 6 P.M., where brigade majors, he ordered, were to read "with an audible voice" the declaration: "We hold these truths to be self-evident, that all men are created equal, that they are endowed by their Creator with certain unalienable Rights, that among these are Life, Liberty and the pursuit of Happiness."

Troops responded with shouts of: "Huzzah! Huzzah! Huzzah!"[11]

That night rowdy troops toppled the statue of King George III onto the Bowling Green, bringing on a rebuke from Washington; he wrote in the next day's orders that pulling down the statue "has so much the appearance of riot and want of order" that "in future these things shall be avoided by the Soldiery."[12]

On the afternoon of July 14, Washington received word that Admiral Howe's flagship *Eagle* had sailed into the harbor flying a white flag of truce to deliver a letter to him. For weeks, the Howe brothers had been widely circulating letters offering a limited peace proposal in hopes of pacifying American soldiers and civilians; Washington correctly guessed that this letter was more of the same: an offer of pardons and the removal of trade barriers in exchange for peace. He immediately called his generals who weren't off island on other duty and told them that he would refuse any letter from the Howes that did not include the honorific of "General" Washington. He then sent three officers—Colonel Joseph Reed, at this point his confidant as well as his aide-de-camp, Colonel Henry Knox, and another aide—out into the harbor to receive the flag.

As the Americans' whaleboat drew near the *Eagle,* a British lieutenant, Philip Brown, welcomed them aboard a barge. Brown took off his hat, bowed, and said, "I have a letter, sir, from Lord Howe to Mr. Washington."

Reed replied: "Sir we have no person in the army with that address."

Brown extended the letter; Reed refused to touch it but read the covering address: George Washington, Esq., &c.—&c.—, New York.

"No sir, I cannot receive that letter," Reed said.

The two sides parted; then Brown brought his barge about and shouted to the Americans, asking by what title did Washington wish to be addressed.

"You are sensible sir, of the rank of General Washington in our army?" Reed said. "All the world knows who General Washington is since the transactions of last summer."[13]

On July 20, Admiral Howe tried again, this time sending his adjutant, James Patterson, to meet with Washington at the mansion on 1 Broadway. Washington arrived for the meeting accompanied by his Life Guards, men picked for the service by their size and good appearance; his gold dress epaulettes covered the broad shoulders of his blue coat, causing Henry Knox to remark, "General Washington was very handsomely dressed, and made a most elegant appearance." Patterson "appeared awe-struck, as if he was before something supernatural."[14]

Patterson again produced the letter addressed to George Washington, Esq., &c.—&c.—, saying that the salutation "implied everything."

"It does so," Washington said, "and anything."

He again refused the letter and, with it, refused to entertain any prospect of peace. Before leaving, Patterson said that the king had given "great powers" to the Howe brothers to negotiate a peace; Washington said it appeared to him they only had the power to grant pardons, and "Those who had committed no fault wanted no pardon." Besides, he said, only Congress—which the king considered to be an unauthorized group of usurping rebels—had the power to negotiate peace.

After hearing from Patterson, Lord Howe wrote to London: "This interview . . . induced me to change my superscription for the attainment of [peace]."[15]

⊹⊱══⊰⊹

On August 1, a detachment of Nathanael Greene's riflemen observed a fresh wave of three dozen ships sailing toward their post on Long Island before tacking behind the protective arm of Sandy Hook.

These ships, some with dangling spars, cracked masts, and pockmarked hulls, had sailed directly from South Carolina, where they had recently been repulsed in an attempt to take Charleston with the loss of more than 200 men. News of the fleet's defeat at Charleston was a balm for Washington's spirits, which had been beaten by a steady drumbeat of bad news from Canada. America's Northern Army had been driven back to Fort Ticonderoga, where one-third of the troops were sick with smallpox and the remainder suffered for lack of provisions. The good news from the Southern Army was welcome indeed.

But the battered fleet also brought even more power for the Howe brothers, as it carried another 2,900 men—including General Henry Clinton, a good and aggressive officer who often clashed with General Howe over tactics, and Lord Charles Cornwallis, a young major general with military school training and combat experience. Another 100 ships straggled in with the first of the 12,000 German soldiers—most of the foreign soldiers hailed from the German state of Hesse, so American referred to all of them as Hessians. With Clinton now on station, the fleet was complete. The Howe brothers were ready for war; Washington was not. "At present, the Enemy can bring more men to a point than we can," Washington observed to General

Charles Lee. "[T]heir numbers . . . cannot by the best Intelligence we can get, fall short of 25,000 Men—Ours are under Twenty [thousand], very sickly."[16]

Camp sickness had grown into a bigger threat to Washington's troops than British bullets. By some estimates, half the 20,000 troops who had flocked to New York by mid-August were sick with dysentery.

On August 15, Washington received word from Nathanael Greene, recently promoted to major general, that he too was sick:

"I am very sorry that I am under the necessity of acquainting you that I am confined to my Bed with a raging fever," Greene wrote. In that same letter, he protested Washington's decision to remove a regiment of Rhode Island soldiers from Long Island to the New Jersey bluffs and to replace them with new troops. Greene wrote that the Rhode Island regiment's "thorough knowledge of the ground" made them indispensable on Long Island.

Greene became so sick that he nearly died. Dr. John Morgan, the army's director of hospitals, ordered the major general moved from Long Island to a house on a ridge in Manhattan. Washington gave Greene's command of the Long Island troops to Brigadier General John Sullivan, just back from a disastrous command of the Northern Army at Albany. Washington's candid assessment of Sullivan, a New Hampshire lawyer before the war, was "he has his wants; and he has his foibles—The latter are manifested in a little tincture of vanity, and in an over desire of being popular, which now and then leads him into some embarrassments." To be fair, Washington also observed that Sullivan possessed "an enterprizing genius"; and besides, Washington noted in that same letter, "His wants are common to us all; the want of experience to move upon a large Scale."[17]

By daylight of August 22, a fresh wind blew from the north, and the day dawned gin clear, revealing that under cover of darkness, three British frigates and two bomb ketches, *Carcass* and *Thunder*, had slipped through the Narrows and dropped anchor in Gravesend Bay. With their broadsides to the beaches the ships were prepared to lob shells at anyone foolhardy enough to oppose the landing of troops on the beaches of Long Island.

A fleet of transport boats followed, some 400 in all, including 75 flat-bottomed boats with hinged bows that dropped onto the beach, allowing artillery to roll right out. For three hours, transports sailed and rowed across the calm, blue waters of Gravesend Bay carrying regiments of red-coated soldiers, Hessian detachments in new blue coats with yellow trousers, kilted Scottish

Highlanders, muscle-rippled draft horses, refulgent brass cannon, all gliding beachward in a beautiful, terrible choreography of war.

By noon, 15,000 British soldiers were ashore on Long Island.

⊹╾═╼⊹

General John Sullivan took the Long Island command on August 20, a command that lasted all of four days before Washington replaced him with Israel Putnam, "Old Put," a semiliterate 58-year-old who was a better storyteller than a general. Putnam, ensconced in Manhattan when it had become clear that Long Island was going to be the target of attack, had felt "miserable" at being passed over for the exciting Long Island command by Sullivan, a less senior general.

On August 25, Washington relented and gave Putnam command of Long Island, telling him to make sure that "your best men should at all hazards prevent the enemy's passing the wood," meaning the wooded ridge stretching away from Brooklyn to the east.

For days, the British and Hessian troops remained encamped in and around Flatbush, forming a line along the base of the ridge rising across Long Island, while their commanders reconnoitered the ground.

At its southern tip, Long Island's sandy beaches gave way to what Washington called "level and open lands" to the village of Flatbush; north of the village, the ground began to rise to the top of a ridge called the heights of Guana. This miles-wide ridge stretched laterally across much of Long Island. The sloping, woody ground was pierced by four passes from west to east: Gowanus Road, Flatbush Road, Bedford Pass, and Jamaica Pass. British troops trying to reach Brooklyn from the south would have to file through one of these passes.

While riding reconnaissance, General Henry Clinton made a surprising discovery: In positioning the American troops, Putnam had failed to protect Jamaica Pass, the easternmost pass through the heights. Clinton suggested that Howe send 10,000 men through this pass under cover of darkness; once these troops climbed to the top of the ridge, they could turn the flank of the line that Putnam had formed across the heights and run them all the way back into the American lines at Brooklyn. Howe, who often found Clinton officious and transparently ambitious, agreed with this plan.

In preparing to receive an attack, Washington often displayed an indecisiveness that he never showed when prosecuting one. Until the very day of battle, he remained unsure whether the British would focus their entire attack on Long Island, or whether they would bring a division up the Hudson River to simultaneously attack his posts there. As a result, he initially sent only six regiments to reinforce Long Island, giving Putnam command of about 6,000 men to face the 15,000 British and Hessians already ashore. On Sunday, August 25, General Howe landed another 4,300 Hessians, giving him nearly 20,000 troops on Long Island; Washington eventually put 9,500 troops at Putnam's disposal—but as Nathanael Greene had observed, none of them knew the ground, and only a handful were horsemen. Washington had recently sent three regiments of light horse back to their home state of Connecticut after concluding that since the horsemen refused to get off their horses and fight as infantry, "they can be no longer of Use here—where Horse cannot be brought to action."[18]

When the last of the Hessians landed on Long Island, General Howe decided the time had come to attack. He would first assault the American right, the westernmost troops, to divert attention while the bulk of his troops scaled the heights through Jamaica Pass. On the night of August 26, nearly 10,000 British and Hessian troops under the command of General James Grant and Colonel Carl von Donop headed up the heights on the west to draw out American lines guarding three of the four passes through the heights.

At 11 P.M., some Pennsylvania riflemen fired on a party of General Grant's advance scouts who were raiding a watermelon patch; the shots from that skirmish announced the Battle of Long Island.

At the sound of the firing, Putnam sent General William Alexander (who claimed some vague ties to an English estate and preferred to be called "Lord Stirling"—an indulgence that his contemporaries granted) and his brigade of 1,600 to form the right side of the American line; to Stirling's left, General John Sullivan formed a line of about 1,500 to protect Flatbush Pass.

By 8 A.M. of August 27, Washington had crossed the East River and climbed from the ferry landing to the forts at Brooklyn Heights; soon he heard rifle fire cracking directly to his south, where Pennsylvania riflemen were trading fire with some of Grant's light troops firing from the leafy cover of an orchard. This went on for about two hours before the timbre of the battle changed to the deeper, full-throated booms of artillery.

The Americans had wheeled two cannon down the hill to cover the Narrows Road on their right; Grant had countered by bringing up four cannon and two howitzers, which pounded the American lines from 300 yards away. The cannon thundered for about an hour before Stirling made a sickening discovery: The vanguard of the British troops that had spent the night scaling the heights through Jamaica Pass, unopposed, was to his rear, cutting off his retreat to the forts at Brooklyn. Before him, Grant's troops formed a battle line ready to march uphill. The time had come for Stirling to try and fight his way through Cornwallis's troops behind him, back to the forts. With Cornwallis controlling the roads, the American troops would have to skirt around the heights, pass through spongy marsh, and ford Gowanus Creek, 80 yards wide and deep now at high tide.

To the east of Stirling, the situation was largely the same; Sullivan's troops, outnumbered and outgunned, turned in retreat from von Donop's Hessians only to find British troops at their rear.

From a hill behind the walls of his forts, Washington watched as his troops tried to make their way back into Brooklyn. With five companies of Maryland men, about 250 in all, Stirling climbed toward the British 2nd Grenadiers and 71st Highlanders hoping to fight his way through, or at least provide protection for the men trying to swim the creek. British cannon poured grapeshot and canister into the creek, which splashed and sizzled around the retreating men like hot hail.

Six times the Maryland companies charged; six times they were turned back. As he watched the fighting from Brooklyn Heights, Washington is reported to have said: "Good God! What brave fellows I must this day lose."[19] And lose them he did: More than 1,000 American troops, including Generals Stirling and Sullivan and scores of other officers, never made it back through American walls. Most of them, such as Stirling and Sullivan, were captured, though 200 were wounded or killed. Washington figured he lost 1,012 men that day; the rest, about 2,500, poured back over the walls with battalions of British and Hessian troops on their heels.

The attackers came within 150 yards of the main redoubt of the American walls before finally heeding General Howe's loudly repeated orders to halt.

"Had they been permitted to go on, it is my opinion they would have carried the redoubt," Howe wrote in an after-action report, "but as it was apparent the lines must have been ours at a very cheap rate by regular approaches, I would not risk the loss that might have been sustained in the assault."[20]

By midafternoon, August 27, the battle was over. Howe drew his troops up in front of the American walls, giving them a chance to rest after marching as far as 10 miles, through the night, uphill, without food, and fighting a battle. From outside, the mile-long stretch of earthworks and abatis (tree sections stuck in the ground with branches sharpened to points) looked formidable, and Howe wanted to probe it for weaknesses. He was in no hurry; as soon as the wind shifted, his brother could sail ships of the line up the East River. Washington would be trapped with half his army. As Lord Percy wrote home to the Duke of Northumberland: "Everything seems to be over with them, and I flatter myself now that this campaign will put a total end to the war."[21]

In his first pitched battle against British regulars, George Washington had done nearly everything wrong. By leaving half of his force in Manhattan, he had engaged nearly all of the British army with only half of his troops. It was not his fault that Greene got sick, but after he did, Washington changed commanders twice in a single week when battle was imminent; he had not made sure that any of his commanders knew the ground they were trying to defend; in a fit of pique, he had previously dismissed his cavalry, when riders could have given him early warning of Howe's presence in Jamaica Pass. Clearly the professional generals—Howe, Clinton, and Cornwallis—had outfoxed Washington, pinning him down with 20,000 troops at his front and his back against a mile-wide river.

But there was one thing about George Washington that Howe never did learn: When cornered, Washington was at his most ingenious.

⊹⊱━⊰⊹

George Washington had not been in a situation this desperate since his troops had lain in the blood- and mud-filled trenches of Fort Necessity. Almost the whole day after the Battle of Long Island, he rode astride a horse whose gray color matched the pewter skies, viewing his lines, riding down to the Brooklyn Ferry to welcome reinforcements and to dispatch them to posts. Among the reinforcements were two Massachusetts regiments drawn from seaport towns such as Gloucester, Newburyport, and Marblehead, men who had been fishing the foggy banks off Cape Cod and Newfoundland since they could walk. They dressed like the sailors they were, in breeches waterproofed with a coating of tar, blue coats, and white sailor's caps.[22]

From the right, or south, of Washington's line, came the *boom* and *crack* of musket and rifle fire, the sounds of skirmishing between some of his regiments and a large party of Loyalists battling for control of a cornfield and its bounty of green corn. Washington usually discouraged long-distance skirmishing as a waste of ammunition, but today he encouraged it to maintain a fighting spirit in his men.

At evening, the sounds of firing ceased, washed away by the sweep of rain. All into the night the rain came down, wetting gunpowder and soaking through clothes to the skin. The men had to stay at their posts, huddled in trenches behind the earthen walls, waiting should the enemy try to storm them. The walls were so long that every man needed to maintain his post round the clock, slouching in trenches that filled with rain, waiting for a dinner, then a breakfast, that never came.

That night, Washington did not sleep. He made headquarters in a mansion known locally as Four Chimneys; by candlelight he wrote to President Hancock at 4:30 A.M., telling him about the skirmishing, a lack of tents, and the rain "which has occasioned much sickness and the Men to be almost broke down."[23] He said he'd send across the East River to Manhattan for more tents, indicating that he planned to hold the forts.

That afternoon, his plan changed. At a council of war, Washington and his generals took stock of their situation: heavy rains, no tents, little food, worn-out men, weak lines, a northeast wind being the only thing preventing enemy ships from coming upriver and cutting off communication with Manhattan. They voted unanimously to withdraw—a thing easier said than done.

To get off Long Island, Washington would have to break down his lines, then turn his back to the enemy to march to the ferry—exposing his flank. To keep Lord Howe from taking advantage of this vulnerability, Washington told no one but his generals of the withdrawal. He decided to move under cover of darkness, with carriage wheels muffled in cloth and men under orders to keep the strictest silence, not even to cough.

At 7 P.M. on August 29, the regiment of Massachusetts fishermen under Colonel John Glover gathered at the ferry landing to man the boats, a collection of flat-bottom rowboats, top-heavy sailboats, essentially anything that would float.

An hour later, the first of nearly 10,000 troops cast off; about then the tide began to ebb and the wind blew a gale from northeast, pushing the lighter sailing ships downriver toward the British fleet. Given the conditions, only 11 of the heaviest, flat-bottomed rowboats could cross. For the next 10 hours, Glover's men crossed and recrossed the shifting currents of a mile-wide river, first through a gale, then after midnight through a thick fog, using nothing but compasses and dead reckoning. Some of them made the crossing 11 times, rowing a distance of 22 miles. They hauled men and horses, kegs of flour and salt pork, gunpowder and cannon, taking all but the heaviest.

The fog that had cloaked their retreat burned off with the coming of day; by 7 A.M, Washington could see the red coats of British troops pouring into the works on Brooklyn Heights. He had taken all of his men off the island but three who had stopped to plunder.

Washington, now 44 years old, had not slept for three nights; he had overseen a battle, ridden two days in a soaking rain, and engineered a near-miraculous retreat. Benjamin Tallmadge, who later managed Washington's secret service, observed: "In the history of warfare I do not recollect a more fortunate retreat. Gen. Washington has never received the credit which was due to him for this wise and most fortunate measure."[24]

The retreat had saved the American army, but no one felt like celebrating.

+≓═╡+

From his headquarters in Manhattan, George Washington wrote to Congress: "Our situation is truly distressing." Entire companies of militia regiments were marching off for home; he had fewer than 20,000 men while his adversary had more than 30,000 plus a fleet of warships; the morale of troops was low, though they had enough energy to plunder. And yet, Washington wrote Congress, he still felt as though he could hold the city: "Till of late, I had no doubt in my own mind of defending this place nor should I have yet If the Men would do their duty."[25]

From his sickbed on the outskirts of New York, Major General Nathanael Greene caught wind of Washington's belief that he could still hold

Manhattan. Greene was incredulous. He wrote Washington: "I give it as my opinion that a General and speedy Retreat is absolutely necessary and that the honor and Interest of America requires it. I would burn the City and Suburbs to prevent the British from using them as winter quarters."[26]

After reading Greene's letter, Washington called a council of war for September 7; Greene was still too sick to attend, and after much debate the assembled generals rebuffed his advice: They would redeploy the troops—leaving 5,000 in Manhattan and 9,000 at King's Bridge, 16 miles north—and try to hold onto New York awhile longer.

Greene drafted a polite but firm petition protesting the decision; six brigadier generals signed it, asking Washington to reconsider. Washington again called for a war council on September 12, and Greene got out of his sickbed to present his case for evacuating Manhattan. (Burning it was out of the question—Congress had forbidden that.)

No minutes of that meeting exist, but judging from dueling arguments submitted by Greene and by Brigadier Generals William Heath and George Clinton, the debate must have been spirited. Greene's argument for quitting Manhattan was that if they didn't, the British could land troops midway up the island, form a line across it, and cut off troops in the city from those up at King's Bridge, severing ties and then conquering each small army.

Heath and Clinton argued that the Howe brothers had not attacked the city because it was so well fortified that they did not dare. "The whole Island," Clinton wrote, "is broken Land very capable of Defence." Abandoning New York would allow the British to expand the war into neighboring states and "greatly Dispirt both the army, and the Country."

Washington was on the fence. Prior to the war council, he had written to Hancock that, on one hand, New York

> was acknowledged by every man of Judgement to be untenable. . . . On the other hand, to abandon a City which has been deemed by some defensible and on whose Works much Labor has been bestowed has a tendency to dispirt the Troops and enfeeble our Cause: It has been considered the key to the Northern Country. . . .
>
> I am sensible a retreating Army is encircled with difficulties, that the declining an Engagemt subjects a General to reproach.[27]

On a vote of 10 to 3—with Washington, as always, abstaining—Greene's argument carried the day with one compromise: The American army would evacuate most of Manhattan, but 8,000 troops would remain in Forts Washington and Lee, the two posts perched on bluffs high above the Hudson on the Manhattan and New Jersey shores.

Now Washington had to move about 12,000 men across King's Bridge, 16 miles away; about half of them would continue on down the Hudson to Fort Lee. If the British attacked while his baggage wagons were rolling and his men were on the march, he would be vulnerable. They did, and he was.

<hr />

The plan that Nathanael Greene most feared—an amphibious landing midway up Manhattan, followed by stretching a line of British and Hessian troops across the island's two-mile width—was exactly what the Howe brothers were working on. To put their plan into action, they would have to move transport boats high up the swiftly flowing East River; to get the boats there without being sunk by American batteries on Manhattan, they needed incoming tides at night, conditions that did not coincide with frequency until mid-September.[28]

While the Howes waited, the Americans debated, finally deciding to evacuate Manhattan at precisely the same time the British were ready to attack it. A brigade of troops marched out of the city on September 13, bound for the mainland across King's Bridge.

"We are now taking every method in our Power to remove the Store &c. in which we find innumerable difficulties," Washington wrote Hancock on September 14. "I fully expected an attack [from the British] would have been made last Night. . . . happy I shall be If my apprehensions of One to Night or in a day or two, are not confirmed by the Event."[29]

Washington did not need unnatural prescience to foresee a looming attack. The day before, four warships had passed up the East River, drawing prodigious fire from the batteries to little effect.[30] Knowing that an attack was imminent was easy; knowing where it would be centered was not. Washington had 16 miles of waterfront to defend, so he formed a chain of sentinels stretching about 5 miles to cover the most likely landing places.

Every half hour the sentinels would pass word down the chain: "All is well." In the absolute quiet of an eighteenth-century night, sailors on the warships in the river could hear and answer: "We'll change your tune by morning."[31]

In the dark of a moonless night, the warships had slipped to within 200 yards of the Manhattan shore; daylight showed them in intimidating glory, big double-decked ships with their gun ports open, broadside to the shore. The sun arced higher into the sky on an unusually hot day for mid-September; at 10 A.M., a fleet of flatboats sprang out from the Long Island shore behind the warships, packed with 4,000 red-coated soldiers, so many that an American private observed "they appeared like a large clover field in full bloom."[32]

For an hour, the flatboats lined up behind the warships, then a pennant slid up the mainmast of *Phoenix* signaling the cannon to fire. All at once the ships touched off their cannon, hitting the American lines with a shock of sound and shell.

"The first broadside made a considerable breach in their works," a midshipman on the *Orpheus* dryly noted, "and the enemy fled on all sides, confused and calling for quarter."[33] The ships fired for 59 minutes with the *Orpheus* alone burning through more than 5,000 pounds of gunpowder. With American resistance blown away, the first of the British and Hessian troops stepped ashore on Manhattan at Kip's Bay.

Washington heard the thunder of ship's cannon from the top of Harlem Heights, where he'd had a good vantage point to watch his troops marching from the city. He rode at a gallop, sweeping down the heights for four miles toward Kip's Bay. He galloped through a scene of confusion—the Connecticut militiamen assigned to oppose the landing had done the natural thing: They had run away. As they fled from the shoreline into the Post Road, they ran into the columns of men streaming north on the retreat, spreading panic.

A half mile from Kip's Bay, Washington crested a hill that sloped down to the landing, a place now called Murray Hill. He quickly realized the tactical advantage of securing this hill, and thanks to Brigadier Generals Samuel Holden Parsons and John Fellows, he had men in place to take it. At the first sound of firing, Parsons and Fellows had marched their Continental regiments toward it, arriving from the west with eight regiments.

General Henry Clinton had also recognized the value of Murray Hill, and as Washington peered down the hill, a wave of British grenadiers was methodically climbing it.

"Take the walls!" Washington shouted to Parsons. "Take the cornfield!"[34]

Parsons's brigade broke in confusion; some ran for the walls, some ran for the cornfield, and some ran for their lives. Fellows's brigade followed suit.

In contrast to the regular British troops, marching in line formation to the beat of a drum with bayonets leveled, the Continentals were running helter-skelter; behind them, where the Post Road crossed over the hill, troops were shedding packs, dropping muskets, and fleeing. Washington dropped back to the Post Road, where he tried to stop the panic and rally his troops. Here, he lost his famous self-control and flashed his infamous temper; details of his conduct vary, but there is no doubt that the mob mentality of panic excited him not to fear but to anger.

Colonel William Smallwood of the Maryland troops swore he saw fleeing men "caned and whipped" by Washington and two other generals; James Thacher, the regimental surgeon, wrote that Washington "drew his sword and snapped his pistols" at fleeing men.[35] George Weedon, then a colonel who had served with Washington in the First Virginia Regiment, wrote that as he stood against the current of men fleeing around him, Washington "struck several officers in their flight, three times dashed his hatt on the ground, and at last exclaimed 'Good god have I got such Troops as Those.'"

William Heath wrote of a similar hat-throwing temper tantrum, and Nathanael Greene noted, "Parsons and Fellows Brigade run away from about fifty men and left his Excellency on the Ground within Eighty Yards of the Enemy so vext at the infamous conduct of the Troops that he sought Death rather than life."[36]

Neither Weedon, Heath, nor Greene actually witnessed the action on Murray Hill, but their stories are consistent; for his part, all Washington would write is that he "used every possible effort to rally [the troops] but to no purpose, & on the appearance of a small part of the enemy (not more than Sixty or Seventy in Number) they ran off without firing a Single Shot."[37]

Washington rode up to Harlem Heights, where he succeeded in stopping his troops' flight. When Clinton's 4,000 men landed on Manhattan, Washington still had 3,000 troops down in the city, awaiting orders to march. General Howe had had no idea that his troop landing would catch Washington in midtreat. He'd ordered Clinton to remain on the high ground of Murray Hill until the rest of the troops—another 9,000 men—had crossed. Landing those troops took much of the day, and while the British massed atop the hill, the 3,000 Americans in New York slipped away up the west side of Manhattan, marching a dozen miles through the heat. The last of the men straggled up Harlem Heights around sunset, literally minutes before the British troops finished forming a line across the island to choke off the retreat. Washington lost about 350 men in the retreat, most of them captured though a few were killed in skirmishes. The loss of baggage was great—tents, kettles, packs, and muskets were left in warehouses, in abandoned wagons, or dropped on the run.

From his new headquarters on Harlem Heights, Washington wrote Hancock: "[T]he retreat was effected with but little or no loss of Men, tho of a considerable part of our baggage occasioned by this disgracefull and dastardly conduct. . . . We are now encamped with the Main body of the Army on the Heights of Harlem where I should hope the Enemy would meet with defeat in case of an Attack."[38]

<hr />

General Washington withdrew his troops to the high ground of Harlem Heights on the night of their retreat, September 14, having them camp in formation in anticipation of an attack.

As he looked out from the heights the next morning, Washington liked what he saw. Finally he was on some strong ground to defend, a narrow, rocky headland that dropped to the Hudson River in the east and the smooth field of Harlem Plains stretching to the west. South of him was a grove called the Hollow Way, a narrow valley through which no one could pass without being raked by the artillery he'd been able to haul out of New York.

That night of September 15, he sent a reconnaissance party of about 120 rangers down the Hollow Way to determine whether Howe's troops were digging in or preparing to advance. The rangers were under the command of Lieutenant Colonel Thomas Knowlton, who had once been singled out by Washington for his daring raid on British barracks outside Boston.

At daybreak, September 16, Washington rode down to visit his sentries atop the lip of the Hollow Way.

"When I arrived there, I heard a firing," Washington wrote to Hancock, a firing of a thousand shots from his men alone.[39] The rangers had passed through the Hollow Way that morning and, while climbing the southern edge of the bowl-shape hollow up Morningside Heights, they had surprised a detachment of British light infantry.

Colonel Joseph Reed, who had ridden out to check on Knowlton, galloped back to Washington and told him that the rangers had stood their ground under fire from nearly three times their number and were now coolly retreating in good order. On their heels came the sound of a British bugler blowing the notes of a fox hunt. For Washington, a proud Virginian who liked nothing better than hunting down a fox, it must have been galling to be treated as if he were the prey.

"Our Men came in & told me that the body of the Enemy, who kept themselves concealed consisted of about three Hundred as near as they could guess," Washington continued in his letter to Hancock. Reed suggested that the troops on Harlem Heights launch a counterattack.

That was all Washington needed to hear. After being dislodged from the works on Long Island and routed in his retreat to Harlem Heights, Washington was eager to attack rather than defend.

"I immediately ordered three Companies of Colo. Weedons Regiment from Virginia . . . and Col. Knolton with his Rangers . . . to try and get in their Rear," Washington wrote in his official report to Hancock. A detachment of 150 New Englanders drawn from Nathanael Greene's division swept down the Hollow Way to divert attention while the Virginians and the rangers tried to sneak around to the rear of the British light infantry detachment. It worked: The redcoats moved down Morningside Heights, advancing on the New Englanders without noticing the Americans skulking through the woods to their right.

Before Knowlton placed his troops behind the British, an American fired on the enemy's right flank, alerting them; the redcoats pulled back 200 yards and re-formed behind a fence. Musket balls splintered the fence as the Americans fired on their position; in the return fire, both Knowlton and Colonel Andrew Leitch, commander of the Virginia troops, were shot down, both eventually dying. Despite losing their leaders, the rangers and Virginians fought on.

A brigade of Greene's troops poured down as reinforcements, and the troops that had arrogantly blown the bugle that morning now turned and ran, retreating up Morningside Heights toward the main camp of the British army. Reinforcements poured in from both sides, and what had begun as a skirmish evolved into the Battle of Harlem Heights, with 2,000 men drawn up on each side of a buckwheat field.

Israel Putnam, Greene, and Reed rode among the troops barking encouragement, although Reed later allowed that it might have been "rash and imprudent for Officers of our Rank to go into such an action."[40] Around 1 P.M., Washington wisely pulled his troops back as British reserves drew up, bringing nearly 5,000 enemy soldiers to the action.

In the battle, neither side gained an inch of ground, and the number of casualties was fairly even: 30 Americans killed and 100 wounded; 14 British and Hessians killed, 154 wounded. Yet for Washington, it was a badly needed moral victory. In his general orders of September 17, he wrote: "The Behaviour of Yesterday was such a Contrast, to that of some Troops the day before, as must shew what may be done, where Officers and soldiers will exert themselves."

And in recounting the battle on September 20, Washington wrote: "This little Advantage has inspirited our Troops prodigiously, they find that It only requires Resolution and Good Officers, to mane an enemy, that they stood in too Much dread of, Give Way."[41]

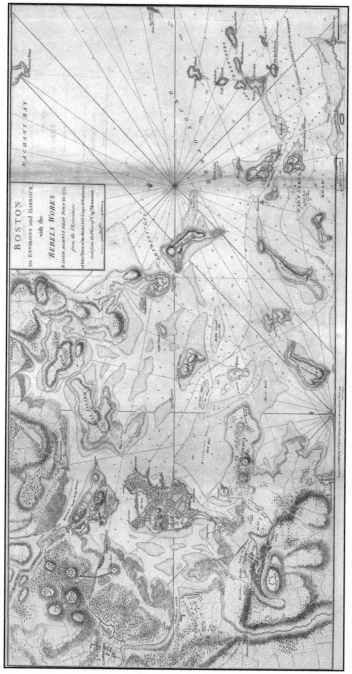

Boston as drawn in 1775 by a lieutenant in His Majesty's Corps of Engineers. The Boston peninsula, tenuously connected to the mainland by a slender neck, was set in a basin flanked by the hills of Charlestown to the north and Dorchester in the south. Courtesy of the Library of Congress.

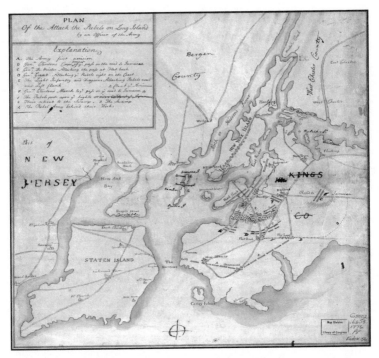

Hand-colored map issued by the London printer John Bowles & Son in 1776, following the British rout of American troops on Long Island. The map, sketched by an anonymous officer in the British army, shows how British troops filed through a pass on the east side of Long Island to flank the Americans, driving them back into their works at Brooklyn. Courtesy of the Library of Congress.

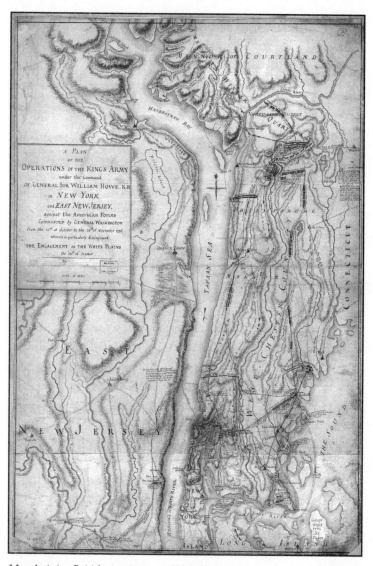

Map depicting British victories around New York in the autumn of 1776, with an emphasis on the Battle of White Plains. General William Howe's troops moved north through Westchester County and drove Washington's troops back across the Croton River. Courtesy of the Library of Congress.

George Washington at Princeton. Painting by Charles Willson Peale, 1779.
Courtesy of the Library of Congress.

The Marquis de Lafayette. Under the tutelage of George Washington and Nathanael Greene, Lafayette grew from a reckless, glory-seeking commander into a mature general who led a conservative, effective Virginia campaign in the months before the siege of Yorktown. Courtesy of the Library of Congress.

"Prayer at Valley Forge," fanciful 1866 engraving by John C. McCrae, depicting Washington in prayer at Valley Forge. Courtesy of the Library of Congress.

Comte de Rochambeau, commander of the French army in America, from an original painting by Charles Willson Peale. Courtesy of the Library of Congress.

LORD HOWE.

Lord Richard Howe, brother of General William Howe and commander of the British fleet. Courtesy of the Library of Congress.

General John Sullivan of New Hampshire. Washington gave Sullivan key commands at the unsuccessful battles of Long Island and Brandywine, and the siege of Rhode Island. His hot temper threatened to break up the nascent French Alliance at Rhode Island. Courtesy of the Library of Congress.

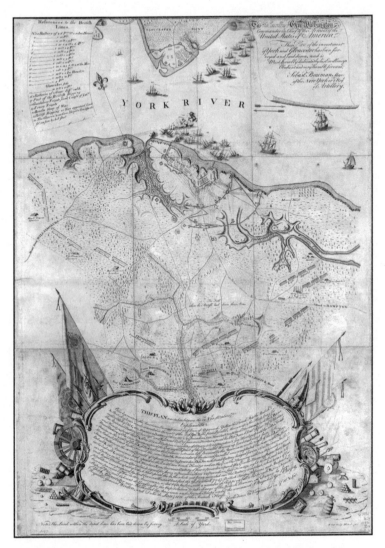

Hand-colored map published in Philadelphia in 1782, showing positions of the French, American, and British troops at Yorktown, Virginia, the decisive battle of the American Revolution. Courtesy of the Library of Congress.

CHAPTER 8

"The Times that Try Men's Souls"

GENERAL WILLIAM HOWE WAS A METHODICAL, CAUTIOUS COM-
mander. As he spied Washington's lines across Harlem Heights in late September 1776, Howe concluded that they were too strong for an uphill frontal
attack. So he turned his thoughts to the New York mainland north of Manhattan and Long Island. If he could move the main body of his troops there,
he could sweep in behind Washington's position on Harlem Heights, cutting
off supplies from Connecticut and trapping the Americans between King's
Bridge and Long Island.

On October 12, 1776, Howe again put his army on the move; from
Manhattan's eastern shore, the troops clambered aboard all kinds of boats—
small flat-bottomed boats, transports, large frigates, even ships of war holding
44 guns—for what promised to be a wild, nighttime ride up the East River
through "Hell's Gate," the swirling, eddying confluence of the East River,
Harlem River, and Long Island Sound.

Miraculously, the fleet made it through, save for one boat holding an artillery company and three six-pound cannons, which sank with the loss of four men.

Howe picked an awful place to land his army—Throg's Neck, a marshy spit of land near Westchester. At high tide, the neck was an island severed from the mainland by a waist-deep ford; a company of Pennsylvania riflemen held the only bridge from the neck, forcing Howe to rethink his plans.

While Howe waited in the marsh of Throg's Neck, Washington schemed atop Harlem Heights. On October 16, he rode down to King's Bridge for a council of war that included General Charles Lee, just returned from his command in the South, and Generals Stirling and Sullivan, who had been exchanged for high-ranking British officials.

The generals agreed that the American army had to leave Harlem Heights, ground Washington had vowed to keep till his death, in order to keep Howe from severing supply lines to their rear. Minutes of the meeting show they also "Agreed that Fort Washington"—the fort at the highest, northernmost point of Harlem Heights—be "retained as long as possible" with a force of 2,000 men.

Howe's blunder in landing at Throg's Neck bought Washington time to react, but not much. On the day Washington was holding war council at King's Bridge, Howe was reembarking his troops for a three-mile sail to Pell's Point, solid ground that would put them on the road to White Plains, a crucial village. White Plains crouched in the center of a web of roads that formed the main route of supplies for the Continental Army. Washington pushed the bulk of his army for White Plains while he rode ahead, arriving there on October 22. Anxious not to repeat the mistakes of Long Island, he rode reconnaissance with some of his other generals.

On the morning of October 28, Washington was riding with General Lee, who pointed to some high ground north of the village and said, "Yonder is the ground we ought to occupy."

"Let us then go and view it," Washington replied, and the scouting party began riding off to the north, leaving behind a rise called Chatterton's Hill, which seemed to rise straight out of the Bronx River. This hill stood southwest of the village, humping up about 180 feet, its sides covered in woods but the top bald and ribbed with stone walls. But before the scouting party had put Chatterton's Hill too far behind, a horseman galloped up. "The British are on the camp, sir," he said.

The news sank in; and Washington said, "Gentlemen, we have now other business than reconnoitering."

Drummers were beating troops to their posts when Washington's party galloped into White Plains. As his army drew up to meet the advancing British troops, Washington said to his generals, "Gentlemen, you will repair to your respective posts, and do the best that you can."[1]

While Washington had been scouting the ground at White Plains, General Howe had continued the conservative ways he'd shown outside Brooklyn and on Murray Hill, drawing up his troops at New Rochelle for a few days to await 4,000 Hessian-German reinforcements, giving him 13,000 men in all.

On October 28, Howe's army moved out in two columns, marching for White Plains, which lay just four miles north of his camp. Washington had deployed to receive them. He did not occupy the high ground that Lee had pointed out because it was north of the village and he wanted to prevent the British from occupying White Plains. He had put about 500 militia on Chatterton's Hill, west of the village. Now Washington quickly reinforced that militia with two cannon and most of his best troops—the Maryland Continentals under Colonel William Smallwood, and two regiments from New York, some 1,600 men in all.

General Howe marched his troops toward White Plains in two columns, the one on the right under Henry Clinton, the left under the command of Hessian General Leopold Philipp von Heister. Washington sent a skirmishing party to head off their advance, but by noon, the British and German troops had managed to drive them back.

Howe quickly recognized Chatterton's Hill, across a river on his left, as the key to that day's battle. He took his time, methodically setting up a 12-gun park of artillery on a nearby rise. On the signal to fire, the cannon roared. Hot shot ignited the dry leaves of autumn; the wooded slope smoked as 4,000 British and Germans forded the Bronx River, split into two parties, and stormed the hill.

The right side of the American line was anchored by militia, a tactical error by Washington. Outnumbered by German troops advancing with leveled bayonets, the green troops broke and ran, exposing the right flank of the

Maryland and 3rd New York Continentals fighting with British regulars storming their post. The two American regiments fought for about a half hour before being driven off the hill, leaving Howe's troops in control of the high ground west of White Plains. The Americans had made them pay, dishing out 313 casualties for 150 received, but had Washington done a better job of deploying his men—putting more and better troops across the hill, not anchoring a flank with militia—he might have taken a higher toll.

By 5 P.M., Howe was looking down from Chatterton's Hill at Washington's vulnerable army; but the days are short in October, and he did not press his advantage before dark.

After the Battle of White Plains, a lieutenant in Smallwood's regiment wrote: "In this affair, as in too many of a similar nature, our Generals show'd not equal judgment to that of the Enemy. We were badly disposed to receive the attack of the Enemy's small arms, and unfortunately much exposed to their Artillery, which flank'd us so heavily as to render the post tenable but a short time."[2]

The next morning, General Howe did not like what he saw. It appeared that Washington's troops had spent the night with shovels in hand, throwing up embankments and strengthening their lines. Again he called for reinforcements, bringing up six more battalions for a decisive attack on Washington's army. It only took a day to get the reinforcements in place; but that night, a hard rain fell, wetting gunpowder and shutting down the artillery. Howe postponed his attack and Washington, sensing danger, withdrew his troops to higher ground about a mile and a half north of White Plains.

General Howe, content with driving the rebels out of New York City and from Long Island, did not pursue.

From his post near White Plains after the battle, George Washington polled 13 of his generals on what to do next. General Howe commanded a huge force of near 30,000 men that he seemingly could move at will. To contain him, the American generals agreed that they needed to divide their force: 6,000 men under Charles Lee would remain on the eastern edge of the Hudson to check Howe should he try to march north from White Plains; General Heath would keep another 3,500 men north of Lee to protect the Hudson

Highlands at Peekskill; and Washington would cross the Hudson with 3,000 to shore up the troops already in New Jersey under Greene.

Lee was so pleased with the arrangement that he declared "I believe my friend Howe has lost the campaign;"[3] but at this point, any eighteenth-century armchair general could have looked at a map of the troop deployments and easily determined which were under the command of a seasoned professional and which were directed by an amateur. General Howe had the mass of his men contained in a formidable fighting force; Washington's troops were scattered helter-skelter up one side of the Hudson and down the other. All of his detachments were vulnerable to defeat in detail—being rolled up one by one by an army of superior force.

By early November, Howe merely had to decide which of several low-hanging fruit to pluck first. On his map, one American detachment literally stuck out above the rest: the 1,800 men in the garrison atop Mount Washington, the highest ground on Manhattan. These were the only American troops still left on the island; Howe did not like having them at his back, and he was determined to turn back to wipe out that threat. An American deserter made his decision even easier by wandering into a British camp with the plans of Fort Washington—the height of its walls, its gun emplacements, the number of men in it. Riders relayed the plans to Howe's camp outside White Plains on November 4, and that day he began his march with Fort Washington in his sights.

A few days later, Washington had a flash of insight about Fort Washington: That garrison had been built to prevent British shipping from sailing up the Hudson; whenever ships came up, the guns of Forts Washington and Lee thundered ceaselessly. And yet, Washington noted, the ships passed those garrisons anyway, with little more than damage to their rigging.

Washington sent a letter down to Nathanael Greene, in command of Fort Lee, 70 miles south, asking: "If we cannot prevent Vessels passing up, and the Enemy are possessed of the surrounding Country, what valuable purpose can it answer to hold a post from which the expected Benefit cannot be had[?] I am therefore inclined to think it will not be prudent to hazard the Men and Stores at Mount Washington, but as you are on the Spot, leave it to you to give such Orders as to evacuating Mount Washington."

Greene wrote back the next day, telling Washington: "Upon the whole I cannot help thinking the Garrison is of advantage—and I cannot conceive the Garrison to be in any great danger."[4] On the morning of November 15, 1776, a British drummer beat for a parley while his officer approached the foot of Mount Washington waving a white flag of truce. The officer, Colonel James Patterson, had a proposal for the fort's commander, a Pennsylvania colonel and rifleman named Robert Magaw: Surrender the fort or risk every life in it. The night before, 30 British flatboats had slipped up the Hudson River carrying troops. Mount Washington was now surrounded.

Magaw sent a message across the Hudson to Greene, up in Fort Lee on the bluffs of the Jersey shore. Patterson "waits for an answer," Magaw said. "I shall send a proper one. We are determined to defend the post or die."[5]

Greene concurred with the decision, sending a letter to Washington, now encamped but six miles away in Hackensack: "I have directed Col. Magaw to defend the place until he hears from me." Greene also sent reinforcements across the Hudson, swelling the number of men at Fort Washington to 2,900 regulars.

As soon as he read Greene's note, Washington thundered off for the scene of the action, grabbing a boat below Fort Lee for a row over to Manhattan. Halfway across the mile-wide Hudson, he met a boat coming the other way with Generals Greene and Israel Putnam, who assured him that "the Troops were in high Spirits and would make a good Defence."[6] The three generals then retired to spend the night in Fort Lee.

At dawn of November 16, Patterson began making good on his threat: British batteries opened up on Mount Washington, driving defenders uphill toward the fort. When the tide was right for landing troops, 8,000 British and German soldiers began a methodical climb up three sides of the hill. On the north and steepest side, 4,000 Hessian soldiers dressed in yellow breeches and blue coats met stiff resistance; they fell by the dozens yet they continued to climb, pulling themselves up by the roots of beech trees through a hail of shot.

Washington wanted a better view of the action. He stepped into a boat with Generals Greene, Israel Putnam, and Hugh Mercer for a row over from Fort Lee. Not 15 minutes after they had landed, the generals found themselves between an advancing party of Scottish Highlanders and another party of Germans. "There we all stood in a very awkward situation," Greene wrote. "We all urged his Excellency to come off. I offerd to stay. General Putnam did the same, and so did General Mercer, but his Excellency thought it best for all of us to come off together, which we did about half an hour before the Enemy surrounded the fort."[7]

The generals were rowed back to the Jersey side of the Hudson, where they watched the fall of Fort Washington. Legend has it that Washington had tears in his eyes.

American troops were driven like cattle into a slaughterhouse; from all sides of the summit they retreated into the fort until they were packed in there so thickly they could not even raise their muskets in defense.

+‡══════‡+

At 4 P.M., the American flag flying over Fort Washington dropped; a white flag of surrender took its place. German soldiers, enraged at the deaths of 58 comrades, wanted to slaughter every American with bayonets, but British commanders would not let them.

The Americans filed out of the fort between two lines of jeering Germans and laid their arms in a pile. British lieutenant Frederick Mackenzie observed: "The Rebel prisoners were in general but very indifferently clothed; few of them appeared to have a Second shirt, nor did they appear to have washed themselves during the Campaign. A great many of them were lads under 15, and old men: and few of them had the appearance of Soldiers. Their odd figures frequently excited the laughter of our Soldiers."[8]

Washington's troops—exposed as a dirty, poorly clothed flock of boys and old men—were herded down to Manhattan, where most were locked up in squalid warehouses or in dank prison ships rotting at anchor in New York Harbor. The British had no plan for feeding so many captives; the commissary of prisoners, Joshua Loring, had no qualifications other than being the husband of General Howe's mistress. Within 18 months nearly 2,000 of the men captured at Fort Washington died of starvation and disease while confined.[9]

Besides the loss of 90 officers and nearly 2,800 soldiers, the Americans left in Fort Washington 34 cannon, 2 howitzers, ammunition, and enough food to feed thousands for a fortnight.

"The Loss of such a Number of officers [and] Men, many of whom have been trained with more than common Attention, will I fear be severely felt," Washington reported to Congress. "But when that of the Arms and Accoutrements is added much more so."[10]

For once, General Howe acted aggressively: Just four days after the fall of Fort Washington, he pushed 5,000 troops across the Hudson River; they landed, undetected and unopposed, six miles north of Fort Lee. By noon, the British troops marched single file up a steep pathway to the top of the bluff; a sentry saw them coming and passed word to Nathanael Greene's aide-de-camp, Thomas Paine.

Greene sent word of the British advance to Washington, over in Hackensack; Washington rode into Fort Lee, assessed the situation, and did not like the odds—he had fewer than 3,000 men, and 5,000 were heading his way. He gave the order to evacuate, orders that came just in time. At 1 P.M., the British marched through the fort's outer walls; inside they found the Americans' breakfast still simmering over smoky campfires.

The "rebels" also left 1,000 barrels of flour, 30 cannon, and 300 tents still standing. With the fall of Forts Washington and Lee, the Americans had lost, in just four days, more than 3,000 soldiers, 46 cannon, 8,000 cannon shot, 400,000 cartridges, and 2,800 muskets.

Washington marched what was left of his troops some 14 miles west, fording two rivers before bedding down across the Passaic. "[W]e have not an intrenching Tool, & not above 3,000 men, & they much broken & dispirted not only with our ill Success but the Loss of their Tents & Baggage," Washington wrote to General Charles Lee. "I have resolved to avoid any Attack."[11]

In his letter, Washington told Lee to cross the Hudson with his 6,000 troops to reinforce Washington's little army. Lee considered the order more of a suggestion than a demand, and he ignored it, believing that he knew better how to use these troops than Washington did.

Washington pushed on into New Jersey, retreating without a firm plan. On November 22, he marched his troops 10 miles through the rain and made a muddy camp in Newark; that night, it rained. The troops, with no tents, curled up on the ground and endured.

+≻━≺+

The Americans camped in Newark for five nights while Washington pondered what to do. He had 1,000 men under General Stirling in Brunswick camped on the Raritan River; if he could link his 3,000 with them, and if Lee would come on from New York with his 6,000, he could match Cornwallis in a battle at Brunswick. But Lee would not bring those troops. Washington was baffled by Lee's refusal to move his men into New Jersey despite his repeated requests for them:

"I confess I expected you would have been sooner in motion," Washington wrote Lee from Newark on November 27. "The force here when joined by yours, will not be adequate to any great opposition, at present it is weak, and it has been more owing to the badness of the weather that the Enemys progress has been checked, than any resistance we can make. They are now pushing this way."[12]

Washington's intelligence was good: Lord Charles Cornwallis was indeed pushing his way with a force that had grown to 10,000 men.

The drums beat in Washington's camp before dawn on Wednesday, November 28, signaling the men to mass in marching formation. They stepped off for Brunswick, 25 miles distant. Troops left behind as a rear guard at Newark marched out of town just as the vanguard of British troops was arriving.

Washington, his horse and clothes doubtlessly mud-splattered from the miry roads, rode into Brunswick around noon. The next day, an express rider galloped into his headquarters with a letter from General Lee to Colonel Joseph Reed, Washington's aide and confidant. Assuming it was official business, Washington broke the seal. Lee had agreed with Reed about what they perceived to be Washington's weakness: indecision.

"I receiv'd your most obliging flattering letter—lament with you that fatal indecision of mind which in war is a much greater disqualification than stupidity or even want of personal courage."[13]

So Colonel Reed had betrayed him. Washington did not need to see Reed's flattering letter to Lee, in which he had written: "Oh! General,—an indecisive mind is one of the greatest misfortunes that can befall an Army" to grasp that he had lost his aide's confidence. Washington dashed off a formally polite, three-paragraph note letting Reed know that he had seen Lee's letter while revealing nothing of his feelings about it.[14]

Lee, meanwhile, still had not moved his troops across the Hudson, explaining to Reed that he intended to ignore Washington's request for troops in order to attack British rangers in New Jersey—a scheme that was stopped by rain wetting Lee's gunpowder.

While Lee was freelancing with the better part of Washington's troops, many of the men with Washington were making plans to march home. The original Continental troops had enlisted for only one year, and on December 1, enlistments would expire for brigades from New Jersey, Pennsylvania, and Maryland. Washington wrote to the Board of War, "we know not to day where we shall be obliged to remove tomorrow."[15]

The next day, December 1, they were "obliged to remove" from Brunswick, as Cornwallis wheeled up a dozen cannon to a bluff above the Raritan River looking down on the town.

"The Enemy are fast advancing," Washington wrote to Hancock at 1:30 P.M. that day; "some of 'em are now in sight. All the men of the Jersey flying Camp . . . have refused to continue longer in service." With British troops in sight and advancing, two brigades of New Jersey troops hoisted their packs and marched off for home.

At 7:30 P.M., Washington sent an express thundering into the darkness with an update for Hancock down in Philadelphia: "We had a smart cannonade whilst we were parading our Men but without any or but little loss on either side." Five American cannon roared back at the dozen British guns on the heights, a thundering fire that kept up until dark. "It being impossible to oppose them with our present force with the least prospect of success, we shall retreat to the West side of the Delaware & have advanced about Eight miles," Washington wrote.[16]

The troops retreated farther into New Jersey, shedding brigades and deserters; Nathanael Greene observed: "When we left Brunswick we had not 3000 men, a very pitiful army to trust the Liberties of America upon." Greene's aide-de-camp, Thomas Paine, began writing his next pamphlet, *The Crisis;* tradition has it that he scratched the first words on a calfskin drumhead: "These are the times that try men's souls. The summer soldier and the sunshine patriot will, in this crisis, shrink from the service of their country."

The remains of Washington's army straggled into Princeton at 8 A.M. on December 2, slept on the ground there that night, then, leaving a rear guard of 1,200, they pushed on for Trenton on the east bank of the Delaware River. Here Washington rounded up every boat up and down the river for 60 miles and began ferrying baggage and supplies into Pennsylvania.

"I hope to have every thing secured this Night and tomorrow if we are not disturbed," Washington wrote Hancock. "After being disencumbered of my Baggage and Stores, my future Situation will depend intirely upon Circumstances.

"I have not heard a Word from General Lee since the 26th last Month, which surprises me not a little."[17]

With his baggage across the river, Washington was prepared to retreat into Pennsylvania, but he did not want to go. He guessed that Cornwallis's goal was Philadelphia, where Congress was sitting, and he did not want to bring the war right to government's door. He decided to make a stand at Princeton, marching 1,200 troops that way from Trenton to join the 1,200 already there as a rear guard, hoping that Lee or Heath could come down from the north with reinforcements.

On the morning of December 7, 1776, Washington's troops trudged toward Princeton, trailing long shadows in the low December sun; about halfway there, a messenger rode up with an urgent letter from General Greene: "This moment a Capt has returnd that went to reconnoiter last Night and it is beyond a doubt the Enemy are advanceing."[18]

Washington could not meet the advancing British troops. He would have to retreat again; he'd have to swallow his pride and give up the entire state of New Jersey. He turned his troops around and withdrew those at Princeton; the last of the men crossed the Delaware at the next day's dawn. At 4 P.M., the vanguard of German troops appeared on the river's opposite bank. Once again, Washington had narrowly escaped; but again, his situation was truly desperate. His men camped that night on the cold clay without blankets or tents while their commander in chief wrestled with what to do next.

+≻==≺+

General Charles Lee finally deigned to move his troops across the Hudson and into New Jersey on December 8, though he had no intention of linking those troops with Washington's.

From Morristown, New Jersey, Lee wrote Washington: "If I was not taught to think that your Army was considerably reinforc'd I should immediately join you, but as I am assurd you are very strong I should imagine We can make a better impression" by remaining behind Cornwallis's troops.[19]

Washington read Lee's letter on the west bank of the Delaware; he could not believe his eyes: "assurd you are very *strong?*" He disabused Lee of that notion, dashing off a letter that read: "my situation is directly opposite of what you suppose it to be, and when Genl Howe is pressing forward with the whole of his Army . . . to possess himself of Philadelphia, I cannot but request and entreat you & this too by the advice of all the Gen; Officers with me, to march and join me with your whole force with all possible expedition."[20]

From Morristown, Lee wrote back: "We have three thousand Men here at present but They are so ill shod that We have been oblig'd to halt these two days for want of shoes." He then lapsed into the third person, telling Washington that General Lee was pondering which of two routes to use to reach Washington, the one skirting western New Jersey that Washington had carefully laid out, going so far as to leave boats there for the Delaware River crossing, or a route that would plunge Lee's troops through the heart of New Jersey, across Cornwallis's line of communications, and place him dangerously close to the left flank of the British army.[21]

Again Washington could not believe his eyes. "I am much surprizd that you should be in any doubt respecting the Route you should take," he wrote to Lee on December 14. "I have so frequently mentioned our situation, and the necessity of your aid, that it is painfull for me to add a word upon the Subject."[22]

This was the last word that Washington would have to write on "the subject" for, as he learned the next day, General Lee had been captured by British dragoons. "Our Cause has receivd a severe blow in the Captivity of General Lee," Washington wrote to his cousin Lund upon hearing the news. "Unhappy Man! Taken by his own Imprudence!"

Lee was indeed taken by his own imprudence—sleeping at a lodging house owned by a widow in Basking Ridge some three miles from the protection of his main army. The next morning, Lee had lingered over a late breakfast while his army marched even farther away. Wearing an old blue coat with red facing and greasy leather breeches, he had been bent over the table, absorbed in writing a letter to fellow general Horatio Gates: "Entre Nous, a certain great man [Washington] is most damnably deficient. He has thrown me into a situation where I have my choice of difficulties: if I stay in this province I risk myself and army, and if I do not stay, the province is lost forever. . . . In short, unless something which I do not expect turns up, we are lost."[23]

Just as Lee signed that letter, the hollow thunder of horses' hooves sounded outside his room. A party of 30 horsemen wearing signature green hunting jackets of the British Legion crashed through the woods and surrounded the house. Leading the charge at the front door was young Banastre Tarleton, 22 years old, a ruthless and aggressive officer out to make a name for himself in the American war. Tarleton threatened to burn the house; Lee skulked out.

Lee had been a regular officer in the British army, and many saw his capture as more damaging to the American cause than even a capture of George Washington, who had never risen higher than the rank of provincial colonel. The dragoons took Lee back to Brunswick, where they toasted the king till they got themselves, and Lee's horse, thoroughly drunk.

Contrary to Washington's assessment, however, Lee's capture did not deal "a severe blow" to the American cause—in fact, Lee's captivity boosted it, for as long as the experienced General Lee was on the scene, Washington's ability and authority would be questioned by most everyone, even by Washington himself. With Lee removed from the picture, and with greater latitude from Congress, Washington made decisions with more confidence, overcoming his tendencies toward deference and indecision and learning to act with decisive authority.

CHAPTER 9

"Victory or Death"

GENERAL JOHN SULLIVAN TOOK COMMAND OF LEE'S TROOPS OUT-side Morristown, and within a week he had them marching into Washington's camp on the west side of the Delaware. Washington had first asked Lee to bring those men on November 17, when they were 6,000 strong; now, on December 20, enlistments for 1776 had expired, and their number had dwindled to about 2,000.

On New Year's Eve, almost everyone's term of service would expire, and Washington would be left with an army of about 1,200. "Ten more days will put an end to the existence of our Army," Washington wrote to Hancock. The courier delivering this letter now had to ride more than 100 miles beyond Philadelphia, as Congress had quit that city in the face of imminent British invasion and moved its business to Baltimore. Because of this, Washington had asked for, and had been granted, greater powers to act without first consulting Congress on such things as appointments of minor officers, arresting people who refused to accept Continental currency, and impressing goods from civilians.

Washington had just about finished drafting his letter to Hancock when he received a brief, melancholy note that had been on the road 13 days from Rhode Island: A large fleet of British ships had sailed into Newport and without opposition dropped 6,000 troops. The Howe brothers now held Newport, a capital city at the head of Long Island Sound; New York; most of New Jersey; and were poised to strike Philadelphia at will. Washington feared that when the river froze, British and Hessian soldiers would emerge from their winter outposts in Trenton, Princeton, and Bordentown, stream across the river, and seize Philadelphia.

Washington wrote to Rhode Island's governor: "It would give me infinite pleasure, if the situation of our Affairs in this Quarter, would allow me to afford you the assistance I could wish, but it will not. . . . How things turn out, the event must determine, at present the prospect is gloomy."[1]

Benjamin Rush, a Philadelphia doctor and signer of the Declaration of Independence, visited Washington at his headquarters on December 23, 1776, and found him depressed. Washington sat at a writing desk, quill in hand, scratching the same phrase onto scraps of paper, a scarce commodity in camp. Rush wrote of this meeting: "While I was talking to him, I observed him to play with his pen and ink upon several small pieces of paper. One of them by accident fell upon the floor near my feet. I was struck with the inscription upon it. It was 'Victory or Death.'"[2]

For Washington, this was not an empty phrase. Before his troops disbanded, he would win a victory over the Hessian forces posted on the eastern bank of the Delaware, or he would die; there was no room for middle ground. The campaign of 1776—which had begun so promisingly with the evacuation of Boston—had become a disaster. On Long Island, he had been outflanked and lost 1,000 men; on Mount Washington, he had lost 2,000; on the retreat from Manhattan and during various skirmishes, he had lost another 1,000; he had also lost the ground—Long Island, Manhattan, and practically the entire state of New Jersey. Only the Delaware River had saved Philadelphia. On Long Island, Washington had nearly lost his army, and near Kip's Bay, he had nearly lost his life; but worse than having his life threatened was the threat to his reputation. He had to do something, something bold and decisive, to get that back. And George Washington decided that he would capture the Hessian soldiers posted in Trenton.

"Christmas day at night, one hour before day is the time fixed upon for our attempt on Trenton," Washington wrote to Colonel Joseph Reed on December 23. "For heaven's sake keep this to yourself, as the discovery of it may prove fatal to us, our numbers, I am sorry to say, being less than I had any conception of—but necessity, dire necessity will—nay must justify any Attempt."[3]

On Christmas Eve, 1776, a procession of officers crunched across the crusty snow outside the Merrick House, the chilly, unfinished fieldstone house where Nathanael Greene was quartered. They came not for a war council to decide what to do but to hear what George Washington had already decided that they would do. The officers assembled there included Greene, two future presidents (Washington and James Monroe), a secretary of the treasury (Alexander Hamilton), and a secretary of war (Henry Knox). Greene and a few others were already privy to the plans that Washington then laid out: On Christmas Day, the troops would cross the Delaware, march under cover of darkness to Trenton, and attack the garrison of 1,400 Hessian soldiers. Once they took Trenton, they would move on and take Princeton, where Major General James Grant, now in command of all British and Hessian troops in New Jersey, had a strong garrison. (This was the same James Grant whose troops Washington rescued from annihilation at Fort Duquesne in the French and Indian War.)

Tactically, the attack plan that Washington laid out was too complicated to have much chance of success. He would split his army into three divisions, which would all make separate river crossings, at night, then somehow simultaneously converge at and below Trenton. It was the plan of an overly ambitious amateur.

+⊨═══⊫+

Christmas Day 1776 dawned blue and cold. The temperature peaked at 30 degrees, and around noon, the main part of the army, about 2,400 men, gathered in camp to begin the march to McKonkey's Landing on the mile-wide Delaware River. These troops, with Washington at their head, would cross the Delaware about nine miles above Trenton, split into two detachments under Generals Sullivan and Greene, and descend on the town as a pair of pincers squeezing the outpost from above; another 700 troops would ferry over directly across from Trenton to hold the bridge at the south end of town, and a force of 1,900 would cross farther south of Trenton to cut off the Hessian garrison in Bordentown from marching north to reinforce Trenton.

In general orders that morning, Washington had been so optimistic about his convoluted plans that he'd ordered his artillery detachment to carry drag ropes for hauling off all the Hessian cannons he was sure they would capture.

Washington's troops marched to within a mile of the ferry landing, where they lined up by brigade, waiting for December's early darkness. As they stood in the cold, Washington ordered officers to read aloud Thomas Paine's latest pamphlet, *The Crisis:*

> These are the times that try men's souls. The summer soldier and the sunshine patriot will, in this crisis, shrink from the service of his country; but he that stands it *now* deserves the love and thanks of man and woman. Tyranny, like hell, is not easily conquered; yet we have this consolation with us, that the harder the conflict, the more glorious the triumph. What we obtain too cheap, we esteem too lightly: it is dearness only that gives everything its value. Heaven knows how to put a proper price on its goods; and it would be strange indeed if so celestial an article as FREEDOM should not be highly rated.[4]

One by one, each brigade marched off toward McKonkey's Ferry, so that by 3 P.M., the entire army was in motion. They crunched across week-old snow that had thawed and refrozen to a sharp glaze. A major, John Wilkinson, saw spots of red in the snow, "tinged here and there," he wrote, "with blood from the feet of the men who wore broken shoes."[5]

By 4:30, the sky was dark enough to conceal the river crossing, and the embarkations began. Once again, Washington relied on his big artillery colonel, Henry Knox, to oversee the business of moving heavy stores: 18 field cannon, 350 tons of ammunition, draft horses, and 2,400 men. The wind blew from northeast, funneling down the Delaware Valley, driving before it large ice floes that had broken from the river's edge. Through the roar of the wind in the gathering dark, Knox's voice rang out, barking orders, loading the artillery and horses, embarking the brigades in correct formation.

Greene's brigades loaded first, stepping gingerly into the boats—big, black boats, 40 to 60 feet long, used in peacetime for hauling iron and pig ore from the Durham Iron Works. At 6 P.M., Washington sent a dispatch downriver to Colonel John Cadwalader, commander of the 1,900 troops supposed to cross the river below Trenton: "I am determined, as the night is favourable, to cross the River."[6]

Colonel John Glover's regiment of Marblehead fishermen poled and steered the freighted boats across the current, battling their way through big floes of ice that clunked heavily against their sides.

Washington, wrapped in a cloak, went over around 7 P.M. to view the landing parties. Ashore in New Jersey, Washington sat on a box that had contained a beehive and watched for hours while his plans slowly went awry. Around 11 P.M., a heavy snow began. Wind whipped the snow and sleet into the faces of Glover's men as they fought off the ice floes, their poles and gunnels glazed in ice. The artillery was supposed to cross first, but the last cannon did not roll up the New Jersey riverbank till 3 A.M.

By the time everyone was across and ready to march the nine miles to Trenton, it was four in the morning, too late to spring a surprise, predawn attack on the Hessians. Washington considered withdrawing but concluded that retreat would be too dangerous; if his troops were discovered midriver, they would be sitting ducks for marksmen on the banks. There was no turning back; they'd have to fight by daylight.

The troops stepped off—thankfully putting the windblown sleet at their backs. After two hours marching in the storm they reached the dark village of Birmingham, where Washington gathered his generals and told them to set their watch by his. He then split his division in two: Greene and Washington led 1,000 men along Scotch Road while Sullivan marched his 1,400 troops down the River Road. The roads were equidistant, four miles, to Trenton.

Washington ordered all lanterns doused, and as they marched the troops kept silence. En route, Sullivan sent a horseman to tell Washington that his men were complaining that their gunpowder was wet. Washington sent a messenger back with an answer: Use the bayonet. "I am resolved to take Trenton."[7]

Peering through the sleet and snow, Washington spied the Hessian advanced post—a cooper's shop on Pennington Road—at exactly 8 A.M. Lieutenant Andreas Wiederhold of the Knyphausen Regiment happened to step out of the guardhouse at that moment and saw Washington's troops heading his way. He thought he was looking at a small party of skirmishers, and called his 20 men to arms.

At 8:03, Washington heard firing to his right, and he knew that Sullivan's troops had matched his column step for step and was now attacking the outpost on River Road. Washington's troops fired from 300 yards; they came on, firing two more volleys, before Wiederhold signaled his men to shoot. The Hessian guard fought, briefly, before realizing that they were vastly outnumbered. He pulled back into the main streets of Trenton, where the main body of troops, barracked between King and Queen streets, was just beginning to stir.

"We presently saw their main Body formed," Washington reported to Congress, "but from their Motions, they seemed undetermined how to act."[8]

The first of the Hessians to spill out tried filing off to their left but soon ran into Sullivan's troops, who drove them back into the town. Knox's artillerymen unlimbered cannon at the top of the two main streets and touched them off. With an explosive roar, cannon cut down the enemy troops with grapeshot as they poured from their barracks. Acrid gun smoke hung in the air, thickening with each blast of cannon and musket, mingling with the snow so that Washington could not see Sullivan's troops sweeping into town to his right.

Washington ordered a regiment of Greene's troops to form a battle line to his left and advance through the fields and apple orchard east of town. With Sullivan's troops sweeping in from the west, Greene's troops sealing off the Princeton Road to the east, and Knox's artillery thundering from the north, the Hessians found themselves in a gauntlet of fire. Grapeshot and musket ball sliced through the fog of gun smoke and snow, buzzing past their heads, in some cases, striking bodies with a sickening *crack*. Colonel Johann Rall, the Hessian officer who had taken the sword of surrender at Fort Washington, dropped from his horse with fatal wounds from two musket balls in his side. About 500 Hessians managed to dash across a bridge across Assunpink Creek at the south end of town before Glover's regiment sealed it off.

"Finding from our disposition, that they were surrounded, and that they must inevitably be cut to pieces if they made any further Resistance, they agreed to lay down their Arms," Washington wrote Congress. Major Wilkinson carried news of the Hessian surrender to Washington, who was just then riding down a snow-slickened King Street, its snow tinged red with blood. Washington firmly grasped Wilkinson's right hand.

"Major Wilkinson," he said, "this is a glorious day for our country."[9]

Washington huddled with his officers for a brief war council to decide: Should they still press on for Princeton to attack the British garrison there? His two youngest generals, Greene and Knox, said they should. The rest said that they should not: The two divisions that were supposed to cross to the south of them had not been able to make the crossing, leaving them exposed to reinforcements from the large Hessian outpost at Bordentown. The victory had been so complete and so necessary to boost morale that they should not jeopardize it. Besides, their troops were cold, wet, and exhausted. Even as they talked, troops were breaking into hogsheads of rum and numbing themselves with drink. At noon they marched out of Trenton, slogging along slushy roads the eight or nine miles to the river crossing, leaving behind 22 dead Hessians and many of the 84 wounded. With them were 918 prisoners and six brass cannon, hauled along by the drag ropes that Washington had insisted on bringing. The Americans had none killed and two slightly wounded, including future president James Monroe.

Again they stepped into the Durham boats to cross the Delaware at night with a cold wind driving ice floes down the valley; this time, three men who boarded the boats never made it alive to the other side. In crossing the Delaware, they froze to death.[10]

＋＞＝＝＜＋

After two river crossings, a battle, and two sleepless nights, George Washington finally slept at his new headquarters, an old yellow house about five miles west of McKonkey's Ferry on the Delaware.

Moving thousands of troops across a freezing river in a deadly storm to attack Trenton had been an act of desperation—but it had worked. Alarmed by what had happened at Trenton, Hessian soldiers fled from their posts in Bordentown, Mount Holly, and Black Horse; Washington saw this as an opportunity to take advantage of the Hessians' panic by following up with another attack.

At 10 P.M. on December 29, after just two days of rest, Washington's men again stood on the cold clay banks of the Delaware awaiting boats to shuttle them across the river. That night it wore a skim of ice too thin to support the weight of men but thick enough to impede the progress of boats.

This crossing took two days. Washington's troops weren't fully assembled in Trenton until December 31, 1776—for many, their enlistments would expire the next day.

After the hard river crossing, in which half of his troops had camped a night in six inches of snow without blankets or tents, Washington rode to inspect a New England regiment of his veteran troops encamped in Trenton. These men had been with him throughout 1776—they had rejoiced at the evacuation of Boston, been driven from Long Island and White Plains, slogged for 80 miles across New Jersey; they looked less like soldiers than like ragged refugees. Washington told them that they had done a good job and he was thankful. If they would extend the terms of their enlistment for just six weeks, he would top their regular pay with a bounty of $10.00. His regimental officers called for volunteers to step forward and a drummer beat a roll.

Not one man moved.

Frustrated, Washington wheeled his horse around in a circle and rode along his men. A sergeant who was present wrote a recollection nearly 50 years later in which he put words into Washington's mouth that likely weren't verbatim, but probably caught the spirit of Washington's words:

> My brave fellows, you have done all I asked you to do, and more than could be reasonably expected. But your country is at stake, your wives, your houses, all that you hold dear. You have worn yourselves put with fatigues and hardships, but we know not how to spare you. If you will consent to stay but one month longer, you will render that service to the cause of liberty, and to your country, which you probably can never do under any other circumstances. The present is emphatically the crisis that will decide our destiny.[11]

Again the drum rolled. This time there were murmurs ("I will remain if you do"), and gaunt veterans came forward till all but the lame and the nearly naked stood in a line. In all, about 2,400 regular soldiers agreed to stay on for six more weeks to help Washington rid the Jerseys of the British. Afterward, Nathanael Greene wrote: "Let it be remembered to their Eternal honor."[12]

Two riders galloped from Trenton into the cold dark of the first night of the new year, 1777, riding hard for eight miles to Crosswicks, bearing a command to Colonel Cadwalader from General Washington: "Some pieces of Intelligence renders it necessary for you to March your Troops immediately to this place—I expect your Brigade will be here by five O'Clock in the Morning without fail. At any rate do not exceed six."[13]

A similar message traveled southeast to Bordentown, where General Thomas Mifflin commanded a few hundred militiamen—Washington was calling in all his troops to Trenton to meet an expected assault. A dozen British dragoons captured near Princeton had revealed that Lord Charles Cornwallis had taken over command of the British troops in New Jersey and planned to lead 8,000 of them the next morning for an attack on the American forces at Trenton.

Colonel Cadwalader's brigade from Crosswicks did not quite meet Washington's deadline; they broke camp at 1 A.M. and marched for six hours, arriving at 7 A.M. on January 2, 1777. They joined Washington as his troops streamed out of town to form the battle line just south of Trenton; Washington had passed through this town several times now, knew the ground well, and he employed that knowledge. He lined his troops along the high ground behind the Assunpink River, setting up an artillery park of 40 guns that commanded the narrow stone bridge that some Hessians had crossed in escaping the last battle. His left flank was the Delaware River; he made sure that his right extended all the way to the only passable ford across the river, three miles away, so that enemy troops could not cross there unopposed and turn his flank, the way they had on Long Island.

To protect his troops while they pulled back to form the lines, Washington sent an advance force to meet Cornwallis north of town: a brigade of Virginia Continentals, some of his best and most experienced troops; plus a regiment of Pennsylvania riflemen and the "German Regiment," comprised of German immigrants recruited to the Continental Army by Maryland and Pennsylvania to show the Hessians how they could succeed in America if they deserted.

The American riflemen fell under the command of Colonel Edward Hand, 32, an Irish-born Pennsylvanian. His riflemen wore loose white hunting shirts and carried long rifles with bored barrels instead of the muskets most soldiers carried. Compared to muskets, rifles fired with deadly accuracy.

At around 10 A.M. on January 2, Hand's men spied Cornwallis's vanguard outside Maidenhead, five miles north of Trenton. The Virginians and the Pennsylvania riflemen did what they could to slow the advancing British, firing from behind walls and woods then dropping back; the German Regiment, however, broke and ran.

Hand's riflemen fell back through the streets of Trenton to the bridge crossing the Assunpink, running back to their side of the span as the British light infantry pressed on. But the riflemen had done their job—they had delayed Cornwallis's vanguard for five hours. With darkness coming, the Americans parted to let the last of Hand's men cross, then they re-formed the line. Henry Knox had his 40 cannon ready for the British assault.

After three blasts from Knox's artillery, the bridge ran red with blood— and the British stopped coming.

Tactically, Washington had done the best that anyone could; still, he faced long odds. He commanded about 5,000 men, all but 1,600 of them militiamen who had never seen combat. To his front, Cornwallis outnumbered him with at least 5,500 British and Hessian troops, all of them experienced, professional soldiers. To his left, Washington was hemmed in by the wide Delaware River.

With the sun now down, Cornwallis decided to postpone his attack on Washington's position until the next morning, when he could see the ground.

"We've got the old fox safe now," Cornwallis told his officers at a council of war. "We'll go over and bag him in the morning."

Cornwallis's quartermaster, Sir William Erskine, felt they should attempt a nighttime attack, saying: "My Lord, if Washington is the general I take him to be . . . you will see nothing of them in the morning."[14]

Washington called a war council to discuss his army's dilemma: fight a superior enemy or risk a retreat, which at best would be demoralizing. But he had found a third option: He'd had four horsemen patrolling a newly cut, little-used road that filed off to the east, and they had not found any British troops along it. Perhaps, Washington suggested, his 5,000 troops could quietly shuffle off into the night along this road, then press on for Princeton. His generals agreed; the retreat was on.

All that night of January 2 into the morning of the third, the American campfires burned brightly, fed by the dry wood of dismantled split-rail fences stolen from local farmers. All that night, too, the sounds of hundreds of soldiers digging trenches spilled over from the American lines. The bright fires, the sounds of shovel and pickax, these were all part of an elaborate ruse. A guard of 500 remained to keep the campfires burning for three hours after the main army's departure; the rest marched in silence. Washington dispatched the baggage wagons south to Burlington; the cannon wheels were wrapped in rags to muffle their heavy roll; and by luck, a January thaw broke that night and the temperatures fell below freezing, giving the wheels hard ground to roll on.

On January 3, 1777, the sun rose into a cloudless New Jersey sky, its bright rays shattered by crystals of frost in the fields and trees. At first light, Cornwallis surveyed the American lines; he saw fresh earthworks, smoldering campfires . . . and nothing else. The old fox had fled the trap.

<hr>

At sunrise on January 3, while Cornwallis was gazing on Washington's empty camp, Washington was pondering a fork in the road just south of Princeton. He sent a brigade of 325 men to the left fork while he rode with a division to the right, which led to the brick buildings of the College of New Jersey.

Washington had not ridden far when one of his colonels pointed out a strange light in the hills to their left—sunlight flashing off the burnished musket barrels of British troops. Washington guessed that this was a small British reconnaissance party; he sent a message to the brigade on his left, headed by General Hugh Mercer, to attack. But before Mercer got this message, he had been attacked—and this was no small party. Two regiments, 50 cavalrymen, and 150 wagons were pulling out of Princeton with reinforcements for Cornwallis at Trenton.

The British spotted Mercer first; they withdrew and, from the cover of a long string of buildings and the winter-bare trees of a snowy apple orchard, they opened fire. Washington heard the shots, off to his left. He galloped toward action where, in the opening salvo of the Battle of Princeton, the British were winning.

Redcoats fired a volley and charged downhill through the orchard, bayoneting the outmanned Americans who stood and fired. Mercer's gray horse took a ball in the leg and fell thrashing to the ground. The general stood and swung wildly with his sword; British troops surrounded him, cracked his head with a musket butt, and seven times they ran him through with a bayonet.

Clearly outgunned, Mercer's brigade ran; untested militiamen bringing up the rear saw them coming through the orchard, turned, and ran with them. Nathanael Greene, in charge of the division on the left, saw the beginnings of a panicky retreat as he thundered downhill from the right.

Greene ordered an artillery captain to haul his two four-pound cannon to the left of the hill to check the British advance long enough for Washington to arrive with reinforcements. Above the roar of the cannon, Washington yelled at his panicked militia, "Parade with us my brave fellows! There is but a handful of the enemy, and we will have them directly."[15]

General Cadwalader brought up a brigade of about 1,100 men who, after a couple of attempts, managed to form a line "in the face of the enemy and under a shower of grape shot," Cadwalader recalled.[16] Two brigades of New Englanders, led by Colonel Daniel Hitchcock, a Yale-educated lawyer, formed next to Cadwalader's troops, who stood next to Hand's riflemen and the Pennsylvania militia now under Washington's direct command. Washington rode out in front of the long line and waved his hat, a signal to come on. He rode uphill, toward the line of British, their coats red against the snow in the morning sun. About 30 yards from the British lines, Washington turned in his saddle. "Halt!" he said. "Fire!"

From both sides muskets thundered, cloaking Washington in a fog of gunpowder. His aide, John Fitzgerald, could not watch. He pulled his hat over his eyes. When the cloud cleared, he saw Washington, again waving his hat to advance.[17]

The British broke and ran. From being the hunted at the Second Battle of Trenton, Washington was now the hunter. As his army took off after the retreating British troops, Washington followed on horseback bellowing, "It is a fine fox chase boys!"[18]

While Washington galloped off after the retreating British, General Sullivan rolled his division up to the College of New Jersey, now Princeton University, and captured the regiment of about 300 British troops that had been left behind to guard the town.

For two hours, George Washington's troops got a break. They grabbed what they could find to eat and drink in the abandoned college town, then word came that Cornwallis was approaching with his 5,500 men. Washington ordered them to move out and again they were marching, 15 miles north to Somerset Courthouse, where they arrived at sunset and bedded down into the snow without blankets or tents; many were without shoes.

Washington woke the men before dawn the next day, January 4, 1777, and marched them toward the British garrison at Brunswick. He wanted to continue his string of successes by capturing that post and taking what he later learned was a British war chest of £70,000. But he was not long on the road before he realized that his plan was beyond human endurance. Brunswick was a 17-mile march away, and Cornwallis was heading there to fortify it. Washington sent Nathanael Greene with a detachment to march for Morristown and prepare barracks there, while he rested the main body of troops and waited for stragglers.

On January 6, the troops staggered into Morristown, a village nestled in a natural castle: The sharp hills of the Watchung range threw up a wall toward New York; behind it, the Passaic River acted as a moat. War had not yet torn up the countryside, so the foraging was good.

From here, Washington could finally take stock of what he'd accomplished. At Princeton, he had captured more than 200 British troops, killed 28, and wounded 58 while losing 40 of his own men. Just weeks before, he had been huddled on the west side of the Delaware with an army on the verge of dissolution; the enemy had been within 19 miles of Philadelphia; Congress had retreated from the capital, and Washington had written to one of his brothers, "the game is pretty near up."[19]

Now the British and Hessian troops had been driven back 60 miles from Philadelphia; they had given up the whole west side of New Jersey, withdrawing into garrisons at Brunswick, Newark, and on the coast at Amboy. In just nine days, from December 25 to January 3, the perception of Washington had changed: None of his officers now saw him as weak and indecisive, as Reed and Lee had; enlisted men who had never seen the young Washington riding in battle next to the doomed General Braddock now had seen him coolly leading the way under fire at Princeton.

The war's tide had changed, and Washington wanted to keep the flow going his way. On January 7, 1777, he wrote orders to two major generals that defined his overarching strategy for the rest of the war. Generals William Heath and Benjamin Lincoln were then stationed at Peekskill, the Hudson River highlands above New York, with a few thousand men, mostly militia. To Heath, Washington wrote: "I beg you will keep up every Appearance of falling down upon New York, as that will be the surest Method of obliging them to withdraw" troops into New York to protect the city.

And to Lincoln he wrote: "the greatest part of your Troops are to move down towards New York to draw the Attention of the enemy to that Quarter, and if they do not throw a considerable Body back gain, you may in all probability carry the City."[20]

These orders began what has often been characterized as Washington's "obsession" with recapturing New York City. From this point until the decisive Battle of Yorktown in Virginia in 1781, Washington always kept a large force within striking distance of New York City, a strategy that was equal parts foolishness and brilliance. Washington's folly was believing that he actually could "in all probability carry the City" when it was bristling with British batteries and surrounded by warships while he, in essence, had no navy. Even the French navy would never dare attack the British position on New York, yet Washington thought he could take it with a few thousand troops under Heath and Lincoln, mostly militia.

Washington's insistence on a presence around New York did oblige the British to withdraw troops and ships to protect the island, thus depriving British commanders of powerful resources they could have used to attack key American, and later French, positions elsewhere. Washington's belief in achieving the impossible made it possible.

+≈═══≈+

George Washington did not plan on spending the winter in Morristown, but the more he looked about, the more he liked it. His troops had comfortable quarters, and the town was located on the main pike between the Hudson and Delaware rivers, putting him in position to move toward New York, Philadelphia, or up the Hudson as the situation might require. So in March he sent for Martha to come to Morristown.

Although the war had taken a turn for the better, Washington was still plagued by innumerable difficulties.

Smallpox was endemic in the 1770s, killing about 100,000 Americans. It spread through an army camp and crippled the first ill-fated Canadian campaign, and Washington was determined to stop it. From Morristown, he insisted that every soldier taking the field in 1777 had to be inoculated against smallpox, a forward-thinking stance in a time when many considered inoculation little more than dangerous quackery. One historian has, with only slight overstatement, called Washington's insistence on inoculation as "the most strategic decision of his military career."[21]

Frenchmen, some of them capable military men but too many mere adventurers, frequently arrived in camp claiming commissions from Congress, claims that put Washington in a bind: He didn't want to brush off men of merit who could provide assistance, but he couldn't risk promoting inferior foreigners over hardworking American officers who'd resent the slight. Ben Franklin, then in France trying to win French participation in the war, passed along to Washington a list of ten men seeking commissions along with comments such as "an old Serjt Major of great distinction," "a youth full of Honor Courage & Zeal," an "old officer patronized by Mr. Turgot."[22]

Washington appealed to President Hancock, writing in late February: "I have often mentioned to you the distress I am every now and then laid under by the Application of French Officers for Commissions in our Service, this evil, if I may call it so, is a growing one, for from what I learn they are coming in swarms from old France and the Islands."[23]

Besides sending men to America, France in early 1777 was secretly sending much-needed military stores: Two French ships dropped 10 tons of gunpowder on the wharves of Philadelphia; another brought 12,000 muskets into Portsmouth, New Hampshire; a ship with 50 brass field cannon arrived in Boston in March, prompting Washington to write: "Glorious News this."[24]

Accompanying the cannon was a French officer named Phillipe Charles Jean Baptiste Tronson du Coudray, who came bearing a promise of a commission as major general of the American artillery, signed by an American agent in France. His appointment was backdated to August of 1776, giving him seniority over Generals Knox, Sullivan, and Greene. Washington got wind of this on May 31 and promptly tried to defuse a potentially explosive situation, writing Congress that, should it approve du Coudray's commission, "a train of ills . . . might convulse and unhinge this important department" by running off three men he considered to be his best generals.

On that same day, Washington also received intelligence that General Howe was massing troops on the New Jersey shore at Amboy, apparently with designs on marching out en route to Philadelphia. Washington had just moved his own troops from Morristown and now had them in tents at Middlebrook—not 15 miles from Howe's gathering troops.

Howe put almost all of his army on the march for Brunswick—some 18,000 men with a long wagon train carrying pontoons for a river crossing. It seemed certain that Howe had designs on crossing the Delaware into Philadelphia, but Washington had his doubts. He thought Howe might be coming directly after him.

On June 13, a vanguard of Howe's troops marched nine miles west of Brunswick, passing to the south of Washington's camp. Scouts observed that the redcoats did not carry the pontoon boats with them, and Washington concluded that Howe's movements were just a ploy to lure him down from the highlands of Middlebrook for an attack. Washington did not take the bait, choosing instead to harass the British troops with a party of riflemen. For five days his riflemen skirmished with small parties of British troops till finally Howe pulled his troops back to Amboy, again staging an elaborate ruse of boarding them on ships before doubling back on Washington, who had advanced but then pulled back, again correctly reading Howe's movements.

<hr />

In the opening months of the 1777 campaign, Washington, now 45 years old, was at the top of his game. Not only had he read and refused Howe's gambit, he even offered insight into the movements of General John Burgoyne up in the Northern Theater. Burgoyne had just captured Fort Ticonderoga, news that struck New Englanders, who feared a strong British presence on their western frontier. But Washington was unfazed. For one thing, the victory at Ticonderoga might puff up Burgoyne, make him overconfident; for another, Washington had received intelligence that Burgoyne was moving down the wooded

Hudson Valley in small detachments, "a line of conduct," Washington wrote, "that is most favorable to us. . . .

"This conduct will certainly give room for enterprise on our part, and expose his parties to great hazard. Could we be so happy, as to cut one of [the detachments] off, supposing it should not exceed four, five of six hundred Men, it would inspirit the people and do away with much of their present anxiety."[25]

This is exactly what happened two months later—New Hampshire colonel John Stark, who had displayed almost reptilian coolness on the Bunker Hill battlefield, led an army of 1,500 against a foraging party of 800 under the command of Hessian lieutenant colonel Friedrich Baum. Stark's men killed and captured almost all of Baum's troops at Bennington in what is now Vermont, and fought off a detachment sent to reinforce them, killing, capturing, and wounding 700 men.

Once Howe's troops really did board ships waiting in the Hudson River between Amboy and Staten Island, Washington was convinced that he knew the general's plans for the campaign of 1777—seize posts on the upper Hudson River in order to link up with Burgoyne.

"There can be as little room to doubt, that Genl. Howe will co-operate with the Northern Army, and make a sudden descent upon Peeks Kill," Washington wrote on July 1. Washington would have to quickly push his troops up into the Hudson River highlands. But first, he had to deal with the wounded feelings of three of his generals—Knox, Sullivan, and Greene—who that day received word of du Coudray's promised commission and sent their resignations to Congress.

Congressmen were furious with the American generals for trying to influence civil authority by threatening to resign. They sent Washington a resolution demanding that the generals apologize; Washington, no doubt siding with his generals, smoothly passed it onto them without comment—and they promptly ignored it. The contretemps passed that August when Congress gave du Coudray a commission as inspector general of artillery, which did not include a line command—leaving Knox in charge of artillery—and was not backdated so that Sullivan and Greene retained seniority. Du Coudray conveniently drowned soon after. Nevertheless, the larger issue of foreign officers winning congressional commissions continued to fester.

Days after pushing his troops on a punishing climb into the Hudson Highlands through the heat of mid-July, Washington learned that Howe's fleet had sailed down the Hudson and disappeared over the horizon. He had no idea where Howe was taking 18,000 men but assumed it must be Philadelphia, now more than 100 miles away from Washington's camp in the highlands of New York. Once again he put the main division of his army on the march, pushing them clear across New Jersey in the summer heat. Greene's troops crossed the Delaware into Pennsylvania on July 28, covering the distance in less than three days; other divisions followed on their heels, pushed so hard that draft horses pulling their wagons foundered and died.

It appeared as if Washington had arrived just in time, for on July 30, the topsails of Howe's large fleet appeared off the "Capes of Delaware"—the bluffs overlooking the Delaware River where it joined the sea. Washington sent out orders for all but the Northern Army and 2,000 troops around Peekskill to hustle across New Jersey, "as the Enemy now seemed fixed" to attack Philadelphia via the Delaware.

Washington steeled for the attack. Then, at 9:30 A.M. on August 1, an express rider sought him out with urgent news: Howe's fleet had turned its stern toward the Delaware Capes and had disappeared out to sea over the southern horizon. The fleet could strike anywhere! Was Howe bound for another attack on Charleston, South Carolina? He could be heading for an amphibious assault of Boston, or, worst-case scenario in Washington's opinion, the entire movement could have been a feint to draw Washington away from the Hudson Highlands, and the fleet was now headed back up the Hudson River to link up with General Burgoyne's northern troops.

Washington sent express riders all over New Jersey, telling every commander currently heading his way to turn the troops around and head for the Hudson hills. Even Nathanael Greene, who had brought his troops all the way down into the Philadelphia suburb of Germantown, was ordered to prepare his troops to march again over all the ground they had just covered. But after a two-day panic, Washington got hold of his senses; he sent out orders for all troops to freeze where they were. He had to have some intelligence of the whereabouts of Howe's fleet.

CHAPTER 10

The Battle of Brandywine

IN EARLY AUGUST OF 1777, GEORGE WASHINGTON MOVED INTO A stone house at a crossroads about 20 miles north of Philadelphia and 20 miles west of Trenton; from there, the troops in tents around him could move south or east as needed. In a letter from this "Camp at the Cross Roads" Nathanael Greene joked: "This is a curious campaign: in the Spring we had the Enimy about our ears every hour. The Northern Army could neither see or hear of an Enemy. Now they have got the enemy about their heads and we have lost ours, compeld to wander about the country like the Arabs in search of em."[1]

This was the situation on August 19, 1777, when a tall, slender teenager appeared at Washington's headquarters bearing a congressional commission as a major general in the Continental Army. His name was Marie Joseph Paul Yves Roch Gilbert du Motier, Marquis de Lafayette—Lafayette for short.

Washington had no idea what to make of this, writing to Congress that the young marquis has misconceived the design of his appointment, or Congress did not understand the extent of his views; for certain it is, if I understand *him,* that he does not conceive his Commission is merely honorary; but given with a view to command a division of this Army. True, he has said that he is young, and inexperienced, but at the same time has always accompanied it with a hint, that so soon as *I* shall think *him* fit for the Command of a division, he shall be ready to enter upon the duties of it.[2]

Lafayette was an enthusiastic, idealistic young orphan of incredible wealth. The British had killed his father in the Seven Years War, and he was bent on revenge. His mother had died when he was 13, and his grandfather had died a few weeks later, leaving him a huge fortune; at 16 he'd married into one of the most powerful families in France. Lafayette arrived at Washington's headquarters thirsting for glory and speaking little English, explaining through an interpreter that he was there to learn, not to teach.

With Lafayette, Washington's exasperation quickly turned to admiration for the young marquis. Lafayette had not come to America in search of a job—he drew an annual emolument of £14,000 sterling, and he was generous in offering horses, equipage, and clothing to the army. But he wasn't just buying Washington's friendship—he had a joyful, guileless demeanor that won people over. Even Nathanael Greene, who in the du Coudray affair had recently offered to resign rather than be subordinate to a foreigner, quickly found Lafayette "a most sweet tempered young gentlemen."[3]

A few days after Lafayette's arrival, the mystery of Howe's whereabouts was finally solved: The fleet had been spotted off Swan Point, some 200 miles up into Chesapeake Bay. After a month at sea, General Howe was going to land his troops in the upper Chesapeake, southwest of the city, and proceed the 55 miles to Philadelphia over land.

Washington put his troops on the march to meet them. On August 23, he wrote Congress with the news that he planned to march his army—now more than 10,000 strong—through the streets of Philadelphia at 7 the next morning. He wanted to make a good impression and was detailed in his instructions for this parade—the drummers and fifers would play a quick step but "with such moderation, that the men may step to it with ease; and without *dancing* along"; camp women were prohibited from marching with the men; officers would ensure "that the men carry their arms well, and are made to appear as decent as circumstances will admit."[4]

For two hours on August 24, the troops trod through the city, trying (without success in John Adams's opinion) to keep in step with the fife and drum. They cut a tolerably good figure—certainly they were numerous and well armed, though they had no standard uniform. Many wore loose white hunting shirts, others the blue or green coats of their home state's regiments; none wore red. Washington had recently banned solid red uniforms after too many incidents of friendly fire.

The troops marched about 6 miles beyond the city, camping that night in Darby while Washington rode on 20 miles to Wilmington, Delaware, where he learned that Howe had begun landing troops at the port town of Head of Elk. This Washington wanted to see with his own eyes. On August 26, he set out with Greene and a small guard to spy on the British troops as they came ashore. Washington and Greene invited Lafayette for the reconnaissance mission to give him a taste of adventure.

Storm clouds rose in the sky as the trio gathered on Grey's Hill, looking down on long boats of redcoats coming ashore; Washington could not even guess at how many troops had landed. On the ride back to camp a storm broke, driving the party into a Tory's farmhouse. Greene and Lafayette spent a restless night, fearing the British would hear word of Washington's whereabouts, but the general rested comfortably in the belief that his guards were numerous enough to fight off any attempted kidnapping.[5]

Howe's troops pitched camp on Grey's Hill, two miles from their landing point; after a month at sea, their draft horses had weakened, and men and horses needed to lose their sea legs. The advance guard of Cornwallis's "grand division" skirmished with some American light infantry at Cooch's Bridge, Delaware, on September 3, and on September 8, the entire British army finally moved, 13,000 strong, setting off a panic in Philadelphia. Families streamed out of the city, driving all of their cattle and carting furniture; Congress, too, fled west to York.

On September 9, the redcoats filed off northwest, away from Washington. He withdrew with them, taking a post on high ground overlooking Chad's Ford, a knee-deep passage across Brandywine Creek, west of Philadelphia. The creek, wide and deep enough to be considered a river, flowed between steep, wooded hills on its way to the Delaware River.

An aide to Washington wrote to Congress on September 10: "The enemy are now lying near Kennett's Square [a village seven miles west of the Brandywine] and in a tolerably compact body. . . . By Light Horsemen this instant come in, the Enemy are in motion and appear to be advancing towards us."[6]

⊬═══⊭

On the morning of September 11, 1777, a heavy fog lay over the Brandywine Valley. Unlike Trenton, through which he had passed several times before coming to battle, George Washington knew nothing about this ground. Locals favored the Loyalist cause and withheld information on the local topography that they gave to Howe. Washington made headquarters in a Quaker's house about a mile behind his lines, which stretched four miles along the east bank of the creek to cover four fords, shallow passages across the creek.

Washington had somewhere between 11,000 and 14,000 men on his side of the creek; on the other side, marching from Kennett Meeting House, Howe had 13,000. With about 25,000 men coming to a clash, the Battle of Brandywine was shaping up as the largest in the American Revolution.

As he awaited Howe's attack that morning, Washington thought that he had all of the creek's fords covered. He was wrong. Within a mile northwest of his right flank, held by a regiment of friendly Canadians, were two more fords. Leaving these fords unprotected was similar to leaving Jamaica Pass uncovered on Long Island. And as he had been on Long Island, General Howe was armed with better intelligence and prepared to exploit Washington's mistake.

The fog burned off that morning, leaving oppressive humidity and heat. By 10:30 A.M., Washington was steeled to receive a body of troops under General Wilhelm von Knyphausen known to be marching toward Washington's front at Chad's Ford. From high in the woods on both sides of the Brandywine, artillery boomed, sending balls crackling through the trees.

At headquarters, Washington waited for the British charge. None came, and he began to suspect that the artillery duel was just a feint to cover a march of the main army to his north and west. At 11, Washington received word from the head of his Canadian regiment, Colonel Moses Hazen, that "a large body of the enemy" had been seen marching north along the Great Valley Road.[7]

If this was true, then the army cannonading Washington's front was just a detachment sent to deceive. Washington could attack and destroy the smaller army before him, then use his combined forces to defeat the rest of the British army. But if the intelligence was wrong, and he attacked the front of the entire British army, Washington could find himself in a bad spot. Twenty-five minutes later, a messenger carried news from General Sullivan, who commanded the right, northernmost wing of the American army. One of his lieutenant colonels had seen 5,000 British troops up in his quarter.

To Washington it appeared that by splitting his troops—with Knyphausen leading a detachment of 5,000 and Cornwallis leading the main army of 8,000 up the Great Road in an attempt to get around the American flank—General Howe had blundered. Washington would press the attack, and Nathanael Greene would lead the charge.

At 1:30 P.M., Greene prepared to spur his horse across Brandywine Creek into the teeth of the British artillery dueling with American artillery; behind him stood about 1,300 men, some of America's best soldiers comprised mostly of veteran troops from Virginia. And then word came from Sullivan that a militia major had ridden miles along the Great Road and seen no sign of the British army up that way—the previous reports must have been false.

The whole of the British forces must be marching straight toward Washington, and he could not afford to splinter his own forces for an offensive. Washington canceled Greene's attack. At that moment a local farmer, Squire Thomas Cheyney, galloped up to headquarters to say he had seen British troops to the north and on the east side of the Brandywine, Washington's side; they were even then marching south to get behind Washington's lines.

"I'd have you know I have this day's work at as much at heart as e'er a blood of ye!" Cheyney stammered. "You're mistaken, general. My life for it you're mistaken. By hell! It's so."[8]

At 2:10 P.M., word came from Sullivan: "the enemy is in my right rear and advancing." Washington was in the jaws of a trap: He faced Knyphausen's force of 5,000 in front of him and Cornwallis moving down from behind with 8,000. He had once again been outmaneuvered by General Howe.

Cornwallis's troops had marched 15 miles through muggy heat, so he gave them a rest before forming their lines. Sullivan withdrew and tried to form his three divisions in a line along the curved face of Birmingham Hill, where he commanded about 3,000 men to face 8,000. His troops were not well trained, could not coordinate their movements properly, and were still unformed when the British attacked.

At headquarters, Washington withdrew Greene and two of his brigades with orders to be ready to march in either direction—north to help Sullivan, or west to help Generals Anthony Wayne and William Maxwell, who had been left at the Brandywine to fend off Knyphausen.

At 4:30 P.M. the thunder of musket volleys sounded to the north, and Washington knew Sullivan's men were under fire. At the sound of battle, Knyphausen fired his artillery at Washington's front, and his troops began to advance on Maxwell and Wayne. Washington instructed an aide to write a note to Congress: "At half after four o'clock, the enemy attacked General Sullivan at the ford next above this, and the action has been very violent ever since. It still continues. A very severe cannonade has began here too, and I suppose we shall have a very hot evening. I hope it will be a happy one."[9]

Then, after leaving orders for Greene's regiments to follow him at quickest step, Washington was off on his charger, galloping up to help Sullivan. When Washington arrived, the American line had been driven back to another hill, now called Battle Hill; the American right was streaming back from Battle Hill, and combined British and Hessian forces were concentrating on the center. Washington tried to rally the right, the way he had at Princeton; the young marquis, who had also galloped to the action, tried to follow Washington's example. Lafayette dismounted and raised his sword high as a rallying post for retreating troops. A British musket ball smacked into his left calf, and his boot filled with blood.[10] The retreating troops stormed past.

Greene arrived with General George Weedon's Virginia brigade just 45 minutes after Washington. In the enervating heat of a late summer's day, he had pushed 1,300 men, each bearing the weight of canteens, bullets, and 10-pound muskets, four miles in under an hour. The Virginians formed the line, allowing the artillery and panicked men to get through before firing on advancing British and Hessian troops.

A British officer described the battle at Plowed Hill as "a most infernal fire of cannon and musquetry. . . . The balls plowing up the ground. The trees crackling over one's head. The branches riven by the artillery. The leaves falling as in autumn" dislodged by the grape shot.[11]

At Chad's Ford, the fighting was also fierce: "the [American] battery playing upon us with grapeshot . . . did much execution," wrote an officer with the Queen's Rangers, which waded through the Brandywine to attack. "The water took us up to our breasts and was much stained with blood."[12] But the Queen's Rangers prevailed, driving the Americans before them on the road toward Philadelphia, where they met Sullivan's troops streaming down from the north. Greene, Weedon, and the Virginia troops held the ground at a crossroads until nightfall, when the shooting stopped and they withdrew.

Washington never did tally his losses for that day, but they were significant. General Howe likely overestimated the American loss at 300 killed, 600 wounded, and 400 captured, a loss of 1,300 men. Howe's own loss stood at 89 killed, 488 wounded, and 6 missing. The Americans had lost more men, had lost the ground, and would soon lose Philadelphia.

+>===<+

Tactically, the Battle of Brandywine was Washington's worst performance of the entire war, worse even than Long Island, because there he had been behind the walls of the Brooklyn forts when his field generals got outflanked— the error was more theirs than his. Washington's mistake at Brandywine was inviting a general action on ground with which he was wholly unfamiliar— and it nearly cost him his army. Had he done a better job of reconnaissance, Washington would have known about the northernmost ford that Cornwallis used to cross the creek, and he would have posted troops there to oppose the crossing.

But even if he had known that Cornwallis was moving down on him from the north, there would have been little Washington could have done to escape the jaws of Howe's trap. The 5,000 troops in front of him at Chad's Ford were well-trained regulars ensconced in a good position. If Washington had attacked those troops Cornwallis could have arrived behind the American army while it was fighting, squeezing it between a vice until Washington was forced to surrender. Though he was often criticized for indecisiveness, at Brandywine this was a virtue. In refusing to act without solid intelligence he prudently recalled Greene's men when they were on the brink of attack, likely saving the American army to fight another day.

CHAPTER 11

Germantown

T HE REDCOATS STILL HAD ONE MORE RIVER TO CROSS IN THAT FALL of 1777—to reach Philadelphia, they needed to ford the Schuylkill River, and Washington resolved to prevent it. Washington has often been called "the American Fabius," a reference to the Roman general Fabius Maximus, who refused to meet Hannibal's superior troops in a pitched battle in order to coax him into a long war of attrition.[1] But, in fact, there was nothing Fabian about Washington's nature, and, with few exceptions, his aggressive nature was usually reflected in his strategy. At almost every step—from the siege of Boston (where the collective wisdom of war councils several times pulled him back from storming the city) through Long Island, Harlem Heights, White Plains, Trenton, and Princeton—the man wanted to fight. Now, with fewer troops than Howe, and no strong ground to dispute the crossing of the Schuylkill's shallow fords, Washington wanted to fight him again.

On September 16, under leaden skies, Washington lined up his troops outside a village called White Horse Tavern in an attempt to stop Howe's inexorable march on Philadelphia. After some morning skirmishes, a long and heavy downpour soaked much of the American army's gunpowder—a contractor had built defective cartridge boxes. With his gunpowder wet, Washington had to withdraw across the Schuylkill.

Still, he left a detachment under General Anthony Wayne on the south side of the river to harass Cornwallis from behind. On September 18, Washington sent Wayne a warning to watch out for ambushes[2] but later learned that Wayne's detachment was taken by surprise in their camp near Paoli, Pennsylvania, after midnight on September 21. Fifty-three Americans died on the spot, their guts spilled by British bayonets; another 40 died of deep wounds in nearby houses in what became known as the Paoli Massacre.

Later that day, Howe put his troops on the march toward Reading—away from Philadelphia toward the west. Many military stores had been moved from the capital city to Reading, and Washington hustled his troops that way to protect them. Then Howe countermanded his orders, putting his troops back on the march toward Philadelphia, successfully faking Washington into marching his troops to the west. Howe found a key river crossing at Fatland's Ford all but undefended and marched across it without loss. Again it was the skillful maneuvering of a seasoned professional outfoxing a reactionary amateur. Within days, the British troops were ensconced in and around Philadelphia, with the bulk of the 12,000 men quartered in the suburb of Germantown.

While Howe was outfighting, outmaneuvering, and outfoxing Washington in Pennsylvania, the American army in the North was faring far better. On September 28, 1777, word filtered into Washington's camp that the Americans had beaten British General John "Gentleman Johnny" Burgoyne at Freeman's Farm outside Saratoga, New York. American forces had driven the British from the field at the farm, killing, wounding, and capturing 600 enemy troops while losing 300. This marked the second triumph of the Northern Army in a month—they'd also killed 200 Hessians near Bennington in what's now Vermont—and Washington ordered a celebratory 13-gun salute followed by a gill of rum (four ounces) per man.

Washington envied the successes to the North and lusted for a victory of his own. On the same day that he ordered the 13-gun salute and a gill of rum for all, he again called a council of war to advise on whether he should attack Germantown, a village of fieldstone houses five miles from Philadelphia.

Even with reinforcements from New York, New Jersey, and Maryland, the Americans could muster only about 11,000 men for an attack on Howe's 12,000 men in Germantown. The majority of officers, and all of the most senior ones, voted that the time was not yet ripe for an offensive.[3]

Then things changed.

On October 2, 1777, Americans scouts intercepted two letters sent by British couriers; from these, Washington learned that Howe had detached 3,000 men across the Delaware River to tackle American forts that were preventing British ships from sailing up the river with supplies for Philadelphia.

Washington called another council of war to tell his officers that Howe's camp at Germantown was now down to 9,000 men; the Americans outside Germantown numbered 11,000. Did the generals now favor an attack? This time Washington's generals were unanimous in voting yes.

+≡≡+

In a hilltop house 15 miles north of Germantown, Washington hatched a plan for taking the British encampment there that was even more complex than his scheme to assault Trenton. As he had at Trenton, Washington would split his troops into four "wings" that were supposed to march through the dark of night and arrive at Germantown simultaneously for a sunrise attack. He expected 11,000 soldiers, a quarter of them militia and many of them barefoot, to march more than 15 miles, at night, and arrive simultaneously on the field to attack 9,000 well-armed regulars camped in battle formation along a three-mile-wide front.

On the morning of October 3, Washington wrote a rousing general order, putting his men in motion for the long, nighttime march on Germantown. In his orders, he openly envied the recent victory of the Northern Army under General Horatio Gates, writing:

> The main American Army will not suffer itself to be out done by their northern Brethren. Covet! My Countrymen, and fellow soldiers! Covet! A share of the glory due to heroic deeds! . . .
>
> Our dearest rights, our dearest friends, and our own lives, honor, and glory and even shame, urge us to fight. And My fellow

Soldiers! when an opportunity presents, be firm, be brave; shew yourselves men, and victory is yours.[4]

As they had at Trenton, Generals Greene and Sullivan would lead the two main columns into town, Greene again on the left and Sullivan on the right. Before stepping off, every man stuck a piece of white paper in his hat so the horsemen delivering messages between columns could identify Americans when they came upon them; each column would be at least a mile from the next, and the entire front would stretch for five miles.

Nathanael Greene's division had to march farther than Sullivan's, 17 miles, so it moved out first, at 7 P.M. He led some 5,000 men plus the Maryland Continentals and New Jersey militia. The Maryland and New Jersey troops would peel off and march even farther east than Greene's division as they represented the farthest left, or easternmost wing, of Washington's attack.

Sullivan's troops, about 3,000 Continentals, moved out around 9 P.M., followed by about 1,500 militia, who would serve as the right or westernmost prong, tasked with keeping the British from escaping across Wissahickon Creek.

Greene's division, the biggest wing of the four-pronged attack, got lost. The local man hired to guide them on a back route to Germantown could not find his way in the dark. When he finally did hit on the right route, Greene moved his men at quickest step. Still, he arrived on the field a good hour after sunrise. The smaller wings on the extreme left and extreme right never made it to the field at all.

Sullivan's column was a little late to the field, but he arrived far earlier than anyone else, about 15 minutes after sunrise. The vanguard of his troops captured British sentries posted on Mount Airy and surprised a few hundred British infantrymen camped about a mile north of the main body of troops. The surprised infantrymen took cover and fired from behind fences and ditches before falling back toward the heart of the village, a two-mile stretch of widely spaced fieldstone houses.

The Fortieth British Regiment, alerted by the pop of musket fire, came forward and soon found itself surrounded. About 120 of its men barged into a solid brick house recently abandoned by Judge Benjamin Chew. They barricaded the doors and windows, then began firing on the rear of Sullivan's troops as they swept past.

A thick fog then settled over the village; smoke from the muskets thickened the fog till men could see no more than 30 yards. Sullivan's men kept coming, driving the British light infantry right out of their camp.

The thick fog acted as a double-edged sword: It aided the American attackers by cloaking them from the British waiting to cut down them down as they advanced along the pike and through fields of ripe buckwheat. What the British could not see they could not shoot; but it also prevented Washington from seeing the arrangement of his men. Sullivan's division was ahead of him, pushing through the fog; but where were the others?

From the sounds of Sullivan's men pushing forward, the battle seemed to be going well, but Washington could not see it; and he did have what he later termed "no small annoyance" in his rear: The British regiment in the Chew house blasting away at his troops. Henry Knox, chief artillery officer, had done a lot of reading about military theory, and he knew that it was bad form to leave an armed "castle" in your rear. He prevailed upon Washington to train the artillery on the thick walls of the Chew house; Washington agreed, and Knox blasted away with three- and six-pound balls. They just bounced off the walls while the troops within trained their muskets on the Americans clustered outside. Fifty-three Americans fell dead on the spot.

Finally, after 45 minutes of battle, Washington heard firing off to his left, the east—Nathanael Greene's division had arrived. One of Greene's commanders, General Adam Stephen, was well known to Washington from his Virginia days. Stephen had been a captain under Washington in the First Virginia Regiment, then had become a political rival in runs for the House of Burgesses. Now he was brigadier general of dubious character; he had often been seen drunk in front of his troops and had been drinking on the march that night.

Stephen commanded Greene's westernmost troops and, without consulting Greene, marched his men toward the sound of artillery fire at the Chew house. General Wayne also heard the cannon firing; and though his troops had advanced into Germantown, he turned them around to see what the blasting was all about. While marching back toward the Chew house, Wayne's men ran into Stephen's men advancing on it, and through the literal fog of war, they began firing on each other.

Knox's artillerymen were being picked off by the British regiment barricaded in the house; American troops under Wayne and Stephen were shooting at each other; Sullivan's most advanced troops called out that their ammunition was almost gone. Howe's troops heard the cries for ammunition and rallied. The Americans panicked, running past their officers along the Germantown Pike.

When Washington gathered his fleeing troops, he marched them 20 miles, 5 miles farther north than they had been that morning, a round trip of 35 miles on foot that included a fiercely fought battle. He settled his troops at a place called Pawling's Mill, where he counted losses: 1,111 men: 152 killed, 521 wounded, and 438 captured. The British lost half that many, 537 killed and wounded, and they held the field at Germantown, clearly a tactical victory for them.

Though he didn't yet know it, in his daring attack on Germantown, George Washington had won a much larger strategic point. Yes, he had lost the ground; but word of his near victory—combined with General Gates's subsequent capture of Burgoyne's entire army at the Second Battle of Saratoga—convinced the French that the American army was strong enough to merit the support of the French navy.

Even before hearing news of France's decision to openly back America the next spring, Washington took this loss as a moral victory, writing to Connecticut's governor: "Upon the whole, our Men are in high Spirits, and much pleased with the fortune of the day, tho' not so completely lucky as could have been wished."[5]

⊢══╉

Now, in early October of 1777, the British held Philadelphia, but the Americans held the water approaches to it—the Delaware and the Schuylkill rivers. If the British could not soon evict the Americans from two forts controlling the Delaware, they would have to quit the city. Troops and civilians in the city were miserably off because supplies could not be shipped in; the city had no flour and only poor beef. With control of the rivers, Washington had reasonable hopes of starving the British out.

On October 8, Washington ordered Colonel Christopher Greene—a third cousin of Nathanael Greene—to "throw" his Rhode Island regiment into the fort at Red Bank, New Jersey, and to hold that fort against an expected attack.

"Upon the whole Sir," Washington wrote Colonel Greene, "you will be pleased to remember that the post with which you are now intrusted is of the utmost importance to America. . . . The whole defence of the Delaware absolutely depends upon it, and consequently all the Enemy's hopes of keeping Philadelphia."[6]

Colonel Greene did the best that he could: On October 22, 1,200 Hessian troops marched on Red Bank, where Greene was lodged with his 400 men. Three times the Hessians assaulted the fort, and three times they were repulsed, their ranks thinned by more than 400: 50 captured, 153 dead, 200 wounded. The Rhode Islanders in the fort lost 14 killed and 23 wounded.

After Red Bank, the Howe brothers decided to bring all of their power to bear on clearing the American presence from the Delaware River. Admiral Richard Howe brought up a fleet of six 64-gun ships; a 36-gun frigate; a 24-gun ship; plus a sloop and galley of 6 guns each. Ashore he had six batteries of 6 guns each and a bomb battery of 3 mortars—almost 500 cannon.

On November 10, they opened up on Fort Mifflin, across the river from the stubborn Rhode Island regiments at Red Bank. Fort Mifflin fell. Now the Howe brothers could focus all of their naval and land forces on Colonel Christopher Greene and his Rhode Islanders in Fort Mercer. They sent Lord Cornwallis with nearly 5,000 troops to march on the 400 men at Red Bank.

Before Cornwallis could get there, Colonel Greene emptied the fort of its food, cannon, and stores, and blew it up. The British now controlled Philadelphia and the water access to it.

With winter setting in, Howe sent to New York for his mistress, Elizabeth Loring. Howe made comfortable quarters for Mrs. Loring, himself, and his troops in Philadelphia while Washington's troops, barefoot and hungry, slept on frost-hardened ground at a field camp in White Marsh.

CHAPTER 12

Valley Forge

IN THE WANING DAYS OF 1777, FROM WHITE MARSH, PENNSYLVANIA, Washington pondered his next move: Should he press on with a winter campaign, or should he put his troops in a winter camp? If they should camp, where would they camp? He also heard word from Philadelphia that General Howe intended to sally out to attack him.

As if Washington did not have enough to worry about, he also fretted about an internal coup to oust him. Since the Northern Army, under General Horatio Gates, had captured Burgoyne's entire army, Gates's star had been rising while Washington's had been falling. People began to question whether Washington was the best choice to serve as commander in chief—although there is no evidence that anyone in Congress other than James Lovell of Massachusetts seriously considered replacing Washington.

As the titular commander of the Northern Army, Gates got credit for flushing the British out of the upper Hudson River valley, and some of that credit swelled his head. Gates, a myopic, uninspiring leader known to his men as "Granny Gates," never deigned to notify his commander in chief about the victory at Saratoga, instead reporting it directly to Congress.

As Gates's army was conquering, Washington's army was floundering, losing at Brandywine, Germantown, and the Delaware River forts. Among those who felt Gates could do a better job than Washington was Thomas Conway, an Irish-born French officer who came over to help win the revolution. At first Washington liked him, and the feeling was mutual. But Conway's impertinence in insisting on a commission as major general did not sit well with Washington; and after watching the general's string of defeats, Conway wrote Gates: "What a pity there is but one Gates! But the more I see of this army, the less I think it fit for general action under its actual chiefs and actual discipline."[1]

One of Gates's aides saw this letter and mentioned it to an aide of General Stirling, one of Washington's most loyal generals. Stirling wrote Washington in November about the slur, twisting Conway's letter to say: "Heaven has been determined to save your Country; or a weak General and bad Councellors would have ruined it."

Washington could not let this go unchallenged. On November 9, he wrote Conway a curt letter expressing annoyance at being called "weak"; Conway protested that he had never said that. The affair might have died there, but Congress then promoted a trio of Washington's harshest critics to key posts, beginning with General Thomas Mifflin, who won appointment to the War Board. Mifflin successfully promoted Gates as president of that board, and on December 13, 1777, Congress promoted Conway to inspector general of the army with rank of major general, putting him in a position to oversee Washington and his staff.

The appointment of this triumvirate opposed to Washington stimulated a fierce loyalty in those closest to him, men such as Knox, Greene, Stirling, and Lafayette. There probably was not, as Washington's devotees claimed, a "Conway cabal" of disaffected officers who wanted to displace Washington; the evidence is as strong that that whole affair was nothing more than vain men praising each other at Washington's expense. What's most interesting about the episode is Washington's deft response to it. Rather than let his critics whisper behind his back, he called them out and turned up the volume. As a leader, Washington did not let resentments fester.

Responding to Washington's curt rebuke, Conway and Gates loudly and falsely tried to blame others, such as Greene and Washington's aide, Alexander Hamilton, for releasing the contents of the offending letter. Washington then wrote Gates that it was his own aide who had read and passed on the contents of that letter.

Though he was not happy about the promotions of Mifflin, Gates, and Conway, Washington never complained to Congress. He was aloof with Conway when the latter inspected his winter camp. When Conway later wrote him that the "cool receptions" he'd received were an insult, Washington did not engage in back-and-forth sniping with him. Instead, he forwarded Conway's correspondence to Henry Laurens, president of Congress, adding:

> If General Conway means, by cool receptions . . . that I did not receive him in the language of a warm and cordial Friend, I readily confess the charge. I did not, nor shall I ever, till I am capable of the arts of dissimulation. These I despise, and my feelings will not permit me to make professions of friendship to the man I deem my enemy, and whose system of conduct forbids it. At the same time, Truth authorizes me to say, that he was received and treated with proper respect.[2]

By exposing Conway's petulance, Washington made him look petty; soon Congress shipped Conway off to Albany to serve under Lafayette while Mifflin and Gates were removed from the Board of War and reassigned (Gates went to oversee the Northern Department, and Mifflin ceased to play an active role in the army.)

━━◄═══►━━

Even as he deftly dispatched the so-called Conway cabal, Washington continued to wrestle bigger problems. All but one of his officers—Casimir Pulaski, a Polish nobleman and experienced cavalry commander—agreed that a winter campaign and an attack on Philadelphia were out of the question; but they differed greatly on where to encamp the troops for the winter. Washington ordered his troops to march on December 10, destination unknown. His was an awesome responsibility: He was leading 11,000 men, many without shoes, all with little food, into the woods to live. He knew that many would die by spring, writing Connecticut's governor: "We must expect to loose a considerable number of Men by sickness and otherways, in the course of the Winter."[3]

Washington led his troops into a gloomy valley called the Gulph. The first night there, it snowed, a few inches of wet slush. The army had not yet ferried its tents across the Schuylkill, so they lay in the snow, many barefoot and without blankets.

They pushed on through a chill rain into Valley Forge, arriving at night on December 20, bedding down in the snow with no supper. Before the British had ransacked it, there had been a village there—a few fieldstone houses clustered near an iron forge that gave the valley its name.

When the tents came up, they covered two miles of the wooded slope rising from the western banks of the Schuylkill to a peak called Mount Joy. Washington wanted the men out of tents and into huts as soon as possible. He divided his men into teams of 12 with orders for each team to build its own log hut of specific dimensions—14 feet long, 16 wide, 6.5 feet high—just 18 square feet per man.

On December 23, the camp commissary reported to Washington that he had "not a single hoof of any kind to slaughter, and not more than 25 Barls. Of Flour." Twenty-five barrels of flour—to feed 11,000 men. Troops turned out to protest the lack of rations, sparking a near mutiny. The army's diet was mostly a paste of flour and water "fire cake"—cooked on the hot rocks of open fires, not much food to fuel the hard work of chopping trees, sawing off branches, hauling the logs, chinking them together with clay. A month of chopping and sawing passed before every man had moved from tent to hut in January 1778.

Moving into dark huts with leaky roofs did little to alleviate the misery of life in Valley Forge. The smoke of 1,000 campfires hovered over a village of squalid huts; herds of skeletal horses nuzzled the muddy snow in vain; horse carcasses rotted in the snow; men, too, died by the thousands. Not surprisingly, there were mutinies, put down by the point of the bayonet.

Then came the snow: For two days in early February 1778 it fell, filling the valley so that no wagons could move, stopping what little food deliveries there had been. Men went without meat; then they went without bread; many went day after day with no food at all.

Washington took great pains to avoid impressing goods from civilians near his camp, for he knew that even those who supported American independence would turn against the cause if the army stole their food, forage, and horses. But on February 12, he ordered Nathanael Greene to lead an impressments party to take "Horses Cattle Sheep and Provender within Fifteen or Twenty miles."[4] Even in this order, he first blamed the need for impressments on the possibility that the British were planning to raid the country, so the Americans might as well beat them to it; he also ordered Greene to make sure that locals were given vouchers for anything taken from them.

Like Washington, Greene had been a stickler for treating civilians fairly; but he zealously carried out these orders for impressments. Greene wrote to a subordinate: "You must forage the Country naked."[5]

Five days of foraging yielded about 50 head of cattle that Greene sent into Valley Forge; from New Jersey, General Anthony Wayne drove cattle across the Delaware then down into the valley. It was enough meat on the hoof to feed the troops for several days.

Martha Washington had arrived in camp just before the snows fell at the first of the month. She wrote to a friend: "The General is well but much worn with fatigue and anxiety. I have never known him to be so anxious as now."[6]

<hr>

February also brought the arrival of another foreign officer seeking an officer's commission: Friedrich Wilhelm Augustus von Steuben, a baron, a former Prussian officer, and a bit of a con man. Steuben brought with him a little Italian greyhound and a 17-year-old boy who could translate the native German's French into English. Steuben himself knew no English, although he proved proficient at picking up the curse words. He carried a letter from Ben Franklin introducing him as the Baron von Steuben, a lieutenant general in King of Prussia's service.

Steuben really was a baron, and had been an officer in the King of Prussia's army, a formidable force; but now at age 48, he had not served in the army for 14 years. He was not in fact a current lieutenant general but a penniless former captain. But he passed muster with Washington, who put Steuben to work drilling the troops.

As a former captain in Frederick the Great's army, Steuben truly did know how a crack eighteenth-century army operated. He chose 100 of Washington's best troops and tried to teach them the innumerable details of the Prussian system: marching, forming the line, wheeling, firing, thrusting, and parrying with the bayonet. He stood in the thawing muck of Valley Forge's parade grounds thinking in German, speaking commands in French, which his translator barked out in English. Often the commands did not translate, leaving the men stumbling about the drill field while the roly-poly baron with a huge medal on his chest cursed in German "Gott damn!" His translator, Pierre Duponceau, remembered that Steuben's "fits of passion were comical and rather amused than offended the soldiers."[7]

His 100 men learned the Prussian system of warfare; others learned from their example, and over the month of March, the soldiers at Valley Forge drilled and drilled until a dozen battalions—some 7,000 men—could move together with precision.

Having Steuben take over the training of troops as inspector general, Conway's old job, offered Washington some relief, but he still had a major operational problem: He had no quartermaster general—the man in charge of supplying the troops. Thomas Mifflin, who had held the post, had not been with the army since the previous July, having resigned in order to take a seat on the Board of War in November. The appointment was Congress's, but in this, Washington and Congress agreed—Nathanael Greene was the man for the job. Besides being a good strategist and field general, Greene had proven to be very good at matters of supply: When Washington needed cartridges for his army at White Plains in the fall of 1776, Greene forwarded 80,000 of them[8]; when his troops were retreating across New Jersey, they lived off stores strategically placed beforehand by Greene; and it was Greene who "forage[d] the country naked" to deliver fresh meat to Valley Forge. Both Washington and a committee from Congress that met at Valley Forge pressed Greene to take the job; in late February, Greene reluctantly accepted, and by mid-March, he had repaired wagons and rebuilt roads so that wagons were once again rolling to distant supply depots and bringing in enough food to keep the army from disbanding.

By the end of April 1778, Washington received news that he'd long been waiting to hear: France, impressed by the victory at Saratoga and the performance of the troops at Germantown, had agreed to sign treaties with the United States, pledging the open support of its land troops and navy.

"I have mentioned the matter to such Officers as I have seen, and I believe no event was ever received with a more heart felt joy," Washington wrote to Congress on May 1. He delayed breaking this news to the troops until

Congress ratified the treaty; then on May 6 everyone lined up on the parade gun for three 13-gun salutes of cannon, each followed by a loud huzzah and toasts of "Long live the King of France," "Long Live the Friendly European Powers," "To the American States." Each man fired his musket a split second before the man to his left, a "running fire" that thundered from nearly 10,000 muskets, reverberating off the spring-green hills of Valley Forge.

General Charles Lee returned to the army that spring, released from confinement in exchange for a British general captured by Rhode Island militia outside Newport. Lee, a native-born Englishman, was an aristocrat whose behavior showed little of the upper class. He was tall, big-nosed, and thin; he could not keep a uniform mended and clean and always traveled with a retinue of small yappy dogs, at least one of which the British allowed him to keep during his captivity. Lee arrived in May with what Nathanael Greene called his "usual train of dogs."[9]

The man sent to escort Lee to camp, Elias Boudinot, noted that nearly two years of captivity had not changed General Lee. After a welcome-back feast at Washington's headquarters, Boudinot showed Lee to his quarters behind Martha Washington's sitting room.

"The next morning," Boudinot wrote, "he lay very late and breakfast was detained for him. When he came out, he looked dirty, as if he had been in the street all night. Soon after I discovered that he had brought a miserable dirty hussy with him from Philadelphia (a British sergeant's wife) and had actually taken her into his room by a back door, and she had slept with him that night."[10]

So now in May of 1778, things were back to normal: General Lee had rejoined the troops, and the men whom General Washington had led into Valley Forge with little more than faith in the darkest days of December—those who had survived—were now better supplied, better trained, and backed by the power of France. Many times in that hard winter the army had been on the verge of disbanding, but Washington had held it together. In many ways this was his finest hour as commander in chief—he had kept his army intact and now Washington was eager to see what it could do.

CHAPTER 13

"So Superb a Man"

In the spring of 1778, George Washington felt torn between three strategies for prosecuting the coming year's campaign: attack the main body of British troops now in Philadelphia; attack the 4,000 enemy troops garrisoned in New York; or keep growing, training, and nurturing his army at Valley Forge throughout the summer. The last of these options seemed least workable; Washington wrote that if he did not take the offensive, the British would go about "spreading their baneful influence far and wide, till their reinforcements enabled them to take the field with some degree of éclat."[1]

That left an attack on either Philadelphia or New York, and he could not decide. In mid-May, the new commander in chief of the British forces, Sir Henry Clinton, made Washington's choice for him. Clinton and General William Howe had not had a good working relationship, with Clinton often and not tactfully arguing for more aggressive measures. Howe was being recalled to England to explain why, with 30,000 troops and fleet of warships, he had not yet won the war. Clinton now had his chance to act.

News of France's entry into the war had reached the British camp as quickly as it had reached Washington's, and the British cabinet responded by ordering Clinton to send 5,000 of his troops to protect British interests in the West Indies, 3,000 to Florida to guard against a potential Spanish threat, and to garrison the remaining troops in New York. To comply with these orders, Clinton had to evacuate Philadelphia; he decided to move his 10,000-man army by land across New Jersey, to New York—more than 100 miles—before redeploying them.

Washington's spies in Philadelphia saw British ships loading heavy cannon, baggage, wood, and water, and by May 17, Washington knew that the British army would soon be on the move. They might be leaving America altogether to protect British islands in the West Indies; or they might head for New York; or they might directly attack Washington at Valley Forge. Washington wrote Henry Knox to be ready to move the artillery at shortest warning and cautioned General Gates—with whom he still had a working (if cool) relationship—to look out for British troops possibly moving toward his posts up on the Hudson River.

What Washington most needed was intelligence of Clinton's plans. He peeled off a detachment of more than 2,000 men, including 50 dragoons and 5 cannon, to patrol the peninsula between the Delaware and Schuylkill rivers above Philadelphia to gather news and harass British troops coming out of the city. He placed the detachment under Lafayette.

In sending Lafayette off with the troops, Washington cautioned: "You will remember that your detachment is a very valuable one, and that any accident happening to it would be a severe blow to this army."[2]

Lafayette established his troops on a place called Barren Hill, about 11 miles north of Philadelphia and a dozen south of Valley Forge. There was no hiding a force of that size, and Howe, still technically in command for one more week, knew they were there. On the night of May 19, Howe sent out three parties: one under General James Grant to get behind Lafayette and cut off his retreat; another to attack Lafayette's left wing; and the third under Clinton and Howe to lead a frontal assault.

Lafayette had done a good job in choosing his ground but had relied on militia for patrols; they failed to see the British troops encircling the American camp through the night, and only at daybreak did an officer named Allen McLane discover the British plan. He warned Lafayette, who managed to march his troops off the hill by using a back road that Grant had failed to notice. When the British troops surged onto Barren Hill from three sides, they found that Lafayette had slipped the trap.

In sending out that detachment, Washington had blundered. He had sent too many men to act as surreptitious scouts and too few to tackle an assault by the British army. Thanks to Lafayette's quick thinking and to the training of von Steuben, who had taught the troops to move in tight platoon formations rather than in long single files, Washington had narrowly averted a disastrous loss to begin the campaign of 1778.

+———+

In mid-June, Clinton's troops began their long-awaited move from Philadelphia, crossing over the Delaware River into New Jersey. Washington could not be hasty in emptying his camp to establish a position in New Jersey to meet them, for if Clinton doubled back and attacked American troops outside Valley Forge, the Americans would be caught outside of their lines in the open field and would have to fight at a disadvantage. Once Clinton committed to the march through New Jersey, Washington would follow along his flanks, sniping at him, not really planning for a full-scale engagement but more than happy to fight one should the opportunity arise.

On June 18, the American troops marched out of Valley Forge at 5 A.M., under strict orders to carry their muskets and kettles and to let no camp women ride on the baggage wagons. The long stay at Valley Forge was ended.

Clinton faced an operational nightmare of his own as he moved his 11,000 men across the sandy plains of New Jersey. His train held 1,500 wagons, a line of men, camp followers, and horses that stretched for 12 miles. Wagon wheels churned the sand into a floury mix, slowing horses and men; an oppressive heat wave draped New Jersey with humid air. After seven days, the British column, bogged down by broken bridges and road obstructions, had traveled only 40 miles.

As Clinton rolled slowly along, Washington's 12,000 troops followed like a pack of predators looking for a weakness. The slow march across New Jersey offered Washington a whole host of tactical difficulties—which roads would Clinton travel? Where best to deploy his own troops to harass the

British? Washington did a good job of keeping scouts on all the roads without dispersing his troops too much.[3]

On June 24 in Hopewell, New Jersey, Washington polled his officers in a council of war: Should they attack Howe's column? Should they get in front of it and invite an attack on them?

In spite of the fact that he had ignored Washington's orders, recklessly allowed himself to be captured, and returned to camp with a mistress, General Lee still held a certain cachet as a former British officer, and he argued strenuously against doing anything at all. With the French now in the war, Lee argued, the best thing to do was let the British pass unmolested till the French navy arrived. By a majority vote of the officers present, Lee's passive strategy carried the day.

A minority, including Lafayette and Nathanael Greene, strongly disagreed. In protest, Greene wrote Washington: "If we suffer the enemy to pass through the Jerseys without attempting anything upon them, I think we shall ever regret it . . . .We are now in the most awkward situation in the World. We have come with great rapidity and we got near the Enemy and then our courage failed us. . . . People expect something from us and our strength demands it."[4]

Washington agreed. On June 24, over the strong objections of General Lee, Washington ordered a detachment to strike the rear of the British wagon train.

<hr />

Washington chose the Marquis de Lafayette to lead several detachments in attacking the British troops, a high-profile assignment for the young marquis. Then General Lee, who at first wanted nothing to do with the attack, wrote Washington that he wanted to lead it because ceding command of such a large force to Lafayette would "of course have an odd appearance," by making it look to the troops as though Washington had rejected Lee for the command.[5]

Washington relented and, after writing an apology to Lafayette, gave command of the attacking troops, nearly 5,000 men, to Lee. On the morning of June 28, 1778, Lee's troops advanced on the rear guard of the British troops on the road to Monmouth Courthouse.

Washington, riding a beautiful white charger given him by the governor of New Jersey, monitored things from a post a few miles behind Lee and a few miles ahead of the main body of his troops. By 10 A.M. the sun, near the summer solstice, hung high overhead, casting a harsh white glare. The temperature that day climbed to near 100 degrees Fahrenheit; from his post, Washington strained to hear the sounds of muskets blasting as Lee pressed his attack.

Around noon, Washington heard the big booms of artillery but not much in the way of musketry; these were not the sounds of the attack that Washington had ordered. He did not know it, but Lee had once again managed to get into trouble. Initially Lee was moving on a rear guard of about 2,000 men under Cornwallis, but the dust of Lee's advance troops of about 6,000 had tipped off the British that a large body of Americans was in the area. Troops that had been filing off away from Monmouth turned around, and General Clinton was bearing down with much of his army—about 6,000.

Lee tried to form his troops to receive the British, but he mismanaged the maneuvers so badly that the troops began to withdraw of their own accord. Lee, who had lost control of his command, had no choice but retreat with them. He had lost his chance to pick off the 2,000 men forming the rear guard, and was retreating from a much larger force. Lee's decision to retreat from superior numbers was justifiable, but it went against Washington's wishes.

By now a clear pattern had emerged in Washington's career: Whenever he defended against a British attack, he lost. From Fort Necessity through White Plains and the Brandywine, Washington had never successfully defended ground when attacked. On the contrary, whenever he had taken the offensive, he had won: Harlem Heights, Trenton, Princeton, even at Germantown where he had lost the day's battle, he had won the larger strategic point of French support.

Washington heard the British cannon, and he received word from a fifer that Lee's troops were retreating. He refused to take the man at his word, riding his white horse to a ridge overlooking a ravine from where he could see his sweaty, exhausted troops moving toward him.

Though he cultivated a cool, diffident demeanor, Washington could flash a nasty temper. As he rode toward the line, Washington saw that his troops were not attacking, as ordered—they were, as the fifer said, retreating.

Private Martin Joseph watched as Washington "crossed the road just where we were sitting. I heard him" ask: "By whose order are the troops retreating?"

The passing troops answered: "By General Lee's."[6]

Washington caught up with Lee and, according to Washington's aide, Tench Tilghman, asked him: "What is the meaning of this?"

Lee stammered, "Sir, sir," then allowed that the entire attack "was against his opinion."

Tilghman observed: "General Washington answered, whatever his opinion might have been, he expected his orders would have been obeyed, and then rode on to the rear of the retreating troops."[7]

A colonel on the retreat told Washington that the British would be on top of his position in 15 minutes; he had 15 minutes to run or to rally. Washington, atop the white charger, was at his battlefield best, displaying the coolness and élan he had shown while riding with Braddock and at the Battle of Princeton. He halted the sweaty, thirsty men staggering toward him and animatedly ordered them to line up behind a long hedgerow overlooking a dip called Middle Ravine.

"I never saw the general to so much advantage," wrote his young aide, Alexander Hamilton. "His coolness and firmness were admirable. He instantly took maneuvers for checking the enemy's advance and giving time for the army, which was very near, to form and make a proper disposition."[8]

The British, as expected, moved quickly onto the field with dragoons, grenadiers, and light infantry. For an hour, the exhausted troops who had marched off with Lee that morning fought a fierce battle, ending in hand-to-hand combat with fixed bayonets before they withdrew across another dip in the ground called West Ravine.

By holding the British off for an hour, the troops had given Washington time to redeploy the 7,000 men of his main army atop the West Ravine. In traveling back and forth to monitor the progress of both positions, Washington rode his white charger to exhaustion; he finished the day astride a chestnut mare.

+>=—=<+

Nathanael Greene, who had been leading a division to the town of Freehold, five miles south, to prevent a flanking action, could tell from the sound of firing that the troops had withdrawn again. He turned his division around, marched back three miles through the heat, and rolled cannon on top of Comb's Hill. He positioned his artillery there then joined the American troops in a long line atop the ravine with Greene on the right, Lord Stirling on the left, and Lafayette commanding troops slightly behind the wings in the middle.

The British continued to press on. Cornwallis led a detachment to assault Greene's position; about 100 Americans fell dead in the attack, but the survivors held the ground.

Clinton himself led an attack on the American left, hoping to turn Stirling's flank; Washington read the maneuver and sent 1,000 men under Colonel Joseph Cilley, who matched the Black Watch Highlanders in bayonet fighting that drove the British back.

By 4 P.M., the battle was over. For the first time, Washington's troops had held the ground against an attack. He had done a masterful tactical job in leading troops, trained by Steuben and clothed by France through a newly efficient quartermaster's department led by Greene. These were not the half-naked undisciplined troops who had fled the battlefield at Germantown into the woods of Valley Forge. Washington now had a fighting force that was worthy of his command.

"Never had I beheld so *superb a man*," Lafayette wrote of Washington that day, and Nathanael Greene reported: "The commander in chief was every where, his Presence gave Spirit and Confidence and his command and authority soon brought every thing into Order and Regularity."

"America owes a great deal to Washington for this day's work," wrote Hamilton, who was nearly crushed to death by his dying horse, which had been shot. "A general rout, dismay, and disgrace would have attended the whole army in any other hands but his."[9]

At midnight, under the relative coolness of dark, Clinton marched his troops from Monmouth Courthouse toward the coast, leaving his dead for the Americans to bury, traditionally an honor, or a chore, left to the victor.[10] Washington counted 249 English and Hessian buried by American troops— 62 dead of heat stroke. About 100 Americans died, 37 of exertion.

Strategically, both sides achieved their objective at the Battle of Monmouth: Washington had harassed the British troops and held the ground, while Clinton rolled on to embark his troops at Sandy Hook, which had been his goal all along. But Washington claimed victory at Monmouth, for when the smoke cleared, he held the battlefield and buried the British dead.

+══ ══+

As a slogan it wasn't very catchy, but its meaning was clear: "Perpetual and undisturbed independence to the United States of America!" George Washington ordered his troops to shout that three times following the "running fire" of muskets he'd ordered his brigades to fire in salute of the Fourth of July. The troops spent the fourth in Brunswick, New Jersey, on the march for the Hudson River, where Washington again planned to attack New York.

Washington's obsession with New York was no longer a quixotic dream—for he would soon have ship support from the French navy under command of Count Charles Hector Theodat D'Estaing. Estaing had been a general before accepting the post as a navy admiral, much to the disgust of experienced naval officers who had to serve under him.

On July 11, Washington heard rumors that the French fleet was off the Virginia coast, and two days later, he received confirmation that a French fleet of 12 warships and 4 frigates was on station and sailing for Sandy Hook, just south of New York. The fleet dropped anchor there in mid-July and then waited, and waited, and waited. Washington sent local pilots out to show Estaing channels for approaching New York; they could not find any. Estaing's ships drew 27 feet of water, 5 feet more than the hulls of the biggest British ships, and there seemed to be no way of getting them across Sandy Hook without running aground.

On July 22, the French fleet weighed anchor and sailed away from Sandy Hook, forcing Washington to postpone his planned attack of New York. He agreed with Estaing that the next best place to attack was the British garrison of 6,000 men on Aquidneck Island, a large island in Narragansett Bay. He agreed to give Lafayette a detachment of 2,000 men to march from his camp above New York to Rhode Island; although he was reluctant to part with his quartermaster, Washington also allowed Nathanael Greene to leave camp for the Rhode Island campaign, since Greene knew well the people and the terrain of his native state. Lafayette would command half of the 10,000 militia and Continentals who flocked to Rhode Island for the attack, Greene would command the other half, and the whole would be under the command of General John Sullivan who, like Estaing, had a reverse Midas touch that turned the most promising opportunities into dust.

The Battle of Rhode Island would be the first test of the new alliance between the French and the Americans, and a lot was riding on the outcome. Washington monitored the situation from White Plains, and by early August, things looked good: Sullivan had 10,000 men camped just across the narrow Sakonnet River from Aquidneck Island, and Estaing had dropped 4,000 French marines on Conanicut, a nearby island, then anchored at the southern tip off Newport, ready to bombard the garrison while Sullivan's troops and the French marines swept in from either side.

But on the very day the battle was to commence, Admiral Richard Howe crested the horizon with a small fleet of British warships. Estaing decided that he had to get rid of that strategic threat to his stern before he could commit to bombing Newport; he plucked his marines off Conanicut Island and sailed over the horizon in pursuit of Howe's fleet.

Even though his ship support had sailed away, Sullivan moved his 10,000 troops onto Aquidneck Island, then watched as a three-day storm raked his men in the field with punishing winds and rain. When the storm cleared, a fleet appeared on the horizon—a look through the spyglass showed Estaing's ships standing for Newport, raising spirits of American troops besieging the city. But Estaing's ships had been crippled, both by the storm and by British broadsides; he had come back only to tell Sullivan that he could not continue the siege. He then sailed around to Boston for repairs, leaving Sullivan exposed on an island with no ship support.

Sullivan, who could be cool on a battlefield but hot-tempered in a drawing room, issued scathing insults to the French in his general orders: "The General cannot help lamenting the sudden & unexpected departure of the French Fleet . . . he yet hopes the Event will prove America able to procure that by our own Arms which his Allies refuse to assist in Obtaining."[11]

This statement—"refuse to assist"—so incensed Lafayette that he nearly quit the American army and returned to France. Sullivan tried to smooth over the affair in his orders of August 26 ("we ought not too suddenly Censure" or "forget the aid and Protection which had been offered by the French" thus far) he wrote, which mollified the marquis.

In fact, Lafayette agreed to ride up to Boston to meet with Estaing in what proved to be a vain attempt to win his support for further pressing the

Rhode Island siege. Lafayette was in Boston when the British, emboldened by the withdrawal of the French fleet, sallied out from Newport and attacked the American troops as they were trying to retreat from the island. Nathanael Greene commanded the right wing of the American troops that day, which included the First Rhode Island Regiment—comprised of African and Narragansett slaves who had enlisted in exchange for their freedom. Men of the regiment successfully repulsed two attempts to turn the right flank and, with reinforcements, drove back a third attempt, allowing the troops to withdraw from the island.

⊢══⊣

In early September, Washington was still fretting about the rift that had developed between the Americans and their French allies. He sent a letter to Greene saying:

> I depend much upon your temper and influence to conciliate that animosity, which I plainly perceive by a letter from the Marquis [de Lafayette], subsists between American Officers and the French in our service. . . . The Marquis speaks kindly of a letter from you to him upon this subject. He will therefore take any advice from you in a friendly light, and if he can be pacified, the other French Gentlemen will of course be satisfied, as they look up to him as their head.[12]

On September 6, a mob in Boston attacked a group of French officers at a bakery, killing one. Greene rode up to Boston to help patch the rift, spending time in the elegant Beacon Hill house of John Hancock entertaining French officers. Thanks to the warm relationship between Greene and Lafayette, the "other French gentlemen" grew satisfied that Sullivan was just an isolated hothead and that in general the American officers held them in high esteem. The French alliance was saved.

With the French fleet in Boston as autumn crept in, it was clear to Washington that he could take no major offensive for the rest of 1778. In November, he ordered his troops into winter camp in Middlebrook, New Jersey, where they spent the winter living in relative comfort inside newly built huts.

CHAPTER 14

"The Womb of Fate"

In mid-December of 1778, Washington got called to Philadelphia to meet with Congress to, as he told Nathanael Greene, "lay before them a general State of the Army."[1] Washington arrived in the city on December 22, then summoned Greene, his quartermaster, to join him there so he could provide a firsthand account of shortages plaguing the army. Congress wanted to push an army up the Hudson River into Canada that winter, but Greene convinced them that this was impossible.

In early January, Washington verbally asked Greene's opinion on what the army's strategy should be for the campaign of 1779.

Greene responded in writing, drafting a letter in his Philadelphia chambers by candlelight in the predawn darkness of January 5: Washington should keep the army in a defensive position in New Jersey; attempt to attack the British in New York City if the opportunity seemed right; and send a detachment into upstate New York to fight the Iroquois Six Nations Confederacy.[2] Five of the six tribes of the confederacy had aligned themselves with Tory militiamen for raids as far south as Pennsylvania's Wyoming Valley.

For most of 1779, Washington followed Greene's advice. He put General John Sullivan in charge of 2,500 men to destroy tribal villages set amid the cultivated orchards and fields of upstate New York.

Like everything that Sullivan touched, the expedition developed problems. Moving thousands of men with artillery through the footpaths of Iroquois country required road building and horses and forage. Sullivan's expedition turned into a long and expensive campaign that did not reach Seneca territory until mid-August.

Eventually, Sullivan did succeed in his objective: Between mid-August and late September 1779, his troops destroyed 60,000 bushels of corn and torched 40 towns, mostly Indian settlements.[3] The strategy stopped Indian raids on the western frontier; it also made a prophet of Tanacharison, the Six Nations chief who decades before had tagged Washington with the sobriquet of "Canonticorius"—devourer of villages.

While Sullivan rampaged through Indian country, the main body of troops remained in huts at Middlebrook until June, when the British sailed 40 miles up the Hudson and captured both terminals of King's Ferry, a river crossing with Stony Point on the west bank and Verplank's Point on the east. Washington authorized General Anthony Wayne—commander of the Pennsylvania line that saw heavy fighting at Brandywine, Germantown, and Monmouth—to conduct a daring, nighttime raid on Stony Point that resulted in the capture of more than 500 British soldiers. Washington destroyed the works at Stony Point and abandoned the post two days after capturing it, reasoning that if he tried to hold the fort there, his troops would be exposed to the same kind of attack that had led to the capture of the British troops. A similar raid on Paulus Hook, across the Hudson from Manhattan's southern tip, led to the capture of a 150 prisoners, but again, the Americans abandoned the post rather than risk defending it. The raids on Stony Point and Paulus Hook were good tactics for building morale and keeping bored troops occupied, but they offered no strategic gain.

+>===<+

The only strategic point gained in the campaign of 1779 was won in October by the British at Savannah, Georgia. King George III had decided to move the seat of the war to the South, where he believed there were more Loyalists.

There the society was fractured, with neighbor fighting neighbor in what had become more of a civil war than a revolution. The king's troops captured Savannah in December 1778 and then clobbered Admiral Estaing as he again tried to link up with American forces to recapture the city. French and American forces totaling about 5,000 tried to storm Savannah in October and were driven back with the loss of more than 800, mostly French marines.

From his headquarters at West Point on the Hudson, where he had retreated into a defensive position, George Washington correctly guessed Great Britain's shift in strategy. Writing to his southern commander, Major General Benjamin Lincoln, Washington said the British "will make a vigorous effort to the Southward. . . . The weakness of the Southern states affords a strong temptation."[4]

The British could not prosecute their southern strategy yet—first they had to secure Jamaica and other valuable islands in the West Indies from French attack—so the campaign of 1779 came to an end with neither side achieving much.

In December, Washington moved his troops into winter quarters at Morristown, New Jersey. The first regiments marched from the West Point Citadel into Morristown on December 2, 1779, arriving in a storm of mixed hail and snow. They pitched their tents in snow and set to work building 1,000 log huts.

A few days later, a heavier snow fell, setting a pattern for that winter of heavy snows followed by bitter cold. A blizzard struck in the first days of January 1780. Teams could not draw sleds through four feet of snow; food stored in magazines outside Morristown could not be hauled in, and as at Valley Forge, the troops went without food. On January 7, starving soldiers waded through waist-deep snow to plunder Morristown's houses and farms. The next day, Washington issued a circular to a dozen county magistrates, apologizing for his men's behavior. Then he appealed for help from the residents of New Jersey.

"The present situation of the Army with respect to provisions is the most distressing of any we have experienced since the beginning of the War. For a Fortnight past the Troops both Officers and Men, have been almost perishing," he wrote. He called upon the "virtuous Inhabitants" of the state to send in cattle and grain. Washington's couched his plea as a request but backed it with the threat of force: "I think it my duty to inform you, that should we be disappointed in our hopes, the extremity of the case will compel us to have recourse to a different mode, which will be disagreeable to me."[5]

People did respond, sending teams to plow roads, flour to bake bread, and cattle for slaughter. By the end of January, Washington could write Congress that the army was now "comfortable and easy on the score of provisions."[6]

But the improvements were short-lived. After five years of war, the Continental currency had nearly no value. Few people wanted to sell food or other goods to the army in exchange for worthless paper.

+━━┅━┅╋

On May 25, 1780, a regiment of the Connecticut troops in Morristown mutinied. They had not been paid for five months, and they were sick of starving. As they shouldered their muskets to march for home, their own officers surrounded them with armed Pennsylvania troops, sending the Connecticut men grumbling back to their camps.

Deserters and spies carried word of the mutiny to the British in New York, then under the command of Hessian general Baron Wilhelm von Knyphausen. The Baron had temporarily taken over for Clinton, who had sailed south for an attack on Charleston. Knyphausen crossed into New Jersey, expecting locals to flock to his flags. Instead, he met an angry New Jersey militia that drove his troops back to Elizabethtown, which was where he was when Clinton returned from his successful capture of Charleston in the South, the worst American defeat of the war. At Charleston, the Americans lost an entire army of 2,571 regular officers and men, plus 800 militiamen. British returns also showed the capture of 5,315 muskets, 15 stands of regimental colors, 33,000 musket balls, and 376 barrels of powder.

Washington assumed that Knyphausen's attack was a feint to draw attention, with a major assault to follow on the American fortress at West Point. He put his army on the march for West Point, leaving a rear guard of 2,000 regulars plus militia in Springfield, New Jersey, under the command of Nathanael Greene.

Clinton was as puzzled by Knyphausen's quirky New Jersey invasion as Washington was, but he decided to take advantage of it. He ordered Knyphausen to advance from Elizabethtown to attack Greene at Springfield. The two sides met on June 23, 1780, the last pitched battle to be fought in the North. Greene's 2,000 troops, outnumbered three to one, withdrew to the hills behind Springfield. They fired on the British from the high ground, driving them back.

A courier relayed to Washington that Greene was retreating in the face of a much larger enemy; Washington turned his troops around to help, but they had marched only five miles when word came from Greene that he would need no help. After burning Springfield, Knyphausen's troops had retreated back into New York.

Greene reported losses of 14 killed and 74 wounded, while observing: "The inhabitants of Elizabeth Town inform us, that they counted eighteen wagon load of dead and wounded"[7] British and Hessian troops staggering back toward New York.

<hr />

A month after the Battle of Springfield, Washington received some more good news: A new French fleet had dropped anchor off Newport with a few thousand soldiers moving into the garrison there that the British had evacuated.

For Washington, this meant one thing: a combined French and American attack on the 12,000 British and Hessians ensconced in New York. Nathanael Greene thought his commander in chief was tilting at windmills, writing to a friend, "Has not the project something *Don Quixotal* in its appearance?"[8] Nonetheless, Greene did his best as quartermaster to gather boats, food, and forage for Washington's planned attack.

In New York, General Clinton also planned an assault: on the French troops in Newport. On July 26, he set sail from New York with 2,000 men, hoping to rendezvous with another British fleet to blast the French. Washington saw the absence of the British fleet as his opportunity to attack New York.

On a 90-degree day, Washington put his men on a forced march toward New York, crossing the Hudson River on July 29; two days later, he learned that Howe and his fleet of warships had returned to New York, forcing him to withdraw across the Hudson. But his movement toward New York had not been in vain—the French fleet had only recently arrived at Newport and was still vulnerable. Admiral Howe had aborted what could have been a devastating attack in part because Washington had moved from his position in the New Jersey Mountains to King's Ferry, threatening New York.

Meanwhile, in Newport, the young Marquis de Lafayette kept badgering Rochambeau to attack New York City, telling the seasoned commander that the attack was also Washington's wish. Rochambeau did not believe it. He suspected Lafayette was using Washington's name to support his own ambitions. Rochambeau and the admiral in charge of the French fleet at Newport decided that they had to speak with Washington in person to discuss their future operations.[9]

From his headquarters in northern New Jersey, Washington wrote Rochambeau with a date (September 20, 1780) and place (Hartford) for the meeting; he also broke what he called some "disagreeable" news from the South: General Horatio Gates had just lost an entire army to Cornwallis in a discomfiting defeat outside of Camden, South Carolina. For the third time in less than two years, America had lost entire armies in the South: at Savannah under Robert Howe; in Charleston under Benjamin Lincoln; and now under Gates at Camden.

Washington set out for his meeting with Rochambeau on September 17, leaving command of the army under Nathanael Greene. Washington met with Rochambeau and a French admiral for two days, achieving little because there were so many variables in all their proposals: Would a second French fleet arrive before the winter campaign? Would Louis XVI agree to attack Canada as part of a winter campaign? The conference produced more questions than answers. In their discussions, Washington emphasized "[t]hat of all the enterprises which may be undertaken, the most important and decisive is the reduction of New York, which is the centre and focus of all the British forces."[10]

<hr />

On Monday morning, September 25, 1780, Washington sent his aides to tell the commander at West Point, Major General Benedict Arnold, that he would be passing through the fortress on his way back to camp and expected to dine at Arnold's house near West Point later that day. The aides delivered the message that Washington was on his way, then sat down to breakfast with Arnold; as they ate, a courier rode up to deliver Arnold a message. A spy, John Anderson, had been caught.

Arnold knew that name as a pseudonym for John André, a British colonel with whom he had been negotiating the surrender of West Point in exchange for a fortune. Arnold had just given André the plans for the fortress and was trying to get £20,000 in return for giving up the fort. Arnold excused himself from the table; he went upstairs and told his young wife, "I have this moment received two letters which oblige me to leave you and my country forever."[11]

Arnold told his guests that he had some business to tend to at nearby West Point; he would be back to meet his Excellency in an hour. Not a half hour later, Washington arrived at Arnold's house. Washington did not know Arnold well—the two men had never fought together, but Arnold's heroism at Quebec and on the battlefield at Saratoga were legendary. Arnold had been wounded at both battles, and at Saratoga, he and Daniel Morgan had been responsible for capturing Burgoyne's army. Arnold was, in Nathanael Greene's words, the idol of America; Washington had recently rewarded him with the command of West Point in appreciation for his hard service.

Washington must have been piqued when he arrived at Arnold's house only to find that the host had just taken his leave. Washington ate his meal, then rode on to West Point to see Arnold and inspect the works. He was shocked at the fort's condition. Without actually sabotaging it, Arnold had let the fort go to ruin.

Washington returned to Arnold's house on the river's east bank to mull things over; then an aide, Alexander Hamilton, handed him a packet that had just come in by courier: the plans of West Point taken from the spy, John André. Washington was uncharacteristically emotional, some said near tears, as he told Hamilton and Lafayette: "Arnold has betrayed us! Whom can we trust now?"[12]

In November 1780, Washington moved his troops into cantonments, groups of winter quarters stretching from Morristown through West Point and a little bit north, to the village of New Windsor, New York, where he made his headquarters. This was a glum time, perhaps the gloomiest of the war. The revolution was entering its sixth year, and even its most ardent supporters were sick of the hardships; the Continental currency was worth less than the paper it was printed on; Arnold, "the idol of America," was a turncoat; the French fleet at Newport was blocked by British warships; and King George's strategy to sever the South had been alarmingly successful. In the South, the British troops had routed American troops under General Robert Howe to capture Savannah in 1778 and had successfully defended that city against French and American troops in 1779; in May 1780, the British captured almost all of General Benjamin Lincoln's army at the siege of Charleston; and three months later, General Horatio Gates lost most of his army outside of Camden.

Congress had handpicked the three commanders who lost armies in the South—Howe, Lincoln, and Gates; on the heels of Gates's defeat in August, Congress told Washington to make the selection this time. In October 1780, Washington chose Nathanael Greene, who had recently resigned as quartermaster after another impolitic argument with Congress about the system of supply. Greene arrived in Charlotte, North Carolina, in December, where, he wrote, the number of American soldiers equipped and fit for duty "does not amount to eight-hundred men."[13] His adversary in the three-state theater, Lord Charles Cornwallis, had a field army of 4,000, plus another 5,000 troops in garrisons stretching from Savannah, through the backcountry, to coastal North Carolina.

On New Year's Day, 1781, the situation became even worse. The Pennsylvania brigade at Morristown, 1,000 men comprised mostly of German immigrants, shouldered their muskets, stole six cannon, and began a march on Philadelphia to demand that Congress give them clothes, food, and nearly a year's back pay—or feel the cannon's wrath. They killed the two officers who stood in their way.

Washington received word of the mutiny from the brigade's general, Anthony Wayne, on January 3, and he hurried off a note telling Wayne to stay with the mutineers but not to get in their way as opposition would only convince them to desert to the enemy.[14] He felt he could not leave the critical fortress of West Point; he monitored the situation from afar, giving Wayne careful advice—allow the mutineers to cross the Delaware to get them away from the corrupting influence of British troops; tell Congress not to flee Philadelphia but to remain and negotiate; remember "a proper degree of generosity . . . will have a tendency to conciliate" the men.[15]

The mutineers refused to cross the river, instead camping in Princeton. The British snuck two sergeants into camp with offers of bribes if the Continentals would come over to the other side; the mutineers, insulted, declared they would not become "Arnolds"[16] and turned the sergeants over to Wayne, who hanged them as spies.

Since the troops were from Pennsylvania, Congress deferred to negotiators from that state; in mid-January, negotiators agreed to let the brigade march home without their back pay but with amnesty. Not a week later, 200 New Jersey troops in Pompton mutinied and marched toward Trenton. This time, Washington was not forgiving. He ordered a detachment of "five or six hundred of the most robust" men to subdue the mutineers.[17] The detachment succeeded, and a dozen of the disobeying New Jersey troops were drafted to serve as a firing squad to kill the two ringleaders. That put an end to the mutinies.

+≡≡≡+

On May 31, 1781, from his headquarters on a bluff overlooking the Hudson, Washington scratched out a letter to Lafayette in Virginia telling him everything about a two-day strategy session that he had just held with Rochambeau in Connecticut. Finally, he wrote, Rochambeau was prepared to send his land forces to the Hudson River for his long-hoped-for attack on New York. "The French troops are to march this way [from Newport] as soon as certain circumstances will admit," Washington told Lafayette.

The attack, Washington wrote, would either force the British to withdraw troops from Virginia to bolster those at New York; or it would force the British to move all their troops from New York to attack Virginia, in which case the Americans would follow them there.[18]

That letter had been on the road toward Virginia only one day when a British ensign captured a bundle of correspondence, giving General Clinton detailed plans of the French and American strategy for the coming summer. Clinton was so pleased by this intelligence that he rewarded the man who captured it with a fortune of £200.[19]

Washington had essentially given Clinton the choice of where to make his stand: Did he want to fight the combined French and American forces on Manhattan, or did he wish to lure them south for a battle in Virginia? Clinton chose New York. He wrote to Cornwallis in Virginia, telling him to march to a deepwater port so ships could retrieve the detachment of 2,000 men he had just received.

Cornwallis, naturally, was not pleased to give back 2,000 men he had hoped to use for an invasion of Virginia; nevertheless, he did as he was ordered, withdrawing his troops from interior Virginia to the York Peninsula for boarding. But, he wrote Clinton in late June, if he had to send those troops back, he was not strong enough to remain in Virginia and would like permission to take his troops back into the garrison at Charleston.

Clinton relented; he wrote Cornwallis saying he could keep the troops in Virginia but, to control the mouth of Chesapeake Bay, he should barrack them at Old Point Comfort on the southern tip of the York Peninsula. Cornwallis had already reconnoitered the point and decided that he had found a better deepwater port for his barracks: Yorktown, an old tobacco port on a bluff overlooking the York River. The first of his 5,000 troops arrived there on August 2.[20]

Clinton was so proud of capturing Washington's letters that he published them in New York. Washington was embarrassed to learn that the letter had been intercepted, but the revelation of his plans did not force him to change them. The French army of 4,400 men, as planned, marched from Rhode Island to a camp outside White Plains, arriving there on July 6.

At the time of their rendezvous, both Washington and Rochambeau knew that a large French fleet was cruising from the West Indies to America to help with the coming campaign. Washington believed that the fleet would most likely help with the reduction of New York, but Rochambeau knew that it would not: He had written the fleet's commander, Francois-Joseph-Paul De Grasse, advising him that the British position on Manhattan was too strong to attack. He strongly suggested that de Grasse set sail for the Chesapeake Bay to attack the British troops in Virginia, as Clinton would least expect an assault there.[21]

For the entire month of July, Washington earnestly prepped for the long-awaited attack on New York, riding reconnaissance, ordering lookouts to stare at the horizon for long hours to spy De Grasse's fleet. Rochambeau, a battle-scarred veteran of more than a dozen sieges, played along. He accompanied Washington on uphill rides to look down on British positions, taking minute notice for a battle that he knew would never be fought.

On August 14, Washington got the news that De Grasse's fleet had set sail from Haiti and was bound not for New York but the Chesapeake. In a letter forwarded from Newport, De Grasse wrote that he could remain on the

American coast only until mid-October; Washington and Rochambeau must "have everything in the most perfect readiness to commence our operations in the moment" of his arrival.[22]

That was a tall order. Moving operations to the Chesapeake meant marching two armies more than 400 miles; it also meant abandoning New York and the Hudson River—the "key slot" to the continent—to the enemy for a long and tedious march of uncertain success.

To Washington's credit, he agreed to do it. In his diary he wrote: "Matters having now come to a crisis and a decisive plan to be determined on, I was obliged . . . to give up all idea of attacking New York."[23]

⊷═⊶

George Washington mapped a route for the French army's march and sent it to their commander, Comte de Rochambeau, with the following note: "I have named no halting day because we have not a moment to lose."[24]

The march began on August 19, 1781, and by September 5, exhausted troops were already staggering into Head of Elk, Delaware—a distance of nearly 200 miles. That day, a courier who had been riding round the clock found Washington's party on the road just outside Chester, Pennsylvania, a port town on the Delaware River. He handed Washington a fat packet with several letters in it, including one from de Grasse: He had dropped anchor at the mouth of Chesapeake Bay with 28 warships plus 4 frigates and 3,000 soldiers. De Grasse would land his soldiers to assist Lafayette's American troops in preventing Cornwallis from fighting his way off the York Peninsula. Cornwallis was in a trap.

Rochambeau was then sailing down the Delaware River to Chester. When his ship docked, Washington stood on the wharf with his hat in one hand and his handkerchief in the other; he was waving both in an uncharacteristic display of joy. Rochambeau stepped ashore and Washington gave him a big hug. A French officer with Rochambeau reported, "I have never seen a man moved by a greater or more sincere joy than was General Washington."[25]

Washington's spirits were also lifted by a steady drumbeat of good news coming in from Nathanael Greene in the South: his forces had driven Cornwallis out of the Carolinas and into Virginia by defeating him in the Battle of

Cowpens and inflicting terrible casualties on British troops at Guilford Courthouse, North Carolina. After driving Cornwallis north, Greene had turned southward and, working with local partisans, begun picking off all of the British backcountry outposts: Camden, Ninety-Six, Fort Watson, Augusta. By mid-summer the British had only two garrisons remaining in the Carolinas and Georgia: Charleston and Augusta.

Washington's joy turned to worry in late August, when word came that de Grasse's fleet had hauled anchor and disappeared out to sea. A British fleet had arrived off the Virginia coast just days after de Grasse, and as at Newport, the French admiral determined he had to strike against this strategic threat to his stern before he could undertake a siege.

Washington gave orders to freeze all soldiers right where they were, refusing to let them embark for the sail to Virginia until he knew which fleet would be masters of the sea. He rode on for Williamsburg, his home state's capital on the York Peninsula, where he again heard good news from de Grasse: He had fought the British off the Virginia Capes and won, capturing two of their frigates. Adding more joy to this news: When de Grasse returned to his anchorage in the Chesapeake, he found that French ships under Jacques-Melchoir Saint-Laurent Comte Barras—de Barras—had slipped into harbor from Rhode Island, bringing with it heavy siege guns to be used in battering Yorktown.

"Our Operations here are fast Ripening to the Point of their Commencement," Washington wrote to a general up north on September 24. "Our Prospects are at present fair and promising. What may be in the Womb of Fate is very uncertain; but we anticipate the Reduction of Ld. Cornwallis with his Army, with much satisfaction."[26]

On September 26, the last of the troop transports sailed in from Head of Elk, and the army was now nearly 19,000 strong: 8,000 American Continentals, 7,800 French land troops, and 3,100 militia. Two days later, they broke camp and marched, sweeping down the Hampton Road to the British garrison at Yorktown.

Yorktown had once been a prosperous tobacco port, but tobacco is hard on the soil; when fields fell barren, the population of this town, set high on a bluff overlooking the York River, dropped. Yet the village still bore traces of its former prosperity with its houses of brick and clapboard neatly arrayed in a grid.

The allied forces pulled up beyond cannon shot of the town and pitched camp with French forces on the left and the Americans on the right, forming a six-mile arc around the village. Across the wide York River, nearly a mile away, a second cantonment of British troops occupied the peninsula town of Gloucester, but they too were hemmed in on a point by French forces and Virginia militia.

Cornwallis had occupied Yorktown for nearly two months, giving him plenty of time for him to dig in: His troops had built a chain of seven redoubts and formidable earthworks linked by trenches. If the French and American troops tried to rush across the overgrown fields of the York peninsula to storm the town, Cornwallis's artillery would cut them to pieces. On the night of September 29, Cornwallis precipitately abandoned his outer entrenchments to concentrate his force nearer the garrison.

The approach to Yorktown called for classic, European siege warfare: French and American troops would have to dig a series of protective trenches zigzagging their way across the open fields until they reached the works and redoubts of Yorktown. Cutting these parallel trenches was a work of complex engineering; Washington had attempted a little siege warfare outside of Boston, but all he really knew about prosecuting a siege was what he'd read in books. It was his fortune to have in his camp two of the best besiegers in the world: Rochambeau was a veteran of a dozen sieges, and the chief engineer, Louis le Bègue du Presle Duportail, was also a master. Rochambeau had agreed to serve as Washington's subordinate on paper; but when it came to engineering the trenches and placing the batteries, Washington possessed enough self-assurance to defer to the experts.

Washington's deference to the experienced French officers did not reduce him to a passive observer—far from it. The man had an insatiable curiosity: Nights he wandered the field with the engineers, studying where best to dig the protective trenches, or "parallels," on their zigzagging course toward the British works. When ox teams had finished hauling all the heavy siege cannon up from the James River, Washington wrapped his hands round a shovel handle and dug the first spadeful in a ceremonial groundbreaking.[27] Fatigue parties of 500 men with shovels and pickaxes worked through the long October nights, and Washington was everywhere. Good leaders make themselves visible at crucial moments. He issued a meticulous list of 55 "regulations" for the miners and their officers, covering everything from the proper order of march on the way to and from the trenches to the practical admonition: No smoking by the gunpowder stores.

After three nights of digging, the works came within 600 yards of the British cannon poking out through the embrasures, or breaks in the earthen walls outside Yorktown. The French and Americans were now close enough to throw up earthen walls for their own gun batteries, and on October 9, the first of the siege guns were in place. The American battery on the right side of Washington's line held three long cannon that could fire 24-pound balls, three 18-pounders, two howitzers, and two 10-inch mortars to lob bombs on top of Yorktown; to the left, the French battery held four 16-pounders plus six mortars and howitzers.

The French guns were in place first; Washington, eager to begin the bombardment, let the French light the first fuse.[28] The signal to fire would be the raising of the American flag above the battery on the right. At 3 P.M., the Stars and Stripes rose up the staff.

"I confess I felt a secret pride swell my heart when I saw the 'star spangled banner' waving majestically" above the trench in which he stood, wrote Private Joseph Plumb Martin.[29]

The French guns roared, followed by shouts, in accented English, of "Huzza for the Americans!" Two hours later, the American guns began firing, sending tongues of flame flaring into the dark. Artillerists trained their first fire on the big cannon ports cut into the walls outside Yorktown to neutralize the British return fire. The French guns were so accurate that they dropped hot shot onto British ships in the James River behind Yorktown, setting them aflame.

Washington ordered rounds fired throughout the night to prevent repairs to the walls. Beneath the crossfire of shrieking, brightly lit shot and shell, fatigue parties dug and dug; more batteries were built, and by the morning of October 11, six more 24-pounders were in place.

On the night of October 12, French and American soldiers began digging their second parallel toward Yorktown while shot and shell lit the skies above them.

"The fire of the enemy this night became brisk," Washington wrote in his diary on October 13, " . . . and more injurious to us than it had been; several men being killed and many wounded in the Trenches but the works were not in the smallest degree retarded by it."[30]

On October 14, the men digging the trenches ran into a problem: The line they were following to their right would soon cut right into two British redoubts—high mounds of earth rising from deep trenches, their slopes bristling with abatis. Atop these redoubts, in cup-shape depressions, stood men with musket, bayonet, and cannon, ready to repulse any attack. To continue digging the second parallel, French and American forces would have to take these redoubts in hand-to-hand fighting.

Washington assigned a party of 400 French regulars under Colonel Guillaume Deux-Ponts to capture the larger of the two redoubts, defended by 120 Hessian and English soldiers. An equal number of Americans under the command of Colonel Alexander Hamilton would storm the smaller redoubt, perched on the edge of a bluff above the York River and defended by 45 men.

Just after sunset, as Jupiter and Venus shone brightly against the night sky, the French and American attackers gathered in front of their trenches about a quarter mile from the two redoubts; between them was a moonscape of bomb craters, some deep enough to "bury an ox in."[31]

Washington appeared before the men. Captain Stephen Olney, assigned to lead a company of 40 Rhode Island soldiers (not the First Rhode Island or Black Regiment, as commonly believed), observed: "General Washington made a short address or harangue, admonishing us to act the part of firm and brave soldiers. . . . I thought then that his Excellency's knees rather shook, but I have since doubted whether it was not mine."[32]

At 7 P.M., a series of six shots boomed from a French battery, the signal that the attack was on. The men plunged across the dark, lunarlike landscape with fixed bayonets. For the Americans, the attack was relatively easy—Olney took a bayonet in the gut that spilled a piece of his intestine (amazingly, he survived), and nine Americans were killed, but they captured the place within 15 minutes.

To their left, the French had a harder time: There the fighting lasted longer and resulted in more casualties with 52 French soldiers dead in the ditches and impaled on the abatis; another 134 suffered wounds. But they prevailed—and by 5 P.M. of the next day, October 16, the two captured redoubts held four howitzers ready to lob bombs into Yorktown.

The French and American forces now had nearly 100 cannon, mortars, and howitzers blasting the little village of Yorktown. Henry Knox, the American artillery commander, figured that the Americans and French fired 15,437 artillery rounds at the British during eight days of bombardment—a round-the-clock average of more than one shot every 30 seconds.

Hardly a pane of glass stood unbroken. Twenty-four-pound balls smashed through roofs; 16-pounders whacked into brick walls and remained embedded there; hot shot ignited wooden houses. Streets were pocked with bomb craters and scattered with body parts—arms, legs, tatters of uniforms.[33]

Finally, on October 17, a British drummer appeared on the long parapet surrounding Yorktown, standing beneath a fluttering white flag. The measure he beat on his drum signaled to Washington that Cornwallis wanted a parley—a negotiation of settlement terms. Firing ceased; an officer appeared on the parapet and was led, blindfolded, behind the American lines to deliver a letter from Cornwallis to Washington reading: "Sir, I propose a cessation of hostilities for twenty-four hours, and that two officers may be appointed by each side, to meet at Mr. Moore's house, to settle terms for the surrender of the posts at York and Gloucester."[34]

Washington wrote back: "An Ardent Desire to spare the further Effusion of Blood, will readily incline me to listen to such Terms for the Surrender of your Posts."[35]

Cornwallis wrote back seeking the same terms that Horatio Gates had granted General Burgoyne at Saratoga: Soldiers could return to England and Germany on the promise of not fighting again in the American theater. Washington called this "inadmissible."[36] Clinton had not given Benjamin Lincoln's troops permission to go home on parole after their capture at Charleston. Washington offered the same terms that Clinton had given Lincoln at Charleston; the captured soldiers, Washington wrote, would be "marched to such parts of the Country as can most conveniently provide for their Subsistence; and the Benevolent Treatment of Prisoners, which is invariably observed by the Americans, will be extended to them."[37]

To negotiate with two British commissioners, Washington sent Colonel John Laurens—whose father had been president of the Continental Congress before being captured at sea and imprisoned in the Tower of London—and Viscount Louis Marie de Noailles, Lafayette's brother-in-law. The four men worked until past midnight of October 19, hammering out an agreement by the fireplace in the widow Moore's farmhouse behind American lines. On the morning of October 19, they had an agreement: Officers could keep their sidearms and, in exchange for all captured American officers, they could return to British-held ports; soldiers would be surrendered as prisoners of war; all were to march out of the garrison with flags furled at 2 P.M.

French and American troops formed a line that stretched for a half mile along the York–Hampton Road, the French resplendent in white uniforms with trim of different colors, all wearing new gaiters for the occasion; the American regulars cut a less uniform figure, wearing the colors furnished by the different states; behind them, many rows deep, stood thousands of Virginia militia. Washington rode through the long line upon a handsome charger with Rochambeau at his side; mounted officers rode behind.

The British came late to the surrender field, and Cornwallis did not come at all, sending General Charles O'Hara in his place. O'Hara, on a horse, led a long and mournful column of 7,241 downcast troops marching beneath bare sticks instead of their flowing regimental colors. One observer wrote: "They marched through both armies in a slow pace, and to the sound of music, not military marches, but of certain airs, which had in them [a] peculiar strain of melancholy."[38]

On reaching the French and American officers, General O'Hara turned to address Rochambeau; the French general waved him off and pointed to Washington. O'Hara turned to Washington—who pointed him to his second, General Benjamin Lincoln, the bow-legged Massachusetts farmer who had been forced to surrender his troops at Charleston. If Cornwallis was going to send a surrogate, that man would deal with Washington's surrogate.

Lincoln directed O'Hara to lead his troops into a field, one regiment at a time, there to lay down their muskets and march back along the road to Yorktown unarmed.

<hr />

The Battle of Yorktown did not end the American Revolution. In fact, the loss of 7,000 men, 12,000 muskets, and 214 cannons prompted King George III to make a bellicose speech to Parliament calling for "firm concurrence and assistance, to frustrate the designs of our enemies."

In the waning days of 1781, Washington and his generals still had a war to fight. Nathanael Greene was camped near the gates of Charleston, holding together a little army that he described as "ragged as wolves" to harass the last British possession in the South; Rochambeau's French force went into winter quarters on the York peninsula to shore up Virginia; and Washington sent the rest of his forces north to establish cantonments, temporary winter quarters in New Jersey and New York as far north as Newburgh, just above the fortress at West Point.

Washington left the camp at Yorktown on November 5 and rode all night for the town of Eltham, Virginia, where his stepson, Jack Custis, lay dying of camp fever, which he had contracted while serving as a general's aide during the siege. Martha was already there; Washington arrived at daybreak, just in time to be with Martha when the last of their two children died.[39]

From Jack's deathbed, Washington rode to Mount Vernon for a brief stay, then onto Philadelphia to confer with Congress on plans for the campaign of 1782. The "primary object of the next campaign," he told Benjamin Lincoln, now a retired general and Congress's secretary at war, was New York.[40] But there was one major problem: The army had no money, and Congress still had no authority to tax the states to raise it.

In an open letter titled "Circular to the States," Washington pleaded with state officials to collectively raise $8 million for the next campaign. "[R]emember the ferment into which the whole Army was thrown, twelve Months ago, for the want of pay and a regular supply of Cloathing and provisions," Washington wrote as a reminder of the previous year's mutinies. "You cannot conceive the uneasiness which arises from the total want of so essential an Article as Money."[41]

Congressional business kept Washington in Philadelphia until late March, when he reached the main army's camp in Newburgh, New York. He did not stay long—first he toured some upstate New York towns to view some outposts, then he was summoned back to Philadelphia to meet with Rochambeau for a strategy discussion. The two agreed that Rochambeau should move his troops north toward New York, which would free Washington to employ his troops for a Canadian invasion.

Nothing ever came of the Canadian scheme: A change in Great Britain's administration led to General Clinton's recall, and in early August, his replacement, Sir Guy Carlton, informed Washington that peace negotiations between American and British representatives had begun in Paris. Washington was not inclined to believe it; as he wrote to Nathanael Greene on August 6: "From the former infatuation, duplicity, and perverse system of British Policy, I confess, I am induced to doubt every thing, to suspect every thing."[42]

Still, with no money to put his army on the offensive and with a hint of peace in the air, Washington allowed the campaign of 1782 to come to a close without taking the field. Again he took winter quarters in a fieldstone farmhouse with four chimneys and a broad, covered porch in Newburgh, New York; and again his officers were upset. Not only had they received almost no pay for four years, their pay had been docked for food and other provisions that they had never even received.

In January 1783, a contingent of officers petitioned Congress for "just recompense for several years of hard service."[43] Though their demands fell on sympathetic ears, Congress sent them back to camp with nothing more than kind words. From his Newburgh farmhouse, Washington wrote to Alexander Hamilton (now a civilian and a congressman) that the just demands of the officers put him in a tough spot: He didn't want his officers to view him as unsupportive, but he didn't want the Congress to see him as unrealistic.

"The predicament in which I stand as Citizen and Soldier, is as critical and delicate as can well be conceived," he wrote Hamilton on March 4. "It has been the Subject of many contemplative hours. The sufferings of a complaining Army on one hand, and the inability of Congress and tardiness of the States on the other, are the forebodings of evil, and may be productive of events which are more to be deprecated than prevented."[44]

Not a week later, Washington's "forebodings of evil" were realized: An officer in his camp had drafted an anonymous address saying that if Congress did not give in to their demands, they should retire to the woods and let the British overrun the country; and if the British declared peace, they should refuse to lay down their arms and take what they were owed by a military coup.

Another circular was passed around camp on that same day, March 10, calling for the officers to meet the next day in the "New Building," a long hall that had just been built for dancing and chapel services. Washington was horrified. In his orders of March 11, he canceled the planned meeting while expressing his "disapprobation of such disorderly proceedings."[45] He recognized the delicacy of his situation—if he was too harsh with officers, he risked losing the most moderate among them. So while killing the unauthorized meeting of that day, he scheduled another meeting of the officers for noon on March 15.

The propagandists seeking to take what was theirs by force declared this a victory, circulating a second address suggesting that Washington's approval of a meeting proved that he was on their side.

At noon of the appointed day, the disgruntled officers gathered inside the freshly cut timbers of the long New Hall. They took their seats; then Washington himself entered, walking the long aisle to the lectern at the front. He turned, and in the silence he spoke: "Gentlemen: By an anonymous summons, an attempt has been made to convene you together; how inconsistent with the rules of propriety! how unmilitary! and how subversive of all order and discipline, let the good sense of the Army decide."

Washington reminded his men that he had been among the first to serve in the army and that, in eight hard years, he had never left its side but to confer with Congress or with Rochambeau. He laid out the two options offered by the anonymous writer of the circular: If the war continues, refuse to fight it; and if there is peace, march into Congress and demand back pay at the point of a bayonet. "My God! what can this writer have in view, by recommending such measures? Can he be a friend to the Army? Can he be a friend to this Country? Rather, is he not an insidious Foe?"

Washington pledged that he would always support the cause of his officers in his dealings with Congress. And now he asked for their support—if they would just be patient, again, and refuse to give in to baser instincts, they would furnish the world with an example of selflessness that would stand for the ages. "[Y]ou will, by the dignity of your Conduct, afford occasion for Posterity to say, when speaking of the glorious example you have exhibited to Mankind, 'had this day been wanting, the World had never seen the last stage of perfection to which human nature is capable of attaining.'"[46]

Washington then reached into his pocket for a sympathetic, if pedantic, letter written by a congressman, Joseph Jones of Virginia. He smoothed the letter and began to read from it, but slowly; Jones's handwriting was smaller than his, and the letters looked like a blue mist. Washington was now 51 years old; his already light hair had gone gray, and he had lost most of his natural teeth. Again he reached into his pocket and pulled out a pair of spectacles that he perched on his nose. "Gentlemen," he said, "you must pardon me. I have grown gray in your service and now find myself going blind."[47]

He finished reading Jones's letter, then he strode down the long aisle and left the officers to conduct their meeting as they saw fit. In his absence, they gave him a vote of thanks; they took a vote of confidence in Congress; and they requested that Washington serve as mediator in their negotiations with Congress. Because he supported his subordinates, when he most wanted their loyalty they supported him. Through his ingenious leadership, George Washing saved America from a military coup.

+——————+

Two weeks after his speech to the officers, Washington received official word from a French officer, the Chevalier de La Luzerne, that a peace agreement had been reached. The war was over. Washington wrote back that day: "Sir: The News of a general Peace, which your Excellency has been so good as to enounce to me, has filled my Mind with inexpressible satisfaction."[48]

Nearly six months passed before peace negotiators in Paris worked out the details of the peace, and two more months passed after that before the last of the British troops sailed from New York, clearing the way for Washington to enter the city on November 25, 1783. He rode astride a fine gray horse next to the civilian leader of the state, Governor George Clinton, on a bay gelding. They were escorted by mounted dragoons of a county militia. A long column of civilian horsemen followed as they rode through columns of cheering people, Washington's first glimpse of the city he had fled in the dark days of 1776.

On December 4, Washington hosted a noontime final farewell of such officers who were present in the city. Not many could make it to the reception at Fraunces Tavern; there were three major generals, one brigadier, a line colonel. They ate, and then Washington lifted a glass of wine for a toast: "With a heart full of love and gratitude, I now take leave of you. I most devoutly wish that your later days may be as prosperous and happy as your former ones have been glorious and honorable."[49] The men drank. And then Washington said, "I can not come to each of you but shall feel obliged if each of you will come and take me by the hand."

Big Henry Knox was the first man to him. Knox held out his hand; Washington extended his then gave him a bear hug—two big men, hugging, with tears streaming unashamedly down their faces.[50] Washington left the tavern for the barge that would ferry him on the first leg of his journey, first to Philadelphia to settle accounts, then to Annapolis, Maryland, where Congress was then trying to raise a quorum for a session.

Washington notified Congress of his arrival in Annapolis on December 18, and Congress agreed to hear from him at noon of their meeting on

December 23. Only 19 or 20 members were present for the session, led by the new president, Thomas Mifflin, a central figure in the long-forgotten Conway affair. At noon, Washington was escorted into chambers and shown a chair; he sat, until Mifflin said, "Sir, the United States in Congress assembled are prepared to receive your communications."

Washington stood, and bowed. He read briefly from a prepared text, concluding:

> I consider it an indispensable duty to close this last solemn act of my Official life, by commending the interests of our dearest Country to the protection of almighty God, and those who have the superintendence of them, to his holy keeping.
>
> Having now finished the work assigned me, I retire from the great theatre of action; and bidding an Affectionate farewell to this August body under whose orders I have so long acted, I here offer my commission, and take leave of my employments of public life.[51]

With a rustle of papers, he handed Mifflin his commission and a copy of his remarks. Mifflin took a few minutes in reading a thanks from Congress, and then Washington was a free man. He lodged that night at a tavern between Annapolis and home, then rode for Mount Vernon where Martha now waited with their two grandchildren. He reached home the next day, just in time for Christmas Eve.

Conclusion

GEORGE WASHINGTON WAS A MAN OF VISION. WHEN THE FRENCH claimed the Ohio Valley, he saw that their claim would lead to North American dominance, and though he was not yet in a position of power he did what he could to stop it; when Parliament attempted to directly tax the American colonies, Washington saw that as a violation of long-held constitutional authority and pledged his life, fortune, and honor to oppose that violation; when the 13 states could not or would not raise money and men to support a strong army, Washington had a vision of a strong federal government that could compel the states to act in unison. This vision put him at odds with the Articles of Confederation and led him to chair what became known as the Constitutional Convention that created the working document of the United States of America.

When in 1789 the new country looked for its first executive, its first president, the Electoral College unanimously selected George Washington, coaxing him out of retirement at his Mount Vernon home in order to create the template for American presidents to follow. He served well, sagely maintaining neutrality in the continued troubles between France and Great Britain, respecting the powers of the legislative and judiciary branches while maintaining the executive power to negotiate foreign affairs.

Throughout his career, both military and political, George Washington showed an excellent sense of timing: He knew when to hold onto his position and, more important, when to let it go. In resigning his commission as a general as soon as the war was won, George Washington demonstrated his enormous respect for placing the civil government over the military; in leaving the presidency in 1797, after serving only two terms, he showed his belief that good government must be greater than any one man. In so doing he became the greatest of men.

✦══✦

But does George Washington belong in a pantheon of books called the Great Generals Series? Arguably he does not. He proved himself to be a great civilian leader, but as a general, he lost more battles than he won. Although he was preternaturally cool on a battlefield, Generals Benedict Arnold and Daniel Morgan were at least his equal as tacticians. And Washington was not even the best strategist of the American Revolution, a title more properly bestowed on General Nathanael Greene.

And yet none of these men could have done what George Washington did. Arnold, obviously, lacked the character to stick with a cause when it looked hopeless, as the revolution often did; Morgan was too rough around the edges to be taken seriously by the elite, merchant-class members of Congress; and Greene had no patience for politics, frequently putting him at odds with politicians who, in civil government, call the shots.

Washington also had experience none of these men had: as a 22-year-old lieutenant colonel of Virginia's militia, Washington had fired the shot that sparked the French and Indian War, a precursor to the Seven Years' War that raged around the world. He saw three years of hard service in that war, eventually rising to the rank of colonel overseeing a regiment of Virginia troops, an experience that taught him how to raise and equip an army from scratch.

George Washington had it all: character, class, and the prerequisite patience and diplomacy to negotiate the army's needs with Congress, an often exasperating exercise. He also brought to the table the intangible quality of leadership. Like most clichés, there is an underlying truth to this notion of Washington as a great leader. Certainly some of his contemporaries—Generals Charles Lee, Horatio Gates, and Thomas Mifflin spring to mind—would have disputed this idea, for they saw him as indecisive, weak, and vain. Yet in other generals who served under him—Nathanael Greene, Lafayette, Henry

Knox—Washington inspired a fierce loyalty that drove them to feats they scarcely could have imagined themselves capable of in the war's early years.

These conflicting views of Washington from his contemporaries prove that he did not spring forth into the world fully formed as a leader of men. He learned his leadership skills the way most of us do, through trial and error—with a lot of error. In his first command, he lost control of warriors who massacred defenseless, wounded soldiers—and arguably covered that up; he recklessly marched his men toward a superior force and placed them in an untenable position where they were soundly beaten, and he inadvertently confessed to assassinating a French emissary. If not for the charitable patronage of Virginia governor Robert Dinwiddie, Washington's military career may have ended early.

But Washington was intelligent, smart enough to learn from his mistakes. It is instructional to witness Washington advising a trained British officer against detaching a small force to attack Fort Duquesne in 1758, just a few years after he had done that same thing with disastrous results.

<hr />

Learning from mistakes is important but is not in itself enough to make a leader great. Every leader needs a fundamental philosophy, a North Star to guide his or her actions. Washington spelled out his overarching philosophy of leadership to officers of his Virginia regiment in 1758, shortly after becoming their colonel:

> I shall make it the most agreeable part of my duty, to study merit, and reward the brave, and deserving. I assure you, Gentlemen, that partiality shall never biass my conduct; nor shall prejudice injure any; but throughout the whole tenor of my proceedings, I shall endeavour, as far as I am able, to reward and punish, without the least diminution.[1]

Washington would govern through meritocracy—he would, and did, reward the deserving and punish shirkers without regard to personal ties and political connections. This represented a distinctly American style of leadership. British generals, hamstrung by a hierarchy of class, could not have based promotions on merit. Someone like Daniel Morgan, a wagon driver in the French and Indian War, could never have become a general in the British army, though he excelled in the American army. By recognizing and rewarding achievement, Washington won the loyalty of his highest achievers.

Washington would also forgive failure. When Greene, his youngest general, made the disastrous decision to keep troops on Mount Washington despite Washington's suggestion that he remove them, Washington kept faith in his young commander. Greene's decision had been reasoned and well intentioned, so Washington accepted the bad result and moved on. Greene felt thankful and matured into Washington's best general.

Without doubt, Washington's strongest innate leadership quality was perseverance, or what is often today called grit. Even as a 20-year-old militia major, he demonstrated this quality in his mission to deliver a letter to the commander of the French forces in the Ohio Valley wilderness. It sounds trite but it's true: For George Washington, success was mandatory. Once he had a vision, nothing short of death would stop him from realizing it.

With intelligence, grit, and an underlying philosophy that emphasized achievement, General George Washington took an army that had no experience, no tradition, no clue, and fought a protracted war against the best, most disciplined force in the world. Yes, Washington lost more battles than he won, but he squarely deserves a place in the pantheon of great American generals, for without his military genius, there would have been no other American generals, indeed, no United States of America.

Notes

Introduction

1. Donald Jackson and Dorothy Twohig, eds., *The Diaries of George Washington, Volume 1* (Charlottesville: University Press of Virginia, 1976), 155.
2. *Diaries*, 1:144–45.
3. *Diaries*, 1:147.
4. *Diaries*, 1:147.
5. *Diaries*, 1:151.
6. *Diaries*, 1:155.
7. *Diaries*, 1:157.
8. *Diaries*, 1:155–57. I chose Gist's retelling of this story over Washington's as it seemed more authentic. According to Washington, the Indian who fired at them was not a single Indian guide but a "Party of French Indians" who ambushed them. He and Gist then somehow managed to separate the Indian who shot at them from his party to capture him; the capture does not seem likely, and it is possible Washington did not want to look like a gullible rube who was fooled by a hostile Indian. Gist's version of a single guide misleading them makes more sense than does Washington's story.
9. *Diaries*, 1:151.
10. *Diaries*, 1:151.

Chapter 1

1. W. W. Abbott, ed., *The Papers of George Washington, Colonial Series, Vol. 1* (Charlottesville: University Press of Virginia, 1983), 70.
2. *Papers, Colonial Series*, 1:71–72.
3. *Papers, Colonial Series*, 1:91, note 8; and exhibit at Mount Vernon Center, January 2009.
4. Edward G. Lengel, *General George Washington: A Military Life* (New York: Random House, 2005), 15. Lengel tallied Washington's survey earnings at £400.
5. Forensic anthropologists working with the Mount Vernon Visitors Center have created figures of Washington's appearance at age 19 and in his mid-forties, when he

took command of the American troops. This description is based on the re-created figure of 19-year-old Washington.

6. Donald Jackson and Dorothy Twohig, eds., *The Diaries of George Washington, Volume 1* (Charlottesville: University Press of Virginia, 1976), 195.

7. Fred Anderson, *Crucible of War* (New York: Alfred A. Knopf, 2000), xxiv. This is an excellent telling of the evolution of the Seven Years' War.

8. Anderson, *Crucible,* 56.

9. Joseph Ellis, *His Excellency: George Washington* (New York: Alfred A. Knopf, 2004), 14. Also: Anderson, *Crucible,* 57.

10. Anderson, *Crucible,* 56–57.

11. Anderson, *Crucible,* 61.

12. *Papers, Colonial Series,* 1:110; *Diaries,* 1:195. Emphasis Washington's.

13. *Papers, Colonial Series,* 1:124.

14. *Papers, Colonial Series,* 1:118.

Chapter 2

1. W. W. Abbott, ed., *The Papers of George Washington, Colonial Series, Vol. 1* (Charlottesville: University Press of Virginia, 1983), 1:117.

2. For an example of his losses playing cards, see W. W. Abbott and Dorothy Twohig, eds., *The Papers of George Washington, Colonial Series, Vol. 10* (Charlottesville: University Press of Virginia, 1995), 222–223. Here Washington logs 63 card games played over two years with a net loss of more than £6.

3. Donald Jackson and Dorothy Twohig, eds., *The Diaries of George Washington, Volume 1* (Charlottesville: University Press of Virginia, 1976), 119.

4. *Papers, Colonial Series,* 1:124.

5. Fred Anderson, *Crucible of War* (New York: Alfred A. Knopf, 2000), 60.

6. Anderson, *Crucible,* 61.

7. *Papers, Colonial Series,* 1:155.

8. *Diaries,* 1:157.

9. *Papers, Colonial Series,* 1:158.

10. *Papers, Colonial Series,* 1:161, note 1.

11. *Papers, Colonial Series* 1:159–161.

12. Anderson, *Crucible,* 63.

13. *Papers, Colonial Series.* 1:168.

14. *Papers, Colonial Series,* 1:168.

15. *Papers, Colonial Series,* 1:252.

16. *Papers, Colonial Series,* 1:191–192.

17. *Papers, Colonial Series,* 1:189.

18. *Papers, Colonial Series,* 1:203–204; 215–216.

19. *Papers, Colonial Series,* 1:209.

20. *Papers, Colonial Series,* 1:226.

Chapter 3

1. W. W. Abbott, ed., *The Papers of George Washington, Colonial Series, Vol. 1* (Charlottesville: University Press of Virginia, 1983), 229–230.

2. Douglas Southall Freeman, *George Washington, Vol. Two* (New York: Charles Scribner's Sons: 1948), 11.

3. *Papers, Colonial Series,* 1:241.

4. *Papers, Colonial Series,* 1:243. Late in his life—probably sometime after the Revolution but before the Constitutional Convention—Washington made emendations and insertions to "The Letter Book for the Braddock Campaign." Whenever possible, I quote the original language that young Washington wrote; when the original language is obscured so that only the updated language is legible, I have bracketed the quotes using these symbols: < >. For more on this, see *Papers, Colonial Series* 1:236–240.

5. Freeman, *George Washington,* 2:46, and 50, notes 104 and 105; also *Papers, Colonial Series,* 1:327.

6. *Papers, Colonial Series,* 1:298–300.

7. Fred Anderson, *Crucible of War* (New York: Alfred A. Knopf, 2000), 95.

8. Anderson, *Crucible,* 95–96.

9. *Papers, Colonial Series,* 1:300.

10. *Papers, Colonial Series.* 1:319–324.

11. Freeman, *George Washington,* 2:64–66.

12. *Papers, Colonial Series,* 1:331.

13. Anderson, *Crucible,* 99.

14. *Papers, Colonial Series,* 1:341.

15. *Papers, Colonial Series,* 1:341.

16. *Papers, Colonial Series,* 1:333.

17. *Papers, Colonial Series,* 1:343.

18. *Papers, Colonial Series,* 1:336, 340.

19. *Papers, Colonial Series,* 1:344.

20. *Papers, Colonial Series,* 1:358.

21. *Papers, Colonial Series,* 1:352.

22. *Papers, Colonial Series,* 1:364.

23. W. W. Abbott, ed., *The Papers of George Washington, Colonial Series, Vol. 2* (Charlottesville: University Press of Virginia, 1983), 176.

24. *Papers, Colonial Series,* 2:256–258.

25. W. W. Abbott, ed., *The Papers of George Washington, Colonial Series, Vol. 3* (Charlottesville: University Press of Virginia, 1984), 294.

26. W. W. Abbott, ed., *The Papers of George Washington, Colonial Series, Vol. 4* (Charlottesville: University Press of Virginia, 1984), 113.

27. Anderson, *Crucible,* 203.

28. W. W. Abbott, ed., *The Papers of George Washington, Colonial Series, Vol. 5* (Charlottesville: University Press of Virginia, 1988), 78.

29. Freeman, *George Washington,* 2: 278–302.

30. *Papers, Colonial Series,* 5:104.

Chapter 4

1. W. W. Abbott, ed., *The Papers of George Washington, Colonial Series, Vol. 5* (Charlottesville: University Press of Virginia, 1988), 106.

2. *Papers, Colonial Series,* 5:126.

3. *Papers, Colonial Series,* 5:243.

4. *Papers, Colonial Series,* 5:361.

5. Fred Anderson, *Crucible of War* (New York: Alfred A. Knopf, 2000), 272; Joseph Ellis, *His Excellency: George Washington* (New York: Alfred A. Knopf, 2004), 74; Douglas Southall Freeman, *George Washington, Vol. Two* (New York: Charles Scribner's Sons: 1948), 335.

6. Freeman, 2:332.

7. W. W. Abbott, ed., *The Papers of George Washington, Colonial Series, Vol. 6* (Charlottesville: University Press of Virginia, 1988), 113–114.

8. *Papers, Colonial Series,* 6:115–116.

9. *Papers, Colonial Series,* 6:120–123. In these dueling interpretations of this skirmish, it is prudent to give Washington the benefit of the doubt: Previous and subsequent events would prove that, under fire, Washington was extraordinarily cool.

10. *Papers, Colonial Series,* 6:123.

11. *Papers, Colonial Series,* 6:178–181.

12. *Papers, Colonial Series,* 6:200.

Chapter 5

1. Most of the burgesses had left: Douglas Southall Freeman, *George Washington, Vol. Three* (New York: Charles Scribner's Sons: 1951), 130; Washington sewing seed: Donald Jackson and Dorothy Twohig, eds., *The Diaries of George Washington, Volume 1* (Charlottesville: University Press of Virginia, 1976), 337.

2. W. W. Abbott and Dorothy Twohig, eds., *The Papers of George Washington, Colonial Series, Vol. 7* (Charlottesville: University Press of Virginia, 1990), 396.

3. W. W. Abbott and Dorothy Twohig, eds., *The Papers of George Washington, Colonial Series, Vol. 8* (Charlottesville: University Press of Virginia, 1993), 178.

4. Clarence Edwin Carter, ed., *The Correspondence of Gen. Thomas Gage, Vol. II* (New Haven, CT: Yale University Press, 1933), 79.

5. *Papers, Colonial Series,* 7:201–202.

6. W. W. Abbott and Dorothy Twohig, eds., *The Papers of George Washington, Colonial Series, Vol. 9* (Charlottesville: University Press of Virginia, 1994), 243.

7. W. W. Abbott and Dorothy Twohig, eds., *The Papers of George Washington, Colonial Series, Vol. 10* (Charlottesville: University Press of Virginia, 1995), 265.

8. *Papers, Colonial Series,* 10:119.

9. *Papers, Colonial Series,* 10:308.

10. Gerald M. Carbone, *Nathanael Greene: A Biography of the American Revolution* (New York: Palgrave Macmillan, 2008), 18.

11. *Papers, Colonial Series,* 10:368.

12. *Papers, Colonial Series,* 10:369. Washington bought the cartouche boxes and sash for a newly formed independent company.

13. Philander D. Chase, ed., *The Papers of George Washington, Revolutionary War Series, Vol. 1* (Charlottesville: University Press of Virginia, 1985), 3.

14. David McCullough. *John Adams* (New York: Simon & Schuster, 2001), 18. Adams described himself as looking like "a short, thick Archbishop of Canterbury."

15. *Papers, Revolutionary War Series,* 1:2.

16. *Papers, Revolutionary War Series,* 1:1.

17. *Papers, Revolutionary War Series,* 1:2.

18. *Papers, Revolutionary War Series,* 1:4.

Chapter 6

1. American losses on Bunker Hill were 441 to 1,150 for the British, according to Mark M. Boatner III, *Encyclopedia of the American Revolution* (Mechanicsburg, PA: 1994), 129. The casualty figures Washington received from Bunker Hill were not

this precise, although by late June he had learned that British losses there numbered more than 1,000.

2. Clarence Edwin Carter, ed., *The Correspondence of General Thomas Gage, Vol. 2* (New Haven: Yale University Press, 1933), 686.

3. Samuel F. Batchelder, "The Washington Elm Tradition," *Cambridge Historical Proceedings for 1925, Vol. 18* (Cambridge, MA: Cambridge Historical Society), 46–75.

4. James Thacher, *A Military Journal During the American Revolutionary War* (Boston: Richardson and Lord, 1823), 37. Reprints of this work are widely available.

5. Richard K. Showman, ed., *The Papers of Nathanael Greene, Vol. I* (Chapel Hill: University of North Carolina Press, 1976), 94. Hereafter *Greene Papers.*

6. For the cultural differences between northern and southern militia, see: Fred W. Anderson, "The Hinge of the Revolution: George Washington Confronts a People's Army, July 3, 1775," *Massachusetts Historical* Review 1 (1999).

7. Philander D. Chase, ed., *The Papers of George Washington, Revolutionary War Series, Vol. 1* (Charlottesville: University Press of Virginia, 1985), 99.

8. *Papers, Revolutionary War Series,* 1:189.

9. *Papers, Revolutionary War Series,* 1:215–216; and Douglas Southall Freeman, *George Washington, Vol. Three* (New York: Charles Scribner's Sons: 1951), 508–509.

10. Frederick Mackenzie. *Diary of Frederick Mackenzie, Volume 1* (Cambridge, MA: Harvard University Press, 1930), 31.

11. boston1775.blogspot.com citing Papers of General John Sullivan.

12. *Papers, Revolutionary War Series,* 1:114–115.

13. *Papers, Revolutionary War Series,* 1:290–291.

14. *Papers, Revolutionary War Series,* 1:290–291.

15. *Papers, Revolutionary War Series,* 1:299.

16. *Papers, Revolutionary War Series,* 1:432–434.

17. *Papers, Revolutionary War Series,* 1:450–451.

18. Frances Dickinson Ackerly, ed., "Diary of a Solider of the Revolution" (Cambridge, MA: Archives of the Longfellow National Historic Site, 2008), 57.

19. *Papers, Revolutionary War Series,* 1:238.

20. *Papers, Revolutionary War Series,* 1:548.

21. Mark Puls, *Henry Knox: Visionary General of the American Revolution* (New York: Palgrave Macmillan, 2008), 15–20.

22. Philander D. Chase, ed., *The Papers of George Washington, Revolutionary War Series, Vol. 2* (Charlottesville: University Press of Virginia, 1987), 385.

23. *Papers, Revolutionary War Series,* 2:434.

24. *Papers, Revolutionary War Series,* 2:449.

25. *Papers, Revolutionary War Series,* 2:564.

26. Freeman, *George Washington,* 3: 573.

27. Philander D. Chase, ed., *The Papers of George Washington, Revolutionary War Series, Vol. 3* (Charlottesville: University Press of Virginia, 1988), 1.

28. *Papers, Revolutionary War Series,* 3:19.

29. *Papers, Revolutionary War Series,* 3:88–89.

30. *Papers, Revolutionary War Series,* 3:103.

31. *Papers, Revolutionary War Series,* 3:179–180.

32. *Papers, Revolutionary War Series,* 3:320–324.

33. *Papers of Nathanael Greene,* 1:195.

34. *Papers of Nathanael Greene,* 1:320–324.

35. *Papers, Revolutionary War Series,* 3:370.
36. Freeman, *George Washington,* 3:600.
37. Thacher, *Military Journal,* 47. For a good, concise account of fortifying Dorchester, see David McCullough, *1776* (New York: Simon & Schuster, 2005), 90–97.
38. Ackerly, ed., *Diary of a Soldier,* 65.

Chapter 7

1. It took Congress 14 years to strike and present this medal to Washington. The original design was so poorly drawn that Lady Liberty appeared to be "leering" at Washington. The obverse or front side of the medal presented to Washington in 1789 looks much like the obverse of the current American 25-cent piece. See Philander D. Chase, ed., *The Papers of George Washington, Revolutionary War Series, Vol. 4* (Charlottesville: University Press of Virginia, 1991), 2–4.
2. Philander D. Chase, ed., *The Papers of George Washington: Revolutionary War Series Vol. 3* (Charlottesville: University Press of Virginia, 1988); also quoted in David McCullough, *1776* (New York: Simon & Schuster, 2005), 80.
3. Clarence Edwin Carter, ed., *The Correspondence of General Thomas Gage, Vol. 2* (New Haven: Yale University Press, 1933), 205.
4. *Papers, Revolutionary War Series,* 3:20.
5. Philander D. Chase, ed., *The Papers of George Washington: Revolutionary War Series Vo. 4* (Charlottesville: University Press of Virginia, 1991), 73.
6. Richard M. Ketchum, *The Winter Soldiers* (New York: Henry Holt, 1999), 89.
7. Philander D. Chase, ed., *The Papers of George Washington, Revolutionary War Series, Vol. 5* (Charlottesville: University Press of Virginia, 1993), 135.
8. *Papers, Revolutionary War Series,* 5:180.
9. Barnet Schecter, *The Battle for New York* (New York: Walker and Co., 2002), 4.
10. *Papers, Revolutionary War Series,* 5:219.
11. *Papers, Revolutionary War Series,* 5:247.
12. *Papers, Revolutionary War Series,* 5:257.
13. *Papers, Revolutionary War Series,* 5:297, 306–306; Mark Puls, *Henry Knox: Visionary General of the American Revolution* (New York: Palgrave Macmillan, 2008), 56; Schecter, *Battle for New York,* 107–108.
14. Puls, *Knox,* 56.
15. *Papers, Revolutionary War Series,* 5:401–402.
16. *Papers, Revolutionary War Series,* 5:682.
17. *Papers, Revolutionary War Series:* 5:21.
18. *Papers, Revolutionary War Series:* 5:336.
19. Philander D. Chase and Frank E. Grizzard Jr., eds., *The Papers of George Washington, Revolutionary War Series, Vol. 6* (Charlottesville: University Press of Virginia, 1994), 162.
20. Troyer Steele Anderson, *The Command of the Howe Brothers during the American Revolution* (New York: Oxford University Press, 1936), 134.
21. Anderson, *Command of the Howe Brothers,* 146.
22. Schecter, *Battle for New York,* 157.
23. *Papers, Revolutionary War Series,* 6:156.
24. Schecter, *Battle for New York,* 166.
25. *Papers, Revolutionary War Series,* 6:200.
26. *Papers, Revolutionary War Series,* 6:223; Richard K. Showman, ed., *The Papers of Nathanael Greene, Vol. I* (Chapel Hill: University of North Carolina Press, 1976), 294.

27. Washington's comments on a possible evacuation of New York: *Papers, Revolutionary War Series,* 6:249; Greene's comments, ibid., 223; Heath's comments, ibid., 302–304; Clinton's comments, ibid., 290–293.

28. Anderson, *Command of the Howe Brothers,* 173–175.

29. *Papers, Revolutionary War Series,* 6:308.

30. Frederick Mackenzie. *Diary of Frederick Mackenzie* (Cambridge, MA: Harvard University Press, 1930), 45.

31. Joseph Plumb Martin, *A Narrative of a Revolutionary Soldier* (1830; New York: Signet Classic, 2001), 30.

32. Martin, *Narrative of a Revolutionary Soldier,* 30.

33. *Papers, Revolutionary War Series,* 6:315

34. *Papers, Revolutionary War Series,* 6:316; also *Battle for New York,* 185.

35. James Thacher, *A Military Journal During the American Revolutionary War* (Boston: Richardson and Lord, 1823), 170.

36. Showman, *Greene Papers,* 1:300.

37. *Papers, Revolutionary War Series,* 6:346.

38. *Papers, Revolutionary War Series,* 6:314,

39. *Papers, Revolutionary War Series,* 6:331–333

40. Showman, *Greene Papers,* 1:203.

41. *Papers, Revolutionary War Series,* 6: Washington's orders of Sept. 17, 320; letter to General Philip Schuyler, 357.

Chapter 8

1. Philander D. Chase, ed., *The Papers of George Washington, Revolutionary War Series, Vol. 7* (Charlottesville: University Press of Virginia, 1997), 51–52.

2. *Papers, Revolutionary War Series,* 7:53.

3. Richard K. Showman, ed., *The Papers of Nathanael Greene, Vol. I* (Chapel Hill: University of North Carolina Press, 1976), 347.

4. Washington to Greene: *Papers, Revolutionary War Series,* 7:115–116; Greene to Washington, ibid., 119–120.

5. *Greene Papers,* I:351.

6. *Papers, Revolutionary War Series,* 7:163.

7. *Greene Papers,* I: 352.

8. Frederick Mackenzie. *Diary of Frederick Mackenzie, Volume 1* (Cambridge, MA: Harvard University Press, 1930), 111–112.

9. Richard M. Ketchum. *The Winter Soldiers.* (New York: Henry Holt and Company, LLC, 1999), 131.

10. *Papers, Revolutionary War Series,* 7:165.

11. *Papers, Revolutionary War Series,* 7:193.

12. *Papers, Revolutionary War Series,* 7:224.

13. *Papers, Revolutionary War Series,* 7:237.

14. *Papers, Revolutionary War Series,* 7:238.

15. *Papers, Revolutionary War Series,* 7:231–232.

16. *Papers, Revolutionary War Series,* 7:245.

17. *Papers, Revolutionary War Series,* 7:255–256.

18. *Papers, Revolutionary War Series,* 7:270.

19. *Papers, Revolutionary War Series,* 7:276.

20. *Papers, Revolutionary War Series,* 7:288.

21. *Papers, Revolutionary War Series,* 7:301.

22. *Papers, Revolutionary War Series*, 7:335.

23. *Papers, Revolutionary War Series*, 7:336.

Chapter 9

1. Philander D. Chase, ed., *The Papers of George Washington, Revolutionary War Series, Vol. 7* (Charlottesville: University Press of Virginia, 1997), 392.

2. George F. Scheer and Hugh F. Rankin, *Rebels & Redcoats* (New York: Da Capo Press, 1957), 211.

3. *Papers, Revolutionary War Series*, 7:423.

4. Thomas Paine, "The Crisis," in Bruce Kuklick, ed., *Thomas Paine Political Writings* (Cambridge: Cambridge University Press, 1989), 41.

5. Richard M. Ketchum. *The Winter Soldiers*. (New York: Henry Holt and Company, LLC, 1999), 248.

6. *Papers, Revolutionary War Series*, 7:439.

7. Scheer and Rankin, *Rebels & Redcoats*, 212, quoting the journal of Colonel John Fitzgerald.

8. *Papers, Revolutionary War Series*, 7:454.

9. Douglas Southall Freeman, *George Washington, Vol. Four* (New York: Charles Scribner's Sons, 1951), 321.

10. Mark M. Boatner III, *Encyclopedia of the American Revolution* (Mechanicsburg, PA: Stackpole Books, 1994), 1115.

11. Scheer and Rankin, *Rebels & Redcoats*, 216.

12. Richard K. Showman, ed., *The Papers of Nathanael Greene, Vol. II* (Chapel Hill: University of North Carolina Press, 1980), 4.

13. *Papers, Revolutionary War Series*, 7:510.

14. Ketchum, *Winter Soldiers, 291;* Langguth, *Patriots,* 426. The phrasing of Erskine's quote varies from account to account but the gist of it is, concerned that Washington would escape, he advocated a nighttime attack.

15. Scheer and Rankin, *Rebels & Redcoats*, 218.

16. *Papers, Revolutionary War Series*, 7:538.

17. Ketchum, *Winter Soldiers*, 308.

18. Scheer and Rankin, *Rebels & Redcoats*, 219.

19. *Papers, Revolutionary War Series* 7:320.

20. Frank E. Grizzard Jr., ed., *The Papers of George Washington, Revolutionary War Series, Vol. 8* (Charlottesville: University Press of Virginia, 1998), orders to Heath, p. 10; orders to Lincoln, p. 11.

21. Joseph J. Ellis, *His Excellency: George Washington* (New York: Vintage Books, A Division of Random House, Inc. 2005), 86—87.

22. *Papers, Revolutionary War Series* 8:455–456.

23. *Papers, Revolutionary War Series* 8:382.

24. *Papers, Revolutionary War Series,* 8:643.

25. John C. Fitzpatrick, ed., *The Writings of George Washington from the Original Manuscript Sources, 1745–1799, 39 Volumes* (Washington, DC: United States Government Printing Office, 1931–1944), 8:448.

Chapter 10

1. Richard K. Showman, ed., *The Papers of Nathanael Greene, Vol. II* (Chapel Hill: University of North Carolina Press, 1980), 143. Hereafter *Greene Papers*.

2. Philander D. Chase, ed., *The Papers of George Washington, Revolutionary War Series, Vol. 11* (Charlottesville: University Press of Virginia, 2001), 4–5.
3. *Greene Papers, Vol. II*, 200.
4. *Papers, Revolutionary War Series,* 11:49–51.
5. Douglas Southall Freeman, *George Washington, Vol. Four* (New York: Charles Scribner's Sons, 1951), 467.
6. *Papers, Revolutionary War Series,* 11:182.
7. W. J. Wood, *Battles of the Revolutionary War 1775–1781* (New York: Da Capo Press, 1995), 103.
8. Wood, *Battles,* 100.
9. *Papers, Revolutionary War Series,* 11:199.
10. Auguste Levasseur, trans. and ed. by Alan R. Hoffman, *Lafayette in America in 1824 and 1825* (Manchester, NH: Lafayette Press, 2006), 539.
11. Scheer and Rankin, *Rebels & Redcoats,* 239.
12. Scheer and Rankin, *Rebels & Redcoats,* 237.

Chapter 11

1. For example, there are three references to Washington's pursuit of Fabian strategy in Douglas Southall Freeman, *George Washington, Vol. Four* (New York: Charles Scribner's Sons: 1951): 363, 435, 505, 586.
2. Philander D. Chase, ed., *The Papers of George Washington, Revolutionary War Series, Vol. 11* (Charlottesville: University Press of Virginia, 2001), 266.
3. *Papers, Revolutionary War Series,* 11:338–339.
4. *Papers, Revolutionary War Series,* 11:373.
5. *Papers, Revolutionary War Series,* 11:426–427.
6. *Papers, Revolutionary War Series,* 11:438.

Chapter 12

1. Richard K. Showman, ed., *The Papers of Nathanael Greene, Vol. II* (Chapel Hill: University of North Carolina Press, 1980), 279. Hereafter *Greene Papers.*
2. Edward G. Lengel, ed., *The Papers of George Washington, Revolutionary War Series, Vol. 13* (Charlottesville: University Press of Virginia, 2003), 119.
3. Frank E. Grizzard Jr., ed., *The Papers of George Washington, Revolutionary War Series, Vol. 12* (Charlottesville: University Press of Virginia, 2002), 613.
4. *Papers, Revolutionary War Series,* 13:514.
5. *Greene Papers,* II:283.
6. Ron Chernow, *Alexander Hamilton* (New York: Penguin Group, 2004), 107.
7. George F. Scheer and Hugh F. Rankin, *Rebels & Redcoats* (New York: Da Capo Press, 1957), 308.
8. Richard K. Showman, ed., *The Papers of Nathanael Greene, Vol. I* (Chapel Hill: University of North Carolina Press, 1976), 325.
9. *Greene Papers,* II:406.
10. Scheer and Rankin, *Rebels & Redcoats,* 313.

Chapter 13

1. David R. Hoth, ed., *The Papers of George Washington, Revolutionary War Series, Vol. 14* (Charlottesville: University Press of Virginia, 2004), 646.

2. Edward G. Lengel, ed., *The Papers of George Washington, Revolutionary War Series, Vol. 15* (Charlottesville: University Press of Virginia, 2006), 152.

3. Douglas Southall Freeman, *George Washington, Vol. Five* (New York: Charles Scribner's Sons, 1952), 15–16.

4. Richard K. Showman, ed., *The Papers of Nathanael Greene, Vol. II* (Chapel Hill: University of North Carolina Press, 1980), 445–447. Hereafter *Greene Papers*.

5. *Papers, Revolutionary War Series*, 15:541.

6. Martin, *Narrative of a Revolutionary Soldier*, 110.

7. Various sources, including Freeman, *Washington*, 5:26–30; George F. Scheer and Hugh F. Rankin, *Rebels & Redcoats* (New York: Da Capo Press, 1957), 330; and Mark M. Boatner III, *Encyclopedia of the American Revolution* (Mechanicsburg, PA: Stackpole Books, 1994), 722.

8. John C. Fitzpatrick, ed., *The Writings of George Washington from the Original Manuscript Sources, 1745–1799*, 39 vols. (Washington, DC: United States Government Printing Office, 1931–1944), 12:144 (hereafter Fitzpatrick, *Writings of George Washington*).

9. Observations on Washington's conduct at Monmouth: Lafayette: Ron Chernow, *Alexander Hamilton* (New York:Penguin Books, 2004), 114–115; Greene: *Greene Papers*, II:451; Hamilton: Fitzpatrick, *Writings of George Washington*, 12:144.

10. Caroline Cox, *A Proper Sense of Honor: Service and Sacrifice in George Washington's Army* (Chapel Hill: University of North Carolina Press, 2004), 163.

11. Order Book of the American Forces in the Battle of Rhode Island, Redwood Library, Newport, RI.

12. David R. Hoth, ed., *The Papers of George Washington, Revolutionary War Series, Vol. 16* (Charlottesville: University Press of Virginia, 2006), 459.

Chapter 14

1. Edward G. Lengel, ed., *The Papers of George Washington, Revolutionary War Series, Vol. 18* (Charlottesville: University Press of Virginia, 2008), 422.

2. *Papers, Revolutionary War Series*, 18:572.

3. *Greene Papers*, IV:26.

4. John C. Fitzpatrick, ed., *The Writings of George Washington from the Original Manuscript Sources, 1745–1799, 39 Volumes* (Washington, DC: United States Government Printing Office, 1931–1944), 16:352.

5. Fitzpatrick, *Writings of George Washington*, 17:362–365.

6. Fitzpatrick, *Writings of George Washington*, 17:449.

7. Richard K. Showman, ed., *The Papers of Nathanael Greene, Vol. IV* (Chapel Hill: University of North Carolina Press, 1986), 41.

8. Richard K. Showman and Dennis M. Conrad, eds., *The Papers of Nathanael Greene, Vol. VI* (Chapel Hill: University of North Carolina Press, 1991), 78.

9. John B. Hattendorf, *Newport, the French Navy, and American Independence* (Newport, RI: Redwood Press, 2005), 68.

10. Fitzpatrick, *Writings of George Washington*, 20:76.

11. *Greene Papers*, VI:320.

12. Ron Chernow, *Alexander Hamilton* (New York: Penguin Books, 2004), 141.

13. George Washington Greene, *Life of Major-General Nathanael Greene, Vol. 3* (New York: Hurd and Houghton; Cambridge: Riverside Press, 1871), 70.

14. Fitzpatrick, *Writings of George Washington*, 21:57.

15. Fitzpatrick, *Writings of George Washington,* 21:71.
16. Fitzpatrick, *Writings of George Washington,* 21:88. In a letter to Washington, General Anthony Wayne wrote: "the Soldiery in General affect to spurn at the idea of turning *Arnolds* (as they express it)."
17. Fitzpatrick, *Writings of George Washington,* 21:24.
18. Fitzpatrick, *Writings of George Washington,* 22:143–144.
19. Frederick Mackenzie. *Diary of Frederick Mackenzie Vol. 2* (Cambridge, MA: Harvard University Press, 1930), 536.
20. Dennis M. Conrad, ed., *The Papers of Nathanael Greene, Vol. IX* (Chapel Hill: University of North Carolina Press, 1997), 142, 178–179.
21. Fitzpatrick, *Writings of George Washington,* 22:208.
22. Edward G. Lengel, *General George Washington: A Military Life* (New York: Random House, 2005), 333.
23. John C. Fitzpatrick, ed., *The Diaries of George Washington, Vol. 2* (New York: Kraus Reprint Co., 1971), 254.
24. Fitzpatrick, *Writings of George Washington,* 23:7.
25. Douglas Southall Freeman, *George Washington, Vol. Five* (New York: Charles Scribner's Sons, 1952), 322.
26. Fitzpatrick, *Writings of George Washington,* 23:132.
27. Joseph Plumb Martin, *A Narrative of a Revolutionary Soldier: Some of the Adventures Misgivings, and Sufferings of Joseph Plumb Martin* (1830; New York: Signet Classic, 2001), 199.
28. Freeman, *Washington,* 5:362 and Fitzpatrick, *Diaries Vol. 2:* 264.
29. Martin, *Narrative,* 200–201.
30. Fitzpatrick *Diaries, Vol. 2:*266.
31. Martin, *Narrative,* 202.
32. Mrs. Williams, *Biography of Revolutionary Heroes* (Providence, RI: Published by the author, 1839), 276.
33. Lengel, *A Military Life,* 341.
34. Freeman, *Washington,* 5:377.
35. Fitzpatrick, *Writings of George Washington,* 23:236.
36. Fitzpatrick, *Writings of George Washington,* 23:237.
37. Fitzpatrick, *Writings of George Washington,* 23:237.
38. Freeman, *Washington,* 5:388.
39. Benson J. Lossing, *Reflections of Rebellion* (1889; Charleston, SC: History Press, 2005), 109.
40. Fitzpatrick, *Writings of George Washington,* 23:455.
41. Fitzpatrick, *Writings of George Washington,* 23:458–461.
42. Fitzpatrick, *Writings of George Washington,* 24:471.
43. Lengel, *A Military Life,* 345–346.
44. Fitzpatrick, *Writings of George Washington,* 26:186.
45. Fitzpatrick, *Writings of George Washington,* 26:208.
46. Fitzpatrick, *Writings of George Washington,* 26:222–227
47. Freeman, *Washington,* 5:467. This is how a captain, Samuel Shaw, recounted Washington's "almost blind" quote a few weeks after hearing it. Forty-two years later, a colonel, David Cobb, recounted the incident with different phrasing, which became the popular account and is used in Fitzpatrick, *Writings of George Washington,* 26:222.
48. Fitzpatrick, *Writings of George Washington,* 26:264.

49. Freeman, *Washington*, 5:467.
50. Freeman, *Washington*, 5:467. In describing the tearful parting at Fraunces Tavern, Freeman cited the memoirs of Colonel Benjamin, who was there, and the *New-York Gazette*, December 6, 1783, reprinted in the *Penn. Packet*, December 12, 1783.
51. Freeman, *Washington*, 5:476–477.

Conclusion

1. W.W. Abbot, ed., *The Papers of George Washington: Colonial Series Vol. 2.* (Charlottesville: University Press of Virginia, 1983), 256–258.

Bibliography

Abbott, W. W., and Twohig, Dorothy, eds. *The Papers of George Washington, Colonial Series, Vols. 1–10*. Charlottesville: University Press of Virginia, 1983—1995.

Ackerly, Frances Dickinson, ed. "Diary of a Solider of the Revolution," Cambridge, MA: Archives of the Longfellow National Historic Site, 2008.

Anderson, Fred. *Crucible of War*. New York: Alfred A. Knopf, 2000.

Anderson, Fred W. "The Hinge of the Revolution: George Washington Confronts a People's Army, July 3, 1775," *Massachusetts Historical Review* 1, 1999.

Anderson, Troyer Steele. *The Command of the Howe Brothers during the American Revolution*. New York: Oxford University Press, 1936.

Batchelder, Samuel F. "The Washington Elm Tradition," *Cambridge Historical Proceedings for 1925, Vol. 18*. Cambridge, MA: Cambridge Historical Society, 1925.

Bell, J. L. boston1775.blogspot.com, 2009.

Boatner III, Mark M. *Encyclopedia of the American Revolution, Third Edition*. Mechanicsburg, PA: Stackpole Books, 1994.

Carbone, Gerald M. *Nathanael Greene: A Biography of the American Revolution*. New York: Palgrave Macmillan, 2008.

Carter, Clarence Edwin, ed. *The Correspondence of General Thomas Gage, Vol. 2*. New Haven: Yale University Press, 1933.

Chase, Philander D., Grizzard Jr., Frank E., Hoth, David R., Lengel, Edward G., eds. *The Papers of George Washington, Revolutionary War Series, Vols. 1—16*. Charlottesville: University Press of Virginia, 1985—2006.

Chernow, Ron. *Alexander Hamilton*. New York: Penguin Books, 2004.

Cox, Caroline. *A Proper Sense of Honor: Service and Sacrifice in George Washington's Army*. Chapel Hill: University of North Carolina Press, 2004.

Ellis, Joseph J. *His Excellency: George Washington*. New York: Vintage Books, A Division of Random House, Inc., 2005.

Fitzpatrick, John C., ed. *The Writings of George Washington from the Original Manuscript Sources, 1745–1799, 39 Volumes*. Washington, DC: United States Government Printing Office, 1931–1944. (Cited volumes 12, 16, 17, 20, 21, 22, 23, 24, and 26.)

Freeman, Douglas Southall. *George Washington, Vols. Two—Five*. New York: Charles Scribner's Sons, 1948—1952.

Greene, George Washington. *Life of Major-General Nathanael Greene, Vol. 3.* New York: Hurd and Houghton; Cambridge: Riverside Press, 1871.

Hattendorf, John B. *Newport, the French Navy, and American Independence.* Newport, RI: Redwood Press, 2005.

Hoffman, Alan R., trans. and ed. Levasseur, Auguste. *Lafayette in America in 1824 and 1825.* Manchester, NH: Lafayette Press, 2006.

Jackson, Donald and Twohig, Dorothy, eds. *The Diaries of George Washington, Volumes 1—3.* Charlottesville: University Press of Virginia, 1976—1978.

Ketchum, Richard M. *The Winter Soldiers.* New York: Henry Holt, 1999.

Langguth, A. J. *Patriots.* New York: Simon & Schuster, 1988.

Lossing, Benson J. *Reflections of Rebellion.* 1889, reprinted Charleston, SC: History Press, 2005

Lengel, Edward G. *General George Washington: a Military Life.* New York: Random House, 2005.

Mackenzie, Frederick. *Diary of Frederick Mackenzie.* Cambridge, MA: Harvard University Press, 1930.

Martin, Joseph Plumb *A Narrative of a Revolutionary Soldier* 1830. Reprint, New York: Signet Classic, 2001.

McCullough, David. *1776.* New York: Simon & Schuster, 2005.

McCullough, David. *John Adams.* New York: Simon & Schuster, 2001.

Paine, Thomas "The Crisis," 1776. Reprinted in Kuklick, Bruce, ed. *Thomas Paine Political Writings.* Cambridge: Cambridge University Press, 1989.

Puls, Mark. *Henry Knox: Visionary General of the American Revolution.* New York: Palgrave Macmillan, 2008.

Schecter, Barnet. *The Battle for New York.* New York: Walker and Co., 2002.

Scheer, George F. Scheer and Rankin, Hugh F. *Rebels & Redcoats.* New York: Da Capo Press, 1957.

Showman, Richard K., Conrad, Dennis M., eds. *The Papers of Nathanael Greene, Vols. I, II, IV, VI, and IX.* Chapel Hill: University of North Carolina Press, 1976—1997.

Sullivan, General John. "Order Book of the American Forces in the Battle of Rhode Island." Newort, RI: Redwood Library, 1778.

Thacher, James. *A Military Journal During the American Revolutionary War.* Boston: Richardson and Lord, 1823.

Williams, Mrs. *Biography of Revolutionary Heroes.* Providence, RI: Published by the author, 1839.

Wood, W. J. *Battles of the Revolutionary War 1775–1781.* New York: Da Capo Press, 1995.

Index

British army. *See also* French and Indian
War; Hessian soldiers; *specific battles;
specific officers:* disease and, 68; free
blacks and, 70; French threat in
colonies and, 53; Loyalists and, 72, 76,
88, 132, 163, 164; northern strategy
for, 164; prisoners of war and, 48,
65–66, 73, 103, 151, 178–79; Scottish
Highlanders, 80, 84, 86, 102, 159;
southern strategy for, 164–65, 170;
strategies in New York campaign, 78,
79–80, 82–84, 85–87, 171
British navy. *See also specific officers:* Battle
of Bunker Hill, 64; described, 76;
French and Indian War, 28; military
strategy and, 126, 127; Newport, 112,
162, 169; New York campaign, 78,
79–80, 82, 83, 91–92, 101, 124; siege
of Boston, 71, 73–74
Brooklyn Heights, 77, 79, 85–87, 89
Brunswick, 104–6, 109, 123, 126, 160
Burgoyne, John, 126–28, 138, 142, 145,
169, 178

Cadwalader, John, 115, 119, 122
Canada, 20, 33, 66–67, 82, 125, 132, 163,
180
Charleston campaign, 82, 166
Clinton, George, 90, 183
Clinton, Henry: character of, 82; New
Jersey campaign, 166–67; New York
campaign, 82, 84, 87, 93, 94, 99,
171–73, 180; Philadelphia evacuation,
153–54, 155–60; siege of Yorktown,
178
colonies: boundaries of, 54; boycotts in,
53, 54; communication between, 75;
Declaration of Independence, 79, 80;
joint decision-making difficulties in, 9,
54; radical, 53; taxes on, 51–54,
55–56, 185
Continental Army. *See also* American army:
battles, 67, 93, 99–100, 119, 140;
enlistments, 106; founding of, 70
Continental Congress: army and, 70; civil
authority of, 74, 127, 147, 186;
commissions, 129–30, 146, 147;
Maryland locations for, 111, 183;
Philadelphia meetings, 56, 57–58, 111,
170; states, and authority of, 180, 185;

Washington and, 56, 57–58, 111, 127,
146–47, 180, 183–84, 186
Conway, Thomas, 146–47, 150
Conway cabal, 146–47, 184
Cornwallis, Charles: Battle of Brandywine,
133, 135; Battle of Cowpens, 173–74;
Battle of Monmouth, 159; battles of
Trenton, 119–21, 196n14; New Jersey
campaigns, 105–6, 123, 143; New
York campaign, 82, 86; siege of
Yorktown, 174–78; surrender and
peace agreement with, 178–79;
Virginia and, 172
Custis, Jack, 51, 55, 69, 180
Custis, Patsy, 51, 55

Dagworthy, John, 38–39
Declaration of Independence, 79, 80
De Grasse, Francois-Joseph-Paul, 172–73,
174
Delaware River: American army crossings,
113, 114–15, 117–18; British army
crossings, 126, 155; forts, 142–43
D'Estaing, Charles Hector Theodat, comte,
160–61, 165
Dinwiddie, Robert. *See also* House of
Burgesses: army and, 24, 36, 37; House
of Burgesses and, 2, 6, 9, 23, 36, 37,
39, 46; Ohio Valley and, 2–3, 5, 9, 16,
22–24; Washington, and patronage of,
187
du Coudray, Jean Baptiste Tronson, 125,
127, 130
Dunbar, Thomas, 31, 35, 36

England. *See* Great Britain

Fairfax, Thomas, 11
Fairfax, William, 10, 30, 41
Fellows, John, 92–93
flag, American, 70
Forbes, John, 41, 43–49
Forks of the Ohio, 9–10, 12–16. *See also*
Fort Duquesne
Fort Cumberland, 29, 30, 35, 38–39, 40
Fort Duquesne, 17, 30, 41, 42, 43–48,
187. *See also* Forks of the Ohio
Fort Le Boeuf, 3, 5–7, 27
Fort Lee, 77, 91, 104
Fort Mercer, 143

British strategies in, 79–80, 83, 154;
Brooklyn Heights, 77, 79, 85–87, 89;
Fort Washington, 77, 91, 98, 101–3,
104, 112; headquarters in, 78, 88;
Hessian soldiers in, 82, 84–86, 91–92,
96, 99, 102; Jamaica Pass, 84–87, 132;
Manhattan, 76, 77, 78, 87, 90, 112,
171–72; re-entry into, 183; retreat
from, 90, 104–7, 112, 195n27; Staten
Island highlands, 78; strategic position
of, 75–76; strategies to recapture, 124,
160, 167–68, 171–73, 180; upstate
campaign, 164–65
North Carolina, 13, 18, 19, 173–74
Northern Army, 82, 83, 127–29, 128, 129,
138, 145, 193n6

Ohio River Valley, 12, 16, 23, 28–34. *See*
also Forks of the Ohio
Orme, Robert, 28, 34

Paoli Massacre, 138
Parsons, Samuel Holden, 92–93
Patterson, James, 81–82, 102
Peal, Charles Wilson, 54–55
Pennsylvania militia, 122, 128, 129,
170–71
Percy, Hugh, 80, 87
Philadelphia. *See also* Delaware River:
British army and, 106, 107–8, 112,
126, 130–31, 137–38, 142–43,
153–54, 155–60; Congress in, 56,
57–58, 111; parade through, 130–31
Princeton, 106–7, 112, 113, 119, 121–22,
123, 157, 158, 170–71
Putnam, Israel, 84–85, 96, 102

Raystown Road, 44–47
Red Bank fort, 142–43
Redstone Old Fort, 13, 19
Reed, Joseph, 79, 81, 95, 96, 105
Rhode Island, 76, 151, 160–62, 177
Rochambeau, Comte de, 168, 171–73,
175, 179–80

St. Clair, John, 29, 32, 33
Schuylkill River, 137–38, 142, 148, 154
Scottish Highlanders, 80, 84, 86, 102, 159
Seneca, 3, 10, 12, 164. *See also*
Tanacharison, the Half King

Seven Years' War, 14, 186
Shirley, William (aide-de-camp), 33–34
Shirley, William (governor), 38–39, 40
siege. *See also* battle
siege and battle of Rhode Island, 160–62
siege of Boston, 67–74
siege of Yorktown, 124, 174–78, 179
Six Nations tribes, 2, 6, 13, 15, 163, 164
Smallwood, William, 93, 99
South Carolina, 19, 82, 168
Southern Army, 82, 165, 170, 193n6
Stamp Act, 51–52
Stanwix, John, 41, 42
Staten Island highlands, 78
Stephen, Adam, 22, 37, 40, 141–42
Steuben, Augustus von, 149–55, 159
Stirling, Lord (Alexander, William), 85, 86,
98, 104, 146, 159
Sullivan, John: Battle of Brandywine,
133–35; Battle of Germantown,
140–42; Battle of Rhode Island,
161–62; character of, 83, 161, 162; on
foreign officers, 125, 127; Long Island
campaign, 83, 84, 85; military
problems and, 161, 164; New Jersey
campaign, 111, 113–16, 122; as
prisoner of war, 86, 96

Tanacharison, the Half King, 3, 10–13,
15–16, 18, 19, 164
Thacher, James, 62, 73, 93
Townshend Acts, 52–54

Valley Forge, 148–51, 155
Van Braam, Jacob, 22, 24
Villiers, Louis Coulon de, 20, 22, 23
Villiers, sieur de Jumonville, Joseph de
Coulon, 14–17, 22
Virginia: British army and, 172; troops, 11,
119, 134, 175, 179, 186; Virginia
Regiment, 12, 17–19, 37–41, 39,
47–48, 187
von Donop, Carl, 85, 86

Washington, Augustine (father), 11
Washington, Augustine (half brother), 37
Washington, George: admiration for, 63,
159; army commissions and, 10,
24–25, 27, 37–39, 43, 49, 59; attacks,
and military strategy of, 67, 71, 135,

137, 153, 157; British army
commissions, 38–39, 40, 49; brushes
with death and, 1, 4–5, 35, 37, 112,
141, 189n8; children and, 51, 55, 69,
180; civil authority of Congress and,
74, 127, 147, 186; as commander in
chief, 58–59; Congress and, 56, 57–58,
111, 127, 146–47, 180–81, 183–84,
186; cool temperament of, 123, 157,
158, 192n9; diplomatic skills of, 125,
127, 181–83; discipline for army and,
36, 39–40, 41, 49, 63, 65, 80, 171;
discipline of, 6; early life of, 11–12;
French in Ohio valley and, 2–3, 5, 9,
16, 22–24, 185; gambling and, 18, 73,
190n2; horsemanship, 62, 157, 158;
House of Burgesses seat and, 44, 50,
51, 53, 55, 141, 192n9; illnesses of, 31,
32, 36, 41, 49; indecisiveness, 85,
90–91, 105, 108, 109, 135, 146–47,
186; on independence, 52–53; Indian
customs and, 10–11; Indian name of,
11; leadership skills, 123, 157, 158,
186–87, 192n9; lessons learned from
mistakes, 47, 98, 187; loyalty to, 49,
146, 159, 182–83, 186–87, 188;
marriage, and relationship between
Martha and, 42, 49–50, 51, 59–60;
medals, 16, 24, 75, 194n1; meritocracy
and, 39, 49, 63, 125, 187–88; military
experience(s) of, 6, 27, 48, 73, 186,
187, 192n9; military rank and
commissions, 10, 20, 24–25, 37,
38–39, 186; military record, 24, 186,
188; military strategy, 47, 100,
123–24, 136, 137, 188; moral
authority of, 109, 159; motives for
military service and, 37, 57, 58–59, 79,
185; natural talent, 11, 58; pageantry
and, 61–62, 130–31, 151, 160, 183;
patience, 6, 65, 74; patrons of, 11, 187;
perseverance, 7, 64, 65, 188; physical
characteristics, 12, 18, 54–55, 62, 182,
189–90n5, 199n47; plantations of, 11,
12, 44, 49–50; portrait, 54–55; as
president, 185, 186; on prisoners of
war, 66; on religious freedom, 66;
resignation from army commissions,
24–25, 49, 184, 185–86; resolve, 7, 65,
74, 79, 112; slavery and, 23, 27, 49,
51, 69; social class and, 11; stamina
and strength, 7, 58, 89; on states and
congressional authority, 185; on taxes,
52, 56, 185; temper, 93, 157; uniforms
and, 10, 55, 58, 62, 81, 131, 192n12;
volunteer aide-de-camp, 28–35; wealth
of, 49, 51, 54

Washington, John (grandfather), 11
Washington, John Augustine (brother), 57
Washington, Lawrence (half brother), 11,
   24–25, 27
Washington, Martha (wife), 42, 49, 51, 55,
   69, 124, 149, 180
Wayne, Anthony, 134, 138, 141, 149, 164,
   170–71, 199n16
Weedon, George, 93, 95, 134, 135
West Point fortress, 165, 166, 168–69,
   170